LEARN OR DIE

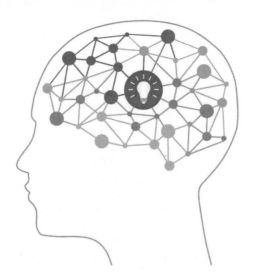

LEARN
OR DIE

Using Science to Build a Leading-Edge
Learning Organization

EDWARD D. HESS

Columbia University Press
Publishers Since 1893
New York   Chichester, West Sussex
cup.columbia.edu
Copyright © 2014 Columbia University Press
Library of Congress Cataloging-in-Publication Data
Hess, Edward D.
Learn or die : using science to build a leading-edge learning
organization / Edward D. Hess.
pages cm
Includes bibliographical references and index.
ISBN 978-0-231-17024-6 (cloth : alk. paper) — ISBN 978-0-231-53827-5 (ebook)
1. Organizational learning. 2. Organizational effectiveness. I. Title.
HD58.82.H365 2013
658.3'124—dc23
2014013370

Cover design: Noah Arlow
Cover image: © Getty Images

To Dr. Lyle E. Bourne, Jr. for elevating my passion for cognitive psychology and for thirty-four years of mentorship, caring friendship, and being an inspiring role model.

CONTENTS

ACKNOWLEDGMENTS

No one publishes a book without lots of help along the way. Let me give thanks.

First, to my parents, Jack and Anita Hess, who gave me the gift of self-efficacy and a love of learning that defined my life.

To my wife, Katherine, who lovingly and unselfishly has always encouraged me to "go for it" even when my doing so disrupted her life.

To my mentors—Coach Charlie Grisham; Professors Charlie Davison, Lyle Bourne, Jr., and Robert Drazin; Judge Harry Michael, Jr.; and Jack McGovern, Peter Norton, Ira Wender, David Bonderman, Tom Aiello, Dick Waite, and Dr. M. O'Neil—for expanding my horizons.

To Dean Tom Robertson and Professors Al Hartgraves, Robert Drazin, L.G. Thomas, and Robert Kazanjian of the Goizueta Business School for giving me the opportunity to enter academia and for supporting my research and writing.

To Jimmy Blanchard, Gardiner Garrard III, Bill Turner, Tom Cousins, and Billy Wren for supporting our Values-Based Leadership Institute at Goizueta Business School.

To Kim Cameron of the Ross School of Business at the University of Michigan whose scholarship and friendship has had an immeasurable positive influence on me.

To Dean Bob Bruner, Jim Freeland, Jeanne Liedtka, and Sean Carr for giving me the opportunity to be part of the Darden Business School at the University of Virginia and to the Batten Institute for funding my research activities for over seven years. To the collegial Darden Faculty who have made me feel at home.

To my research associate, Katherine Ludwig, whose professionalism, high standards, intellectual integrity, research skills, and growth mindset have contributed immensely to this book, making it a great learning experience.

To Myles C. Thompson, publisher at Columbia Business School Publishing and Economics, for his belief in this work and in me.

To Bridget Flannery-McCoy, editor at Columbia University Press, whose consummate professionalism and developmental editing made this a better book for our readers.

To the CEOs of all the organizations, too numerous to name, who have given me the opportunity to research their organizations and learn.

To Kaaren Hanson of Intuit, Rich Buckingham of W.L. Gore & Associates, and Dr. Gary Klein for your generosity of spirit and time, making it possible for me to bring your wonderful stories to our readers.

To Ray Dalio of Bridgewater Associates LP, a learning organization visionary and a learning leader who "walks the talk," for the opportunity to both learn about and tell the Bridgewater story with such "radical transparency."

To Drs. Katherine L. Acuff, Rita Yaroush, and Lyle Bourne, Jr. for their very helpful critique of chapters of this book.

To three special friends who for decades have always been supportive of my learning forays both good and not so good: Joe Street, Lyle Bourne, Jr., and Terry Brown. Love you, guys!

To my two sparkling granddaughters, Sarah and Caroline, for the reminder that learning can be joyful and for not letting me forget the learning power of the word: "Why." Stay curious, my dears!

LEARN OR DIE

The Science of Learning

1

Learn or Die: Building a High-Performance Learning Organization

Learn or Die: Is this just a snappy title or is it a business truth? My research, teaching, and consulting with private and public companies has led me to believe that now, more than ever, organizations and individuals must either be continuously learning, adapting, and improving, or risk professional obsolescence.[1] Why—and why now?

First, many organizations rely on operational excellence—getting better, faster, and cheaper—as the key part of their business models; many also rely on innovation to drive growth. The former requires relentless, constant improvement; the latter requires discovery and experimentation. What is the fundamental process underlying both efforts? It is learning.

> Both operational excellence and innovation are dependent on learning.

Second, organizations cannot learn unless the individuals within them learn. Individuals must continuously learn to stay relevant and competitive—jobwise—in a fast-paced, dynamic, global environment characterized by high levels of uncertainty, ambiguity, and change.[2] This environment requires exploration, invention, experimentation, and adaptation, all of which require learning.

Third, globalization and technology continue to increase the speed and reach of change. Today new competitors can arise almost anywhere in the world and, through technology, can reach your customers from thousands of miles away. Technology, especially SaaS (software as a service), reduces the capital needed to start and build businesses, thereby diminishing another historic barrier to entry. Technology empowers consumers to buy—with a few clicks—from anyone, anywhere. Such developments necessitate faster adaptation, and adaptation requires institutional learning processes such as critical thinking, critical conversations, and experimentation.

> Environments of uncertainty, ambiguity, and change require exploration, invention, experimentation, and adaptation, all of which require learning.

This increasing pace of change creates volatility that diminishes the life cycle of most competitive advantages, products, and public companies, as well as the tenures of public company CEOs. As a result, strategy making necessarily becomes more dynamic and distributed. Data-driven decision making becomes necessary to manage risks.

> In more volatile environments, organizations need institutionalized learning processes to enable speedier adaptation.

The amount, accessibility, and speedy creation of data require an organization to constantly learn to stay relevant. The more data, the faster knowledge is created, and the more unlikely it is that only one person has the answer. Organizations need processes for collaboration and constructive debate that rise above politics and egos. Thinking better, communicating better, making better decisions, and having a healthy regard for what one doesn't know are essential.

> The organizational response to changes requires better and faster learning by more people.

The Science of Learning

This book is about learning. How do people learn best? What types of organizational environments enable or inhibit learning? What are required learning processes? What capabilities do individuals need in order to learn better and faster? *Learn or Die* was written for individuals, team leaders, managers and leaders of any organization, and can be read from two different perspectives. First, from an individual's perspective: "How can I become a better learner?" Second, from an organizational perspective: "How can I enable better learning in others and within my company?"

The concept of a business learning organization is not new. It has been around at least fifty years. Its big boost came after the publication of Peter Senge's landmark 1990 book *The Fifth Discipline: The Art & Practice of the Learning Organization*,[3] and there have been scores of books published on the subject since. So why do you need this book?

The answer is that in the past twenty-five years, the science of learning has advanced materially, especially in the fields of neuroscience, psychology, and education, and—from an applied perspective—in areas of study surrounding high-reliability organizations and high-velocity, change environments. Those advances in the understanding of how people learn, the role of emotions in learning, and the environmental factors that inhibit or enable learning need to be brought more fully into the business world in an accessible applied manner. That is the purpose of this book. *Learn or Die* aims to synthesize that science and answer these two questions:

1. How does one become a better and faster learner?
2. How does one build an organization that is more adaptable and learns better and faster than the competition?

This book is not an academic treatise. It does not attempt to present a comprehensive review or summary of every stream of research that touches on learning. Instead, it presents syntheses of the key concepts that relate to two questions set forth above. With that in mind, I made judgments about relevance and importance in deciding what material to cover and include. Those judgments were based on my years of study and a review of over 450 academic articles and sixty books across the applicable disciplines, and were also influenced by my educational experience in the fields of cognitive and educational psychology and my thirty years of experience in the business world. They were further informed by my twelve years of teaching, researching, writing, and consulting with executives and managers to help them improve their organizations' learning and effectuate change in their organizations. Finally, the content was reviewed by two leading cognitive psychologists: one a leading academic researcher and author; the other a leading applied researcher and author. Overall, my goal is to present the most relevant findings across academic silos, with a focus on the information that you can implement and act on in your day-to-day operations and strategic planning.

Because *Learn or Die* is about learning, let us start with a question. Guess what CEO made the following statement: "We live in a much more competitive . . . environment. This means that we have to learn faster and better than our future adversaries [competitors]. Stated a bit differently, we must prevail in the competitive learning environment."

Before you guess, let's consider the content of this quote for a moment. What data supports the notion of faster overall business volatility? Here are a few data points to consider:

- In 1980 the average tenure of a company listed among the S&P 500 was over thirty years. Today it is about eighteen years and projected to continue declining.[4]
- In the past decade almost one half of the membership in the S&P was replaced.
- Today the average holding period of corporate stocks is less than twelve months.[5]
- Today the average tenure of a Fortune 500 CEO is only 4.6 years.[6]

Add to this data the dominance of "short-termism" in the capital markets and you have some powerful trends at work.

So who said it? You may have thought it was the CEO of a tech company, or an investment firm—but it was General Martin E. Dempsey, chairman of the Joint Chiefs of Staff, when he was commanding general, U.S. Army Training and Doctrine Command.[7] The Army has been funding major applied research for at least ten years to operationalize the concept of "Adaptive Leaders"—leaders who can continually learn. As this example suggests, learning organizations can be present in any industry. I believe that every organization, small or large, for profit or not for profit, public or private, in any industry or sector, would benefit from becoming a better learning organization. I suggest that the statement could have been made by any of the CEOs of the organizations examined in this book.

Building a Learning Organization

My objective with this book is to give you a blueprint by which you can improve your learning and your organization's learning and build or transform an existing organization into a learning organization. Through a synthesis of the research on learning, management, and education, and building on my own experiences and on the established science of the field, I've come up with a formula for building what I call a High-Performance Learning

HPLO = Right People +
Right Environment +
Right Processes

Organization (HPLO). An HPLO requires the right kinds of people, in the right learning environment, using the right learning processes, to continually learn faster and better than the competition.

Part I of the book focuses on the science of learning and research in other fields. It helps us answer the questions of who are the right people, what are the key elements of a good learning environment, and what are some of the key thinking and communicating processes that increase learning. We will look at learning from a cognitive, emotional, motivational, attitudinal, and behavioral basis. We will focus on our natural proclivities not to learn, and find out how to mitigate them. We will explore good learning behaviors and discuss the organizational system that can generate those behaviors. That will require us to look at the motivations, attitudes, and behaviors of organizational leaders and managers, and to examine the practices of learning organizations like IDEO, W. L. Gore & Associates, Room & Board, and the U.S. Army. The last chapter of part I presents an interview I did with Dr. Gary Klein, a scientist with more than forty years of experience as a research psychologist. His research and reflections on decision making and learning shed new light on many of the topics I discuss throughout part I.

Part II takes an in-depth look at three exemplary learning organizations—all different, and all with different lessons. The first company explored in chapter 9 is Bridgewater Associates, LP (Bridgewater), the largest hedge fund in the world and the consistent market leader in producing high returns for its investors. The chapter goes into depth in describing the unique learning "machine" that underlies Bridgewater's stellar success. Bridgewater is probably the most advanced learning organization I have studied—by that I mean that its learning culture and processes are consistent with what is known in the science of learning. Bridgewater has confronted our "humanness" better than most organizations I have studied or worked with; the only other organization that I have found that relies as heavily on the science of learning is the U.S. Army.

Chapter 10 is about Intuit, Inc. (Intuit). Intuit is also an interesting story—one of a consistently high-performance company that has decided to become an even better learning company by changing its culture and leadership model to facilitate a decision-making model based on learning experimentation. What fascinates me about this is that Intuit was not motivated to undertake this major transformation by any kind of crisis— rather, it did so simply because it realized a transformation was necessary to continue to excel in the rapidly changing business environment. Intuit has taken on a difficult task of changing behaviors that have worked well in the past in order to work better in the future. We will focus on how that has required its most senior leaders to change their behaviors, too.

Chapter 11 is about United Parcel Service, Inc. (UPS), a more than 100-year-old behemoth of operational excellence. The company's culture and employee-centric policies have driven continuous adaptation and relentless constant improvement over ten decades of existence. In this chapter we will explore how UPS has created that type of organization.

These three companies demonstrate that there are different ways to build a learning organization. While the foundational science and principles are the same, the implementation is more like a work of art sculpted by the leaders (artists) of the organization.

A Way to Learn

I expect that many of you believe you are good learners. This book may raise questions about that. As you read about our reflexive ways of thinking, the rigidity of our mental models, and the strength of our ego defense systems, I ask that you keep an open mind. I expect that the science of learning will challenge many of your beliefs about how to learn and how to enable learning in your organizations. At the end of each chapter you will find three reflection questions. A book on learning should follow learning best practices, and taking the time to reflect and record one's reflections when confronted with new ideas is a practice that has been shown to encourage learning.

As you read through the book, you will encounter several consistent themes. Two of those themes are (1) learning individually and organizationally is a change process that has to be facilitated emotionally and by the institutionalization of critical thinking and collaboration processes; and (2) the quantity and quality of learning is impacted greatly by the attitudes, beliefs, and behaviors of leaders and managers. My hope is that there is something here that will capture your attention and can help you learn more and be more.

Stay curious, my friends!

2

Learning: How Our Mind Works

Learning involves assessing relationships between stimuli and their effects.[1] If I eat this berry, will it nourish or poison me? More broadly, our learning is geared to systematically match causes to their effects. As we have more experience with stimuli or classes of stimuli, we learn probability—"if this, then likely that." In other words, I might learn that if I eat one berry, then I'll likely still be hungry, but if I eat a few handfuls of berries, I'll likely feel full. The relationships we assess between stimuli and effects become more contextually nuanced over time.

As our catalogs of stimuli and their effects grow, we develop stories that link them together so we don't have to remember them all individually. When it came to literal survival, for example, ancient man may have come up with this kind of story: When the sky gets dark, it usually rains; often when it rains, there is lightning; when there's lightning, often there is fire and destruction. In the context of today's business survival, we might string together the following story: when a cold front moves in, it usually rains; when it rains, business slows down, because people don't want to be out walking in bad weather.

When we gain confidence with our stories and categories, they become our reflexive, more automatic shorthand for interpreting the world. That is, they become our internal operating system, similar to the software operating systems hidden in our computers. Both systems are a web of invisible (unconscious) network linkages. Our brains' network linkages are mediated through neurons and operate electrically and chemically. Unlike a computer's software operating system, however, the human operating system functions in an environment that includes emotions and consciousness.

Our operating system runs automatically and unconsciously and shapes our perceptions, attention, cognitive processing, learning, emotions, and behaviors. The problem is that our operating system is not always right. Developed and shaped by our lifetimes of experience, our operating systems are more difficult to rewrite than a computer's operating system. Unlike a computer's software code, our operating systems are heavily protected by our existing beliefs and views of the world—called our "mental models," and our ego defense systems—the ways in which we deny or distort reality to protect ourselves from anxiety or our fears.

Because our human operating systems have successfully allowed us to navigate the world, including our jobs, it takes special effort to change them, which is exactly what is needed in order to learn. Understanding how people learn, as well as what environmental factors promote and inhibit learning, needs to be embedded in the design and operation of a learning organization.

Learning and Cognition

How people learn most effectively is a question that has been asked for millennia.[2] Historically, students engaged in mental inquiry with notable teachers, and several of the most enduring methods of facilitated learning are still in use today. From the ancient Chinese and Hebrews, for instance, came what is now known as the case method, in which a prototypical example is studied in detail. Many of today's business schools use this approach. From the Greeks came the Socratic dialogue; in this method, the instructor questions his students in an unending search for truth. The point is to get to the basis of the students' views by asking continual questions until a contradiction is exposed, thus proving the fallacy of the initial assumption.[3] Although the Socratic method is the bane of many a law student, it remains a central part of legal teaching. The Romans, as the classic text *The Adult Learner* puts it, "were more confrontational; they used challenges that forced group members to state positions and then defend them."[4] In some professional service firms today mentors utilize this teaching method with younger professionals.

The basics of learning by critical inquiry, critical debate, subjecting one's views to testing, and environmental feedback have stood the test of time. For many nonprofessional service firms, the use of training and development programs, rather than reliance on a wise mentor, is the answer to corporate learning. Many of these programs are designed to develop a long list of desired competencies. These programs vary in quality. The most effective are grounded in the science of learning. Fortunately, we now know more than ever before about the psychology and neuroscience of learning and can employ this in creating a learning organization.[5]

Our human learning mechanics or "machines" involve our sensory, nervous, and motor systems; our brains and minds; and the complicated network that links everything through electrical and chemical communications. Our learning machines have evolved to be efficient, which is not necessarily what is desired to promote the learning of new ideas or the fostering of innovation or constant improvement.

To operate the human learning machine takes a disproportionate amount of energy. Although the brain comprises only 2.5 percent of our body weight, it uses 20 percent of the body's energy.[6] As a result, the human learning machine prefers to operate in a low gear—on autopilot—as much as possible to conserve energy. Nobel laureate and author of the bestselling book *Thinking, Fast and Slow*, behavioral economist Daniel Kahneman stated: "Laziness is built deep into our nature."[7] Kahneman went on to explain the difference between our two ways of thinking: "System 1" is quick and automatic, with little or no effort or voluntary control, while "System 2" is slow, effortful, and associated with deliberate attention and concentration.[8] The terms "System 1" and "System 2" originally were advanced by psychologists Keith Stanovich and Richard West.[9] It is a useful, pragmatic way to differentiate reflexive, instinctual, auto-pilot type of thinking from more deliberate, intentional thinking. Like most dichotomies, it probably is not a true dichotomy, but rather a continuum.

Other terms that describe basically the same concepts as System 1 and System 2 thinking are Edward De Bono's "vertical" vs. "lateral" thinking, Chris Argyris' "single-loop" vs. "double-loop" thinking, and Shane Frederick's "intuitive" vs. "reflective" thinking. Another way of explaining it is that System 1 refers to our intuitive system, which is typically implicit and emotional, while System 2 is reasoning that is conscious, explicit, and logical.[10]

Our System 1 autopilot-like thinking relies on our existing views of the world—our mental models—and our learned emotional responses to stimuli and processing shortcuts, which are called "heuristics." Through feedback, we have learned a repertoire of what to do and what not to do in different situations. For example, in early childhood we learned that it is not appropriate to scream or yell in public, and as we got older, we developed a more nuanced understanding—do scream and yell at a football game, don't speak at all at a symphony. These mental models, stories or views are based on experience, assumptions, and inferences that may or may not be true. System 1 encompasses our quick "nonthinking" responses, impressions, feelings, and impulses.[11] We naturally seek to confirm and affirm. This automaticity makes learning hard.

Because our minds are fast, efficient seekers and processors of validating and confirming information, we tend to be confirmation-biased learners. Moreover, we have a strong, ego-defense system that defends and protects our existing views of ourselves. As another backup, if we do happen to process information that "disagrees" with our mental models, we are likely to rationalize that information to make it fit with what we already know—a phenomenon called "cognitive dissonance." That is our "humanness."

Taking our cognitive and emotional processing to a higher level is called System 2 thinking. System 2 occurs when, for example, we are weighing alternatives and trying to make a hard decision, or when something goes wrong and we are trying to figure out why. This type of thinking should occur when one is doing a root cause analysis of a problem or evaluating different strategic scenarios. This happens in business, for instance, when one is trying to truly understand customer needs or assess one's competitors. In order to learn as an adult, in many cases we have to sense, attend to, process, and make meaning from anomalies, contradictions, surprising results, and failures that don't fit with what we think we know—and this requires System 2 thinking. The difficulty is that it's very hard to perceive and process those differences because we have to overcome our reflexive System 1. To switch into System 2 takes mindfulness and the development of a heightened sensitivity to those different results, contradictions, and aberrations that may or may not be meaningful to us.

System 1 thinking clearly has its benefits, such as when we are engaged in doing simple repetitive tasks that we have done hundreds of times or when we can't explain it but we just intuitively feel that someone is lying. But how do we manage our thinking so that we don't block out disconfirming data or data that challenges our views when necessary? Our preference for System 1 thinking is strong. It's dominant for most people almost all the time. To overcome it takes hard work. It generally takes a team effort, because as Kahneman explained: "It is easier to recognize other people's mistakes [in thinking] than our own."[12] Overcoming our proclivity to use fast, confirmation-type System 1 thinking requires individuals to make transparent—to "unpack"—the assumptions and beliefs underlying their judgments, conclusions, opinions, and beliefs and subject them to testing against evidence or data.

It takes processes, tools, and checklists (some of which I discuss in chapters 6 and 7) and the help of other people who have the right motives, in an environment where critical debate, permission to speak freely, permission to admit mistakes, and permission to be vulnerable are the behavioral norms and not penalized. Abraham Maslow, one of the leading founders of the humanistic psychology movement, stated that an individual engages in learning "to the extent that he is not crippled by fear and to the extent he feels safe enough to dare."[13] I cover the topic of fear, a big learning inhibitor in a business environment, in more depth in chapters 4 and 5.

To overcome the weaknesses or limitations of individual System 1 thinking is one purpose of a learning organization. It takes the right people, in the right environment, using the right critical thinking processes and the right critical communication processes. I discuss each of these variables in chapters 4 through 7.

Learning Requires Overcoming Our "Humanness"

Learning involves a diverse set of operations, including perception of stimuli, attention, encoding, pattern matching or recognition, short and long-term memories, recall, training, feedback, practice, and managing emotions and ego. We develop efficient and effective learning skills through practice, practice, and more practice.[14] Learning well is not done carelessly. Learning skills are improved through intentional practice with contemporaneous feedback that focuses on improving specific weaknesses. We have to learn "how" to learn.

Many assume that what we encode in our memories is a recording of events. However, our perception of events is not perfect. We distort our memories of them with mistakes in our perceptions, biases, emotions, and the influence of others. Likewise, our memory recall is imperfect. Recalling a bit of information is not like taking down a book from the shelf. Instead, recall is a *reconstruction* process. We don't remember an event by replaying a film in our minds. Rather we recreate memory by combining bits and pieces together into what we "think" was the likely story.[15] That reconstruction process requires us to fill in the blanks, and we "guess" what happened based on our past experiences in those contexts.

Unlike the sense of wonder a child has in learning new things, learning for an adult with years of accumulated experience, biases, and emotional filters is often narrowed. This is particularly the case when new information challenges our mental models. Learning is the process of modifying or completely changing our mental models based on new experiences or evidence. In essence, learning is the "making of meaning" of new or contradictory evidence and incorporating it into our mental models. That means we have to deliberately focus on the data, bring our existing knowledge out of long-term memory into working memory, and be able to reflect on the data and incorporate it into our mental models. That is hard. To do it we need to be open-minded and not allow our biases or ego defenses to inhibit this process.

Mental models and System 1 thinking can be efficient in that they help us function in information overload environments, but they are counterproductive in situations in which we confront new information that is different from what we believe. As Jack Mezirow puts it, "We have a strong tendency to reject ideas that fail to fit our preconceptions."[16] To change our mental models requires critical reflection and evaluation of the assumptions that underlie our mental models.[17] Mezirow calls this "transformative learning"—"becoming critically aware of one's own tacit [unconscious] assumptions . . . and assessing their relevance for making an interpretation."[18] I revisit this process in more detail in chapter 7. Learning requires us to make meaning of new information or information that conflicts with what we believe. To do that effectively requires us to be open-minded and to uncouple our ego from our beliefs.

We also are highly selective in the stimuli we process. People with different histories of experiences likely attend to and process a different subset of stimuli arising from the same new data. Each of us focuses on what seems particularly relevant in the data and can be effectively blind to the rest.[19] Two employees working for the same company may be exposed to the same new data, but unless there are rigid organizational mental models in play, each will process information in ways that confirm his own existing knowledge. Having a diverse group can be a learning enabler by helping identify cognitive blind spots.

Cognitive blindness to different interpretations of the information is one reason change is so hard for people, and it's why, absent a life or death situation, organizational change or transformation is so difficult. It's why smart people make bad decisions, and it's why companies miss competitive shifts or new trends.

Good System 2 thinking is necessary to learn and to make good decisions. We have already learned that we are defective thinkers and, in many cases, resist learning if learning requires us to change our views of the world or our view of ourselves. Well, it gets even more complex. Much of this book focuses on factual learning. Learning skills or how to do something is also an important type of learning. Skill learning takes deliberate learning, and it takes lots of practice. For example, learning how to think using critical thinking processes is a skill that I discuss in chapter 7.

Even when we take our thinking to a higher level, we still unconsciously take thinking shortcuts—heuristics—that can diminish the quality of our thinking. In addition, "cognitive biases" affect our thinking.[20] We tend to be impulsive and make insufficient investments in deep processing. We tend not to consider alternatives, and we tend to think narrowly and fail to challenge assumptions or examine other points of view. We can also be careless and imprecise and think in a disorganized fashion.[21]

It is beyond the scope of this book to tackle cognitive biases in depth, but two outstanding and accessible short books for business managers and leaders in this area are Bazerman and Moore's *Judgment in Managerial Decision Making* (Wiley, 2009) and Mauboussin's, *Think Twice: Harnessing the Power of Counterintuition* (Harvard Business Press, 2009). However, there are a few common types of cognitive biases that are important to keep in mind.

We already discussed "confirmation bias" in the context of System 1 thinking—a predisposition to seek confirmation of what we believe or what we want to exist. Even when we're being deliberate and use System 2 reasoning, this bias often leads us to make decisions that are in line with what we've done before. We tend to latch on to the first decision option that feels right without deeply exploring alternatives. Because thinking more fully and deliberately is hard, we tend to quit thinking too soon.

"Availability bias" has us reaching for the easiest option. We tend to use information that is the most readily available or easy to recall, especially if particularly strong emotions were involved in sensing and processing that information.

The "self-interest bias" influences us to make decisions that advance our personal interests in situations where the data may dictate a different rational decision.

"Anchoring biases" tend to "chain" us to a particular item and prevent us from fully exploring other options. Once we have focused on a key data point, it's hard for us to move far away from that anchor.

On top of the operation of this stew of biases is our "superiority illusion." Of course the decision is a good one—I made it! We become emotionally invested in our decision, defending and protecting it.

Managing How We Think: Metacognition

As the preceding discussion demonstrates, it is extremely hard for us to ward off the automaticity of System 1 thinking and to mitigate our biases when engaging in System 2 thinking. The process of managing how we think is called metacognition, and focusing on this can help us understand how we think and teach us what strategies work best in various circumstances.[22] Sometimes when we make an automatic System 1 type decision, it just doesn't feel right. That may be an emotional cue telling us we need to take this decision up to System 2's higher, more intentional level of thinking. Metacognition skills allow us to recognize those situations that require us to switch from System 1 to System 2 thinking in order to apply critical inquiry and thinking processes. Metacognition is a crucial learning skill. Being aware of and managing how we think is critical to learning. Therefore, a key question is this: How do we learn when to take control of our thinking and pause our automatic thinking and move our thinking to a System 2 level?

We can better control our thinking using a few key strategies:

- Learning what types of decisions require intentional reflection or critical debate;
- Being sensitive to emotional cues; and
- Engaging in real critical inquiry or debate with colleagues to stress test our thinking.[23]

As each of these strategies emphasizes, you have to be aware of what types of situations or decisions have important enough consequences that you need to think more slowly and deeply. To do this you need to deliberately think about how you think. Each day, you could "mentally rehearse" the upcoming day by thinking about what instances, meetings, occurrences, or events may need System 2 thinking. Each night, you could take fifteen minutes and "mentally replay" the day, evaluating what occurrences probably needed System 2 thinking. You could create an ongoing checklist of the types of issues, problems, or situations that likely require System 2 thinking.

This is one good way to personally improve your learning. But for many of you reading this book, it is not just about "you." Your thinking could affect hundreds or thousands or even hundreds of thousands of employees and their families. Bringing your best thinking to bear at the right times is very important. The ability to constantly stress test the critical assumptions that underlie your mental models about your business's strategy, operating model, differentiating customer value proposition, and competitive space is critical.

Years ago, I suggested that every public company needed an "Executive Vice President of Dissent" whose sole job was to continuously stress test underlying assumptions and to perceive and attend to data that served as early warning signals of potential challenges to the business model, strategy, and competitiveness. I was trying to institutionalize a process to mitigate our humanness.

Other Saboteurs of Learning: Ego and Fear

As one moves up the promotion chain to senior management, one's self-confidence tends to increase as well as one's self-image, which can lead to intellectual and/or personal arrogance. Often, one's views about business become more entrenched as promotions validate one's knowledge base. Sometimes validated expertise in one technical area wrongly leads people to assume they are experts in other areas. If a senior manager views life as a competition that he is winning, then he has a self-interest in continuing to enforce his views rather than in open-mindedly listening to other perspectives. That inhibits personal and organizational learning.

Our ego—the view we have of ourselves—can be a major barrier to our learning. In many cases, learning comes from mistakes or failures or other people disagreeing with us, which means that in order to learn, we often have to admit that we were wrong. This is hard for many people because doing so "makes them look bad" or "makes them look stupid" or subjects them to potential "harm"—bad grades, bad performance reviews, no bonus, job loss, loss of colleagues' respect, and so on. Overcoming the strength of our ego-defense systems requires deliberateness, mindfulness, and management of our feelings and emotions. Fear is a huge inhibitor of learning. Fear of failure, fear of looking bad, fear of embarrassment, fear of a loss of status, fear of not being liked, and fear of losing one's job all inhibit learning. To grow, we have to acknowledge that none of us is as smart as we think we are. As Ray Dalio, founder of the largest hedge fund in the world, has been known to say: "We all are dumb shits."

Confronting the power of fear in inhibiting learning is a prime focus of the learner-centric learning theory that grew out of the humanistic psychology movement. This movement occurred over sixty years ago as a countermodel to Skinner's behavioral stimulus-response model and Freud's psychoanalytic theories. Carl Rogers and Abraham Maslow were two of the movement's leaders. According to Rogers, the only things we learn significantly are those things that we perceive as being involved in the maintenance or enhancement of ourselves. The educational situation that most effectively promotes this kind of significant learning is one in which "(a) threat to the self of the learner is reduced to a minimum and (b) differentiated perception of the field is facilitated."[24] In other words, we learn best when we are not fearful and when we trust that our "teachers" truly care about us as individuals and want to help us individually make meaning of new information by relating it to our past experiences and knowledge.

These ideas underlie the field of perceptual psychology that was formally advanced in the early 1960s by Arthur W. Combs, who studied under Carl Rogers.[25] Combs stated: "We know that when people feel threatened (a) their perceptions become narrowed to the threatening events and (b) they are forced to the defense of their existing perceptual organizations."[26] He also said that a greater openness to experience offers many advantages, including more data, and with more data, one is more likely to be right, make better decisions, and better tolerate ambiguity.[27]

Chris Argyris, a renowned Harvard professor and authority on learning, explored similar ideas in his article "Teaching Smart People How to Learn." In it he focused on our propensities for self-defensiveness by explaining the universal human tendency to design our actions according to four basic values:

1. To remain in unilateral control;
2. To maximize "winning" and minimize "losing";
3. To suppress negative feelings; and
4. To be as "rational" as possible by defining clear objectives and evaluating our behavior in terms of whether or not we have achieved them.[28]

Argyris went on to explain that the purpose of all these values is to avoid embarrassment, vulnerability, or feelings of incompetence—feelings that put us as individuals in postures of "defensive reasoning" in which we tend to hide the assumptions underlying our behavior and avoid objectively testing those assumptions. All of this, says Argyris "inevitably short-circuits learning."[29] Maslow, Rogers, Combs, and Argyris teach us that learning occurs best when we are not fearful and when we are not defensive. Only then can we be open to new information and undergo the transformative process of learning described earlier by Mezirow.

As we become better learners and more open to testing our views of the world and of ourselves, our stories and mental models become more complex and nuanced and we are able to sense and recognize more complex patterns. We are able to move up the knowledge ladder. As Edward de Bono writes in his book *Lateral Thinking: Creativity Step by Step*, "[The] self-organizing, self-maximizing memory system is very good at creating patterns and that is the effectiveness of the mind."[30] As we move up the knowledge ladder we may have the opportunity to reach expertise.

K. Anders Ericsson, who was a young psychology professor in the cognitive psychology department where I studied decades ago, is a world expert in how experts learn. His research showed that the difference between expert performance and very good or good performance is not innate ability, IQ, or genetic differences.[31] The difference is lots of practice—a special kind of practice. Deliberate, focused practice was the difference in those who became experts in Ericsson's studies. Ericsson found that becoming an expert required an average of 10,000 hours of focused practice. Think about that for a moment: To be an expert thinker or an expert leader takes *10,000 hours of deliberate, focused practice*. Ericsson's work built on and provided more specificity to the earlier research by his mentor Nobel laureate Herbert Simon, who, together with William G. Chase, found that becoming an expert took about ten years.[32]

What constitutes deliberate practice? It's a focused, designed, and repeated practice with a teacher or coach that involves working on one specific aspect of performance relentlessly with contemporaneous feedback and repetition.[33] How does deliberate practice apply in the world of business? Its emphasis on working on very specific weaknesses with a coach or mentor is directly applicable to manager and leader development. When you get to chapter 10 and the Intuit case, you will see how Intuit's founder Scott Cook and CEO Brad Smith talk about their continued work with mentors and coaches, openly admitting that they have areas to improve.

Also, in chapter 9, you will notice how Bridgewater has institutionalized the diagnosis and transparency of personal weaknesses.

Deliberate practice techniques can be used in other organizational environments, too. For example, the U.S. Army used deliberate practice techniques to design its "Think Like a Commander" adaptive thinking training that we'll discuss in later chapters. [34]

My Story: Learning to Think

Thinking about your own learning story is a good way to move into the content that follows, and it will help you understand how to apply the information this book has to offer in your own life and company. Because we can't talk face to face, I will begin. I hope you will reciprocate by thinking deeply about your learning story to date.

I am fortunate in that I had over twenty-one years of education that included two advanced graduate degrees. You might assume that, given all this schooling, I understood a little about the most effective ways of learning during my college and postgraduate education. Not so.

During my time in school and in my first twenty years of work experience, I became an "expert" at speedy thinking, because I was right enough of the time to prosper. I thought the speed of my thinking was a competitive advantage, so I became a turbo-charged fast thinker and never slowed down to drill down, question, or critique issues. I just went with my very quick flow—believing erroneously that I was a good thinker.

I might have been exposed to some of the concepts described in this chapter, but I did not internalize them until I hit my mid-forties and "hit a wall." It took two big setbacks (my first significant failures in life)—occurring in the same week—to shake my self-confidence (or arrogance) enough to make me realize that I didn't have as much figured out as I'd thought. Those setbacks encouraged me to think deeply, over time and with a coach, about certain assumptions that were foundational to my mental models. It was not easy. I had to admit that I was not as "good" a thinker—or even a person—as I'd thought. I was still the kid who sat in the front row of my elementary school classes and raised his hand the fastest every time, wanting to show everyone how smart he was by earning the teacher's praise. I had to change. I had to become more humble, more open-minded, a better listener, more emotionally intelligent, and a real (not a pseudo) critical thinker. Yes, I had a lot of work to do. The process was humbling but needed.

As a result, I began to work on being a better thinker. I learned to really listen. I learned to suspend my judgments and my rapid formation of answers in order to be in the moment, sensing people's emotional cues, and focusing on what was and was not being said. I learned to stop interrupting people so much by counting to ten after a person stopped speaking and before I spoke. I became more direct at dealing with people issues. I learned that it was not all about me. I started mentally rehearsing upcoming key meetings and mentally replaying them after to learn what I could have done better. I learned the power of apologizing to employees when I had inadvertently hurt someone's feelings. As a leader, I learned the power of saying: "Please; Thank you; I was wrong; I don't know; I am sorry; and How may I help you?"

Over time I changed. And what happened? My teams performed at even higher rates of excellence, making the firms I worked for more successful. By becoming more authentic and less dominating, I unleashed organizational loyalty and productivity that made the last ten years of my corporate life much more rewarding financially and, just as important, emotionally rich and meaningful. I became a better thinker, leader, and learner.

That last sentence is important. I became a better thinker by becoming a better learner. To become a better learner, I had to quiet my ego. That had a big impact on my leadership style and effectiveness.

Some years later, I continued my study of cognitive psychology for a possible book on cognitive strategy. I was convinced that our cognitive limitations often lead to ineffective strategy making. That period of study reignited my passion in continuing to learn to become a really good thinker. No, I have to be honest—to try to become a *great* thinker. My next big step occurred after a health scare. It propelled me to become even more mindful, empathetic, and positive emotionally.

What is your learning story? Do you think about how you think? Do you think about your learning processes? Do you really think enough?

Reflection Questions

1. What did you read in this chapter that surprised you?
2. What are your top three takeaways that you want to reflect and/ or act on?
3. What behaviors do you want to change?

3

Emotions: The Myth of Rationality

Have you ever heard someone say: "Don't be so emotional—just be logical"?[1] Have you ever been in a business meeting when someone said: "Let's leave emotions out of this discussion"? Those statements assume that there is a dichotomy between logic and emotions. That dichotomy is false. Cognition and emotions are inextricably intertwined in our mind and behaviors; the two appear to be dynamic, interactive, and interdependent.[2]

Research has shown that emotion and cognition jointly contribute to the control of mental activities and behavior.[3] The areas of the brain that primarily process and regulate emotions are networked with the parts of the brain that primarily are associated with cognitive functions. These parts not only communicate with each other but in some cases overlap. Emotions are a potential moderator of all kinds of "thinking" processes—from perception and attention to implicit learning and implicit associations.[4] Thus, when it comes to making decisions, we should be considering the interaction of our cognition and our emotions, rather than expecting to use only the former and completely ignoring the latter.[5] Let me put it this way:

Can you be totally logical or rational? No.
Can emotions ever help you make good decisions? Yes.
Can emotions ever lead you to make bad decisions? Yes.

According to leading neuroscientists Mary Helen Immordino-Yang and Antonio Damasio, the interaction of emotions and rational thought processes gives emotions a potent modifying role in how we see the world, learn, and make decisions. They call this interaction "emotional thought."[6] Moreover, they say that neurobiological research has shown that certain aspects of cognition, such as learning, attention, memory, decision making, and social functioning, are "both profoundly affected by emotion and in fact subsumed within the processes of emotion."[7]

So, if cognition and emotion are inherently integrated, is it possible to leave emotions out of the discussion? Of course not.

What does this mean? It means that our emotions play a role in both our reflexive System 1 thinking and our more deliberate System 2 thinking.[8] For example, emotions created by a particular experience or task influence what we will recall from memory later, and thus influence our reflexive, autopilot-like System 1 thinking. Emotions, in effect, can code the relevance of certain events to us and likewise can impact the likelihood of recalling those events. Moreover, the mood we are in and our attitudes toward the tasks at hand, as well as the moods and emotions of others, can influence both System 1 and System 2 thinking.

That is why it's unrealistic to believe that we can keep emotions out of our thinking and decision making altogether. What we should instead focus on, and what I'll explore further in this chapter, is how and when we need to mitigate the negative effects that emotions can have on our thinking, collaborating, and learning. Many times, our emotions serve as early warning signs that something is wrong or that we're entering an area that could be risky. At other times, our emotions can overtake our thinking and hinder our deeper analysis of the issues. Emotions also can mask underlying beliefs and assumptions that are the root cause of our decisions and behaviors. Have you ever experienced a "gut feeling" that the decision you were about to make was not the right one? What underlies that feeling is an emotional response—and a better understanding of that response will allow you to determine whether you should "go with your gut." In chapter 8, the well-respected researcher and author Dr. Gary Klein recounts his personal story about "going with your gut feeling."

There is a mind-brain-body connection at play as well. Bodily sensations can trigger emotions that impact cognitive processing, and thoughts can trigger emotions that impact the body.[9] For example, lack of sleep or hunger or even an uncomfortable chair can affect the ability to work or learn. Likewise, chronic stress or anger can both impair clear thinking and have short- and long-term effects on health. And the flip side of this is the physiological impact of emotions, which gets "broadcast" throughout the brain by a cascade of hormones and chemical neurotransmitters that in turn affect the body. Our heart rates may go up, we may perspire or feel queasy, our breathing rate might increase—all of which signals an emotional response.

Rather than rejecting the role of emotions in our so-called disembodied, rational processes, we must acknowledge and manage them to have better outcomes. We have to accept the science. Even if we think we're very rational people and are not outwardly emotional, our emotions still impact our thinking, communications, and behaviors, as well as our approaches to problems, new situations, and decisions. Much of the effect goes on automatically and subconsciously. Our challenge is to be more aware of our emotional states and proactively manage their effects on our thinking and learning—to increase their positive effects and decrease their negative effects as best we can.

Controlling and Comprehending Emotion

Just as System 2 requires us to be aware of and intentionally slow down our thinking, in many cases we need to slow down our emotions. We have to take control of our emotions physiologically and mentally, so that we can prevent emotions from hijacking our thinking and behaving. Taking deep breaths or taking a walk to reduce the physiological stress can "tame" emotions. Although we can't completely "turn off" our emotions, we can deliberately try to think rationally about the situation, causing the emotional reaction to "turn on" cognitive areas of the brain that can "tamp down" emotions. We can control our reactions to emotions that we sense.[10] In many cases this could help us make better decisions and be more open-minded. Another way to become more attentive and attuned to our body's messages and feelings is to practice "mindfulness," a topic I discuss in more detail in chapter 6.

In addition to being aware of our emotional reactions, it is important to understand what they are telling us in a particular situation. At a very basic level, emotions provide instinctual, "good vs. bad" or "approach vs. avoidance" information.[11] Emotions also convey more nuanced categories of information—that of "valence" and "arousal."[12] Arousal gives us information with respect to the exciting-calm spectrum, and tells us how fast we need to act or the importance of the stimuli.[13] For example, an unsavory looking character approaching us in a dark, deserted area likely would elicit high arousal. In a business context, a performance review or a real-time critique by a difficult or unfriendly manager can elicit highly negative emotional arousal that impacts one's listening, processing, and interpretation of what is being said.

Valence refers to whether the stimuli creating the emotional response are pleasant or unpleasant and conveys information about "value." For example, we would have a different emotional response to a loved one approaching us than a hostile boss. One situation creates positive emotions and the other, negative.

This is important because positive emotions generally enhance our cognitive processes, while negative emotions tend to restrict and narrow our cognitive processes.[14] Another way to state this is that positive emotions generally enable higher-level, System 2 thinking, while negative emotions generally inhibit higher-level thinking in favor of a more reflexive, System 1 response.

The Power of Positive Emotions

The evidence is quite strong that positive emotions enhance and enable cognitive processing, thinking, and learning. The next chapter presents evidence that positive work environments also generally enhance learning because they enable positive emotions.

In the past twenty years, the field of positive psychology has blossomed, coinciding with the rise of cognitive, social, and affective neuroscience. The positive psychology movement has led to extensive study of psychological well-being, resiliency, the relationship between psychological well-being and health, positive deviance, and a focus on positive organizations.[15] Professor Barbara L. Fredrickson's research on positive emotions is foundational to the positive psychology movement, and a better understanding of her work can help in understanding the power of positive emotions in our professional lives.

Decades of research had already provided support for the notion that negative emotions served an evolutionarily adaptive purpose because they caused us to behave in very specific, anxiety-fueled, self-protective ways that were necessary for our survival—for example, flight or fight.[16] Fredrickson's research and her "broaden-and-build" theory posits that over the long term (millennia), positive emotions also were evolutionarily adaptive because they helped build our survival resources by increasing our awareness, which in turn facilitated exploration, a broader scope of attention, and an increased breadth of behavioral responses, intuition, and creativity.[17] Positive emotions are associated with openness to new ideas, better problem solving, openness to disconfirming information, less rigid thinking, better recall of neutral or positive stimuli, and mitigation of ego defenses.

Alice M. Isen was another prolific researcher of the impact of positive emotions on cognition, motivation, and even workplace interactions.[18] Isen found evidence that positive emotions (and positive emotional environments) generally enhance or expand our cognitive processing and decision making, because they improve our ability to evaluate ambiguous and neutral data and disconfirming information; relate new information to existing knowledge; see alternative interpretations or explanations of data; and reduce conflict in face-to-face negotiations.[19] She also found that people who feel positive going into a situation are likely to be more thorough in using decision processes and less likely to take huge risks. All of the foregoing benefits of positive emotions are crucial to supporting a learning organization.

Another important finding from the research on positivity is that with training, individuals can increase the quantity of positive emotions they experience daily and decrease the quantity of negative emotions.[20] Because positive emotions enable learning better than negative emotions, this is important for any organization. What are some of the ways in which individuals can increase their levels of positivity? According to research, expressing gratitude every day to at least three people, smiling more, keeping a daily journal in which you record positive emotional events, and taking time to think about the good things in your life each day have been shown to increase positive emotions.[21]

The strength and applicability of positive psychology is evidenced by a major initiative of the U.S. Army called the Comprehensive Soldier Fitness (CSF) initiative.[22] CSF's goal is to train more than 1,000,000 soldiers to increase psychological strength and positive performance. As part of CSF, the Army enlisted the founder of the positive psychology movement, Professor Martin E.P. Seligman. Drs. Barbara Fredrickson and Sara B. Algoe are leading one of the working groups and designing a program to train soldiers to be emotionally resilient. Based on scientific evidence that increasing people's levels of positive emotions increases their likeliness to be resilient, the training includes learning about emotions and their effects on the body and mind; learning how to manage emotions; reducing the frequency of negative emotions; and increasing the frequency of positive emotions. Although the CSF project is in its infancy, it is important to acknowledge it because the CSF represents a significant commitment by a major organization that for decades has been on the forefront of both funding and applying cognitive psychology learning research.

In contrast to the positive effects of positive emotions, negative emotions tend to have a detrimental effect on cognitive processing, decision making, and learning. They force us to narrow our focus in order to allocate more of our cognitive resources to deal with perceived threats—whether physical or emotional. In environments where bodily harm to oneself or to others is a risk, such narrowed focus is good and protective. In most organizational environments, however, this narrowed focus is inappropriate and can adversely affect learning. This is especially the case when it comes to emotional threats, which are an attack on our ego and activate the ego-defense system.

In organizational environments, persistent negative emotions, such as anxiety or fear, are toxic to learning. Fear and anxiety impair comprehension, creativity, and retrieval from long-term memory.[23] They cause people to interpret neutral or ambiguous information more negatively because they sense more risk—whether real or perceived.[24] Research on anxiety and decision making shows that anxiety generally increases the probability we assign to potential negative outcomes, our aversion to risk in general, and our tendency to recall negative events from memory.[25]

For example, if we are anxious about a new work challenge or because we've been asked to change how we perform our jobs, we have a tendency to fear the worst by disproportionately recalling only negative experiences involving similar situations from our past. We might try to avoid what we perceive (often unreasonably) to be a risky situation. In that case, we'll be less likely to float innovative ideas because of our tendency to hunker down, avoid risk, and just survive.

Professor Gregory S. Berns calls fear the "mother of all stresses."[26] This is because fear activates our stress-response system maximally and "can override every other system in the brain. The stress system is not rational."[27] The limbic system in our brain is a major part of our stress-response system. In appropriate fear situations—a train is coming!—the triggering of the limbic system and the subsequent stress response increases our chances of survival. We don't need to think rationally about getting out of the way of an oncoming train—an automatic System 1 response works. The downside of the stress-response system, however, is that an inappropriate or over-blown fear can cause the limbic system to overtake or hijack our thinking and every cognitive process, resulting in very poor decision making and diminished cognitive processing.

Underlying most of our learning inhibitions or inadequacies is fear of something. Fear often is what underlies our inability to change behaviors that we want or need to change. What are we afraid of? We're afraid that our colleagues will find our ideas weak or even stupid. We're afraid that we'll lose our jobs. We're afraid that we'll fail. We're afraid that we won't be liked. We're afraid that we'll look bad or be embarrassed.

Unfortunately, it is challenging to overcome a fear response. We can't mentally run or hide from fear. We often acutely remember past fearful events, and the fear response that accompanied them, for a very long time. They are etched into our brains. Those memories prime us to have fear responses almost instantaneously when faced with similar circumstances. Such responses are not precise and may be triggered even if the actual stimulus is not ordinarily something to be feared.

If we cannot completely eliminate anxiety or fear responses, then the question becomes: How do we manage or mitigate the subsequent inappropriate cognitive and physiological reactions? There are at least two techniques to diffuse a fearful or anxious response: (1) reframing the situation to something less fearful and/or (2) logically reducing the magnitude of a situation's perceived, potential, harmful effects.[28]

To reframe a fear response is to recast a fearful situation into a nonfearful one. This takes some work, but it can be done by thinking about other plausible interpretations of the fearful situation. For example, you might say to yourself, "Yes, I'm afraid to give this speech to the district managers, but this is a great learning opportunity."

To logically reduce the magnitude of a fearful situation is to downplay the downside or probability of negative outcomes,[29] as in saying to yourself: "OK, I might look stupid, but we're all just brainstorming and every idea can't be a gem. Others might be in the same boat." I talk more about how to illuminate and mitigate emotional inhibitions to learning in chapter 5.

Understanding and Managing Our Emotions

Emotions are central to how we perceive and interact with the world. They are intertwined with sensing, perception, encoding experiences in memory, memory retrieval, thinking, making decisions, creativity, considering alternatives, motivation, demeanor, life outlook, our body sensations, and our physiological responses. Certain kinds of emotions—fear, anxiety and stress—can override our cognitive systems. Critical to understanding the power of emotions is understanding that they are malleable, and that we can take steps to avoid these types of overriding emotions. We have some control of how we interpret our emotions and how we manage their impact. The challenge is to learn how to manage our emotions so that they can work in our favor and not to our detriment.

Managing emotions is one aspect of emotional intelligence (EI). Emotional intelligence, generally understood, is the ability to be aware of and manage one's emotions. It is analogous to metacognition—one's ability to be aware of and to better manage how one thinks. Over the years the concept of EI has led to the development of a four-branch model:[30]

1. Perceiving Emotions—the ability to recognize and appraise verbal and nonverbal information.
2. Using Emotions—the ability to access and/or generate emotions that facilitate cognitive processes such as creativity and problem solving.
3. Understanding Emotions—the ability to cognitively process and gain knowledge of the feelings of self and others.
4. Managing Emotions—the ability to regulate emotions in oneself and others.[31]

Each of these four branches contains several underlying competencies for a total of seventeen abilities. EI is like one's IQ in that it is not fixed and can be improved. Many school systems today teach EI competencies. In the business world, however, anecdotal evidence suggests that EI is discussed more than it is operationalized. I won't go into all seventeen EI abilities here, but if you want to be a better learner or be part of a better learning organization, I suggest you dig into all the abilities and the work of Peter Salovey, John Mayer, and David Caruso, including the Mayer-Salovey-Caruso Emotional Intelligence Test (MSCEIT). A learning organization should prioritize these seventeen abilities and seek to teach and role model them.

One of the EI abilities I find particularly interesting in the four-part model is the ability "to generate emotions to facilitate judgment and memory," which falls under the "Using Emotions" branch. I take it to mean that we can actively bring to consciousness positive emotions or memories to change our emotional state for the purpose of getting into a better frame of mind to make decisions. Asking a team: "Are we ready to start?" is too vague. It is better to ask if everyone is in a good frame of mind and feeling good, or to start each meeting with a positive story.

Neuroscientist Richard J. Davidson has another model that addresses the role of emotions in an organizational environment. It is based on determining a person's unique "emotional style" and comprises six dimensions:

1. Resilience: how slowly or quickly you recover from adversity.
2. Outlook: how long you are able to sustain positive emotions.
3. Social Intuition: how adept you are at picking up social signals from others.
4. Self-Awareness: how well you perceive body feelings that reflect emotions.
5. Sensitivity to Context: how well you regulate your emotional responses to take into account the context in which you find yourself.
6. Attention: how sharp and clear your focus is.[32]

Davidson's model uses a diagnostic tool that can place us on a continuum along these six dimensions. This model can help us understand our emotional proclivities, leading to better EI and better management of our emotions. This diagnostic, along with the MSCEIT and Carol Dweck's Growth Mindset diagnostic (discussed in the next chapter), are all interesting approaches for anyone looking to hire the kind of people suited to populate a best-of-class learning organization.

Conclusion

As it turns out, we all are rational and emotional (or emotional and rational) thinkers and learners. So what does that mean for our purposes? It means that the processes of individual learning and the processes necessary to become a learning organization are much more complicated than just learning to think better and to make better decisions. People are emotional. Organizations are emotional environments.

How we behave and communicate with other people directly impacts those people—their willingness to learn and the effectiveness of their learning. If we behave in a teaching moment with another employee in a way that creates negative emotions, that person's ability to learn is in most cases diminished. If other employees witness that bad behavior, their ability to learn also will be negatively impacted. Emotions can be triggered by consciously or unconsciously attending to stimuli that we perceive or that we expected but did not perceive. Those stimuli can be perceived by any of the senses. For example, a manager's body language; failure to acknowledge; failure to make eye contact; multi-tasking; tendency to interrupt; negative attitude, words, tone or facial expressions; loudness; rudeness; meanness; insensitivity; or incivility could trigger emotions among employees that inhibit learning and create avoidance tendencies. Cultures of fear, or environments where any mistake is punished, usually inhibit learning.

We know that positive emotions and a positive emotional environment generally promote better thinking and learning. If you are a manager or leader of an organization, you have to be concerned with your emotional state because it impacts your learning. And you have to be concerned about your emotional state and your behaviors because they impact other people's learning. This chapter's message can be summarized with the following pithy statement: *Positivity is a powerful, enabling force in learning.*

The chapter's other message is that in order to maximize our learning we have to be sensitive to and manage our emotions. Just like System 2 thinking requires intentional hard work, being sensitive to and managing our emotions to prevent them from inhibiting or suboptimizing learning takes deliberateness. As Ray Dalio says, "Don't let your emotions hijack your thinking."

Reflection Questions

1. What did you read in this chapter that surprised you?
2. What are your top three takeaways that you want to reflect and/or act on?
3. What behaviors do you want to change?

4

Learning: The Right People

Building a learning organization is a lot like building a house.[1] A house needs a supporting foundation, electrical and plumbing systems, a roof, and an insulated structure. These components must be integrated and aligned to work together to produce the desired results. The same applies to the components necessary for building a learning organization. In chapter 1, I introduced the concept of a High-Performance Learning Organization (HPLO) the formula for which has three key components— the Right People, the Right Environment, and the Right Processes that enable and promote learning. Each of the next three chapters focuses on one of these key components. This chapter focuses on the first component: people.

A learning organization needs employees who have the right motivation for and approach to learning—a learning mindset. Effective learning organizations hire and develop people who like to learn and who proactively seek to learn. Fostering learning by employees requires managers and leaders who are not only good learners themselves, but also are good learning facilitators (teachers) and role models. There has been significant research done over the last few decades on the characteristics of good learners; this chapter explores some of this research and presents some of the science behind an individual's inclination and motivation to learn.

Learning Mindsets

Psychologists have spent decades researching how different approaches to motivation, goal seeking, and achievement among individuals affect learning; my concept of a "learning mindset" comes from this research. There are three areas of research that are relevant for our purposes—the first focuses on a human being's basic motivational needs; the second on individuals' beliefs about how they will perform in learning or challenging situations; and the third on how individuals set their goals and define achievement.

The first area of research concerns a human being's basic need to survive and have a meaningful life. As Freud explained,[2] we seek or approach pleasure or positive experiences and avoid painful or negative experiences. This is a foundational concept in psychology. From our own experiences and from the experiences of others, we learn what produces positive and negative results. Using inputs from our sensory, cognitive, and emotional systems, we "approach" those positive things and "avoid" or run from negative things. "Approach or avoid" applies to learning, facing new challenges, and handling situations characterized by ambiguity or uncertainty.

If we have had positive or negative experiences with learning in childhood or in the context of work, it will impact our inclination to learn going forward. For example, imagine that your manager encourages you to try doing a task in a new way. You try for the first time and it does not work out well, leading your manager to ridicule you in front of colleagues. That feedback makes it unlikely that you will look favorably on trying new ways of doing things at work in the future; you will seek to avoid new approaches because of your prior negative experience.

At the time they are hired, employees will have ingrained beliefs about learning and about being taken out of their comfort zones. Those beliefs have come from their prior experiences, both positive and negative—in school, work, and other life situations. Understanding how these experiences have shaped learning beliefs is one of the purposes of behavioral interviews in hiring.

Although this foundational "pain versus pleasure" understanding of learning can be helpful, recent research streams have moved beyond looking simply at approach and avoidance and have delved into the question of what, beyond pleasure and pain, motivates our behavior. There is a rich set of theories regarding motivation.[3] Particularly important in defining a learning mindset is Edward L. Deci and Richard M. Ryan's "self-determination" theory.[4] Their theory posits that we human beings have the innate psychological need for (1) autonomy—some choice and control over our actions; (2) effectiveness—a feeling of competence and sense of accomplishment; and (3) relatedness—a sense of mutual respect and reliance with others.[5]

For example, if an employee is asked to change a current process, it is likely that she will perform better if she has input into how and when the change happens. Moreover, she'll likely be more motivated if the change is within her capabilities and if she's been given the tools to make the change. Having input meets one's needs for autonomy. Feeling that one has the ability and has been given the necessary tools to perform meets the need of effectiveness. All of this will enhance learning and make the transition to a new process more effective.

Likewise, if the learning experience produces a sense of relatedness or affiliation with a community, it generally will be viewed as more positive, thus increasing the likelihood that additional learning will be pursued. In the work environment, relatedness needs are met by being part of a great team and/or working for an organization where the employee feels respected and whose mission the employee respects. Using the above example, if the employee understands the purpose of the change and how it contributes to the overall mission of the business, the need for affiliation is also more likely to be met.

Related to the notion of effectiveness described under Deci and Ryan's theory of self-determination is Albert Bandura's theory of "self-efficacy." According to Bandura, a professor at Stanford University and one of the most renowned psychologists in the world, self-efficacy is our belief in whether we can or cannot do something. Most simply, if we believe we can, we are more likely to try. The strength of this belief is determinative of our learning optimization and how we approach new or challenging situations. It influences our perceptions, cognitive processing, goals, and vulnerability to stress.[6]

If we have a strong sense of efficacy we will tend to:

- approach difficult tasks and view them as challenges rather than threats;
- be persistent and sustain strong commitments to our goals;
- attribute failures to insufficient effort or bad learning strategies;
- work even harder in the face of difficulties; and
- rebound quickly after failures or mistakes.[7]

By contrast, if we have a low sense of efficacy in a given context we generally will:

- avoid difficult tasks that are perceived as personal threats;
- have low aspirations and weak commitments to the goals we choose;
- dwell on personal deficiencies, obstacles and potential adverse outcomes;
- attribute failures to personal deficits;
- give up quickly in the face of difficulties; and
- have difficulty rebounding from mistakes or failures.[8]

We build confidence in our efficacy by being put into challenging situations that we have the potential to handle well—those in which we have the requisite capabilities and tools. As our confidence grows, we are more willing to take on even more challenging tasks.

Efficacy beliefs, Bandura says, also influence how we view threats. If we believe that we can manage threats, then we are less likely to be distressed by them. But if we believe we can't manage them, then we will likely experience high anxiety, dwell on our coping deficiencies, view many aspects of our environments as fraught with danger, and magnify possible risks. All of this creates stress that can impair functioning.[9] In a work environment, examples of threats could be a breakdown in production; a major product recall; an employee engaging in destructive behavior; or a top customer threatening to take her business elsewhere. How we respond to these challenges depends on our belief in our ability to handle the situation.

Learning organizations need managers and leaders with self-efficacy. Learning organizations need to hire individuals with self-efficacy. Learning organizations need to have development plans for all young employees that include developing self-efficacy. Self-efficacy is very important in business environments characterized by change, ambiguity, and uncertainty. If more and faster change is the norm in a business, having employees, managers, and leaders who believe they can adapt and cope could be a competitive advantage. If employees have strong self-efficacy, they are more comfortable tackling new challenges or exploring and discovering new ways of doing things. They are more comfortable being put into uncertain environments, and they approach situations requiring creativity or innovation well. They seek to learn from mistakes or failures and do not attribute the causes to their self-image. Thus, they are more resilient as learners.

The theories of self-efficacy and self-determination can help managers understand how employees will react to challenges and threats, and can also help them frame new challenges in the most productive way possible.

The third area of research that is relevant to managers trying to identify learning mindsets among employees concerns how individuals set their goals and define achievement. This line of research has produced a series of dichotomies—among them extrinsic versus intrinsic motivation and performance versus mastery goal orientation.[10]

A quick note of caution before exploring these two sets of categories further. Dichotomies can be instructive as a pragmatic shorthand or either-or way of classifying people. But it's important to note that these dichotomies exist along continuums, and how people behave along the continuums depends in part on the task at hand and the context. Although the categories are black and white, in reality most people operate within shades of gray. Dichotomies also tend to "brand" people just like IQ does, and this may be unfair. We now know, for example, that IQ is not fixed— we can continue to learn and physically change our brains throughout our lives. Because our brains have plasticity, meaning our neural pathways and processes can continue to change, fundamental aspects of intelligence can be improved.[11] Likewise, there is evidence that approaches to learning and achievement can also change, thus changing a person's "classification" within a dichotomy.

Generally, however, people are motivated to learn for either intrinsic or extrinsic reasons. Intrinsic motivations can be verbalized as: "I love to learn because it makes me feel good" or "I learn for me." Learning in and of itself is the reward. Extrinsic motivations can be verbalized as: "I love to learn because of what it gets me from others—grades, rewards, acknowledgement, fame, love, respect." Extrinsically motivated learners give the external world a lot of power over their lives and self-images, and they work very hard to receive "pats on the head" from others. Learning is a means to an end, with the end being the approval or acclaim of others. Because others define their self-worth, they strive to avoid disappointing people—by, say, getting bad grades or making mistakes. Therefore, they prefer to avoid too much risk and to stay in a safe zone of capability.

Extrinsically motivated employees can be very motivated to succeed and can be quite competitive. They can generally be more self-oriented than team-oriented. They worry about who gets credit. Research has shown that in extreme cases, these types are more likely to hoard information and more likely to cheat to win.

The internal versus external reasons to learn are also tied into another dichotomy: mastery goal-orientation versus performance goal-orientation. Learners are either "masters" or "performers." Masters seek to develop competence through learning and improvement, while performers seek to demonstrate competence by showing others how smart they are or by out-performing others.[12] A theoretical model that I find quite useful because it incorporates both intrinsic versus extrinsic motivation and mastery versus performance dichotomies comes from decades of research by Professor Carol Dweck of Stanford University. Her model is one of "growth" versus "fixed" mindsets.

Dweck has found that the types of students who have a performance or fixed mindset are driven to perform for the purpose of receiving good grades and external rewards and react defensively when they make mistakes or fail. They believe intelligence and aptitude are fixed—(e.g., people are either good at math or they aren't). These types of students not only neglect to seek out challenging learning problems because they believe their aptitudes are fixed, but they also actively avoid them. Why? Because the primary drive is to receive affirmation and positive feedback that confirms their intelligence. They avoid situations or opportunities where failure is likely, because failing threatens the fixed view of their self-image. They create an internal culture of fear—fear of challenges and fear of stretching themselves—and they have difficulty cognitively processing negative feedback, because they have an automatic emotional response to defend, deflect, or deny. These performance-oriented or "fixed" mindset people have their egos all tied up in being right and looking right—not in learning.

By contrast, Dweck has found that students who have a mastery or "growth" mindset are internally driven to master tasks or subjects, and they believe that a person's intelligence and aptitude are not fixed, but can grow with effort. They tend to seek challenges and opportunities to extend their skills. If they make mistakes, they overcome them by working harder. These students view mistakes and failures not as negative feedback about them-selves, but rather as negative feedback about their learning strategies or the amounts of effort they expended. Mistakes or failures are not as debilitating to these students' egos as they are to performance-oriented students. Mastery-oriented students tend to have a more secure view of their self-worth. They believe they can learn, and they seek out and thrive in situations where there are opportunities to learn.

Dweck quotes the noted sociologist Benjamin Barber: "I don't divide the world into the weak and the strong, or the successes and the failures. . . . I divide the world into the learners and nonlearners."[13] Of course, this isn't to say that one cannot move from one mindset to the other. Indeed, one of the most important things to realize when considering learning styles is that our learning mindset can change. I know, because mine did.

Looking back, I understand that I grew up being a performance-oriented learner—although, of course, I wouldn't have thought that at the time. I performed to get great grades and make my parents proud—especially my father. I was performance driven all the way through law school. I worked very hard and did well.

However, my mindset shifted when I attended the Master of Laws in Taxation program at New York University School of Law while practicing law in New York City. There, I studied under some of the intellectual tax giants in the field, including Jim Eustice, Victor Zonana, and Steve Gardner, all of whom wrote scholarly articles and books, taught, and actively practiced tax law. They were among the best in the world at their craft. They exposed me to the thrill of learning for learning's sake and to the inner joy of striving to be an expert in my craft. My motivations changed under their tutelage from performance-oriented to mastery-oriented.

My early experience practicing law also greatly influenced how I reacted to negative feedback, which helped me to shift away from a performance mindset. I had a mentor, a partner, who was "Mr. Feedback." He taught me that negative feedback was necessary to become the best in a field. (Thank you, Peter.) He taught me to pause and reflect rather than automatically defend, deflect, or deny. He taught me that it wasn't about me, but rather about producing the best legal memorandum or brief that could be written in a particular case. As I advanced in my career, I came to realize how difficult it can be to get this kind of constructive feedback. Rather than getting the kind of specific, constructive feedback that can help us improve our skills, most of us will receive guarded or politically correct feedback that is fairly useless in practice. Thoughtful and constructive feedback is a valuable thing, especially when you can foster your mindset to absorb and not deflect it.

Hiring and Training the Right People

Overall, to be a great learning organization, you need to select and then cultivate people who like or even love to learn. You want people who are curious enough to keep on learning. Constant improvement is table stakes in today's business environment. For an organization to constantly improve, it needs people who are willing to constantly improve. It needs good learners.

Dweck's research shows that people with an intrinsically motivated, mastery approach to learning, as evidenced by a growth mindset, are better learners and are not as afraid of negative feedback, failure, difficult tasks, uncertainty, and new situations. Bandura's research finds that people with a strong sense of self-efficacy are likely to be more resilient and adaptable. If you give those people a sense of control over some parts of their job, this is even better because they have some autonomy and some power to control their destiny—very important, according to Ryan and Deci's research on self-determination. If people feel a sense of belonging to a great learning team or organization, then you have met their relatedness needs. If you put people with these productive learning traits into a positive emotional environment, then you are on the way to building a learning organization.

Of course, existing organizations cannot just clear out their ranks of people with a fixed learning mindset in favor of new hires with a growth mindset. The key question becomes: Can you teach people to move away from fixed thinking and develop a growth mindset?

As evidenced by my personal story, I believe you can. Dweck thinks so too. The premise of her book *Mindset: The New Psychology of Success* is to provide practical guidance for how to do this.[14] She (and I) are not alone in believing a person can learn to become a better learner. Professors at the Harvard Graduate School of Education believe you can teach thinking dispositions.[15] Their list of key thinking dispositions is quite good and includes being open-minded and exploring alternative views; generating multiple options and being inclined to probe; having a zest for inquiry and the tendency to question the given and demand justification; and having an alertness to the need for evidence and the ability to weigh and assess reasons.[16] They believe that all these dispositions can be cultivated and strengthened.

The U.S. Army is far ahead of most businesses in trying to operationalize the science of learning by applying this research to its Adaptable

Leadership transformation program as well as its Comprehensive Soldier Fitness program. One of the Army's major focuses is on "hardiness"—this isn't a term that's used by the researchers I mention above, but it has some very interesting resonances with Bandura's self-efficacy model, Deci and Ryan's self-determination model, and Dweck's growth versus fixed mindset model. The Army describes the concept of hardiness as follows:

> Hardiness is a psychological style associated with resilience, good health and performance under a range of stressful conditions. People high in hardiness have a strong sense of commitment to life and work, and are actively engaged in what's going on around them. They believe they can control or influence what happens, and they enjoy new situations and challenges. Also, they are internally motivated and create their own sense of purpose.[17]

The Army's concept of hardiness incorporates Bandura's concept of self-efficacy in its assertion that people with this quality "believe they can control or influence what happens." With its references to "performance under a range of stressful conditions" and having a "strong sense of commitment to life and work," the Army's concept also seems to fit with the Deci-Ryan self-determination model of autonomy, effectiveness, and relatedness. Finally, by describing those high in hardiness as the kind of people who "enjoy new situations and challenges" and "are internally motivated," the Army's concept also fits within Dweck's model.

The Army has found that candidates who score high on hardiness are highly adaptable and make the most successful Special Forces candidates.[18] The Army's Leadership Training is directed toward producing leaders who can adapt to new and challenging situations and uncertainty—that is, learn. The U.S. Army Special Forces believes that adaptability—learning—is predicated on self-efficacy, resiliency, open-mindedness, mastery achievement motivation, and tolerance for ambiguity and uncertainty. Key adaptive skills are metacognition, problem solving/decision making, interpersonal skills, and self-awareness. Adaptive leadership training emphasizes discovery learning, mastery not performance orientation, and deliberate practice.[19] All of the foregoing incorporates the key concepts of this chapter and chapters 2 and 3. If you are interested in learning more about the Army's Leadership Training, see the bibliography for some of the key reports.

Theory X Versus Theory Y Manager Mindsets

To be a learning organization and to encourage learning mindsets, it is critical that the organization's managers and leaders have learning mindsets. This, along with their conscious or subconscious beliefs about employees, impacts managers' abilities to be good learning teachers or facilitators. It's crucial to devote attention to "managerial mindsets," because a manager's behavior toward and with employees is driven in part by his or her own underlying mindset about employees. Most managers and leaders I have worked with either are not conscious of their own mindsets, or they have trouble being truthful about them. Paying more attention to the managerial mindset can help in the transition to a learning organization.

In a 1957 speech, Professor Douglas McGregor of MIT advanced the thinking about managerial mindsets when he challenged the assumptions underlying the dominant management model since the Industrial Revolution—an autocratic, "command and control" style of management. He posited that managers and leaders had underlying assumptions about the nature of employees that fit either into what he called "Theory X" or "Theory Y." This idea is important to our quest to enable learning, because leaders and managers who understand their beliefs about people can improve the quality of their engagements with others—and this will directly impact learning.

Theory X

Theory X[20] managers, as McGregor defines them, basically believe that employees are inherently lazy, not very bright, gullible, and self-centered. They believe employees generally lack ambition and resist change. They believe management's job is to use rewards and punishments to direct, motivate, control, and even modify employees' behaviors in order to get organizational results. Theory X management beliefs underlie statements like:

- If you give employees an inch, they will take a mile.
- Being nice to employees just means they will take advantage of you.
- Employee-centric practices are inconsistent with high accountability.

- Employees are lucky to have a job, and if they don't want it, plenty of others will.

In my many talks with managers, no one has ever admitted to being a Theory X manager. But if I ask open-ended questions about employee motivation and the manager's management style and means used to produce results, I hear Theory X answers. I am convinced that Theory X beliefs make learning conversations, feedback conversations, collaboration, trust building, and high employee emotional engagement difficult.

OK, Theory X does not look promising, so what is Theory Y?

Theory Y

McGregor's explanation of a Theory Y[21] mindset is not as clear or as elaborate as his explanation of Theory X. I find it helpful to think about Theory Y as the opposite of Theory X.

Theory Y managers believe that employees have the capacity to assume responsibility, continue to develop, and contribute to the organizational good. Because of past experiences in Theory X organizations, these capacities are stunted for many employees. Management's job is to create the environment and opportunities for employees to grow and to align personal growth and organizational growth.

McGregor's work challenges every one of us to answer this question: What are my assumptions (implicit and explicit) about the most effective way to manage people?[22] And as a follow-up: What would my employees say about my assumptions?

Gallup, Inc., which has spent years researching and doing employee engagement testing, has developed twelve key questions[23] that I consider a good indicator of whether the employees are operating under a Theory X or a Theory Y manager. Consider the following:

- In the last seven days, have I received recognition or praise for doing good work?
- Does my supervisor, or someone at work, seem to care about me as a person?
- Is there someone at work who encourages my development?
- This last year, have I had the opportunities at work to learn and grow?

Would the answers to these questions differ qualitatively between employees with Theory X managers from those with Theory Y managers? I think so.

A High-Performance Learning Organization requires its employees to be learners. To be an HPLO, the CEO and other leaders and managers must role model learning behaviors and attitudes and actually teach, facilitate, and enable learning. Theory X leader and manager mindsets would seem to inhibit that teaching, facilitating, and enabling. Theory Y leader and manager mindsets would seem to facilitate learning.

Conclusion

This chapter focused on the people part of the HPLO formula. We approached this element from three different perspectives: the learning mindset of employees; how meeting self-efficacy and self-determination needs enables learning; and the mindset that managers and leaders have about employees. We learned that intrinsically motivated people with a strong sense of self-efficacy, who approach learning with a mastery mindset and as an avenue for personal growth, are more likely to seek learning opportunities and to be resilient learners. This is especially true in situations characterized by change, uncertainty, and ambiguity.

We also learned that managers and leaders who have Theory Y mindsets about employees better enable learning than managers and leaders with a Theory X mindset. In chapter 2 we discussed that learning requires one to incorporate new learning into one's mental models or views of the world and, in some cases, one's view of oneself. That transformative process is made easier if the learning experience itself meets one's basic needs for autonomy, relatedness, and effectiveness. In a work environment, transformative learning is more likely to occur when workers have some input into the learning process; have the necessary capabilities and are given the necessary tools to accomplish the task; and when the reason or purpose for learning is made meaningful from both business purpose and personal growth viewpoints.

Having the Right People is necessary to create an HPLO, but it is not sufficient by itself. You also must have the kind of work environment and processes that enable and promote learning. I explore the second element of the HPLO formula—the Right Environment—in the next chapter.

Reflection Questions

1. What did you read in this chapter that surprised you?
2. What are your top three takeaways that you want to reflect and/or act on?
3. What behaviors do you want to change?

5

Creating a Learning Environment

Chapter 4 focused on the Right People, the first element of the formula for a High-Performance Learning Organization (HPLO).[1] As I stated in the conclusion to chapter 4, having the Right People with the right learning mindsets along with Theory Y leaders and managers that enable and promote learning is necessary but not sufficient to be an HPLO. Those people need to be in the right environment that enables and promotes learning. The Right Environment, the second element of the HPLO formula, is more than just having a learning culture; the culture has to be supported by an infrastructure that includes particular leadership behaviors, HR policies and processes, and measurements and rewards that together enable and promote good learning behaviors. In other words, you need a whole learning system. Peter Senge was right when, in explaining the necessary disciplines for a learning organization, he said: "Without a systemic orientation, there is no motivation to look at how the disciplines [elements] interrelate."[2]

My systems approach to learning focuses on enabling and driving learning behaviors at all levels of an organization—employees, managers, and leaders. Asking questions, for example, is a good learning behavior. Likewise, a manager taking the time to explain to an employee why a new process is necessary—and implementing this transition in a way that meets the employee's needs for autonomy, relatedness, and effectiveness—is a behavior that enables learning. Once you define those behaviors that enable and promote individual learning, you have to design your culture, leadership model, HR policies, measurements, and rewards to drive those behaviors.

My approach comes from my research projects[3] in which I studied the characteristics of consistently high-performing public and private companies that relied primarily on a strategy of organic growth. That research led me to introduce the concept of a "growth system" that drives growth behaviors, a concept I presented in my book *Smart Growth*.[4] I believe a similar approach is necessary when one is trying to build a learning organization. Operationalizing learning requires an environment that drives the desired learner, manager, and leader behaviors. This chapter presents research in education and business that helps us further define some of the key ingredients of a good learning environment.

A Good Educational Learning Environment

The field of education has been researching good learning environments for decades. Recently it has become even more sophisticated by taking into account the plethora of new research in the areas of social and affective neuroscience. Findings from this field can also often be applied directly to the workplace, and this is a good place to start in determining how to build a learning environment.

The current consensus is that a good educational learning environment[5] is one that fosters intrinsic motivation and gives students some autonomy and control over their learning. It's an environment where there are good role models (teachers) for learning and creativity, and where the style of teaching meets the diverse needs of learners (i.e., learner-centric). In a good educational environment, the learning process resembles a journey of discovery in which the learner plays the main character and is encouraged to be creative and socially and authentically connected to the learning community. It's also one where learners experience a combination of positive support and positive challenges.[6] The best combination for learning is one in which learners feel socially differentiated and unique, as well as socially integrated and authentically connected members of a community. Other well-respected works in the education field published since 2010[7] confirm that good learning environments are those that support learner-centricity with a focus on mastery learning and growth (versus performance) mindsets, are emotionally positive, recognize students as individuals, and offer psychological safety.

Clearly, the work that's been done on good educational learning environments dovetails with some of the research I discussed in previous chapters regarding learning mindsets, self-efficacy, and self-determination theory. There are some fundamental common themes that can provide the foundation for how to best create a good workplace learning environment. First, it should be an emotionally positive environment that mitigates learning inhibitors such as stress, fear of failure, negative emotions, and ego defenses. Second, it should encourage mastery learning and intrinsic motivation, and be learner-centric (i.e., employee-centric) in that it would seek to engage learners (i.e., employees) emotionally by treating them with respect, dignity, and trust. It should encourage a growth mindset of discovery and exploration, self-efficacy, and experimentation. Third, it should characterize mistakes not as personal failures but as the result of bad learning strategies or too little effort. It should not punish employees for making learning mistakes or failures in nonassessment situations, so long as they learn from those mistakes or failures. Managers should role model learning behaviors, giving employees permission to speak freely and honestly. Fourth, the environment should meet the fundamental needs set forth in Deci and Ryan's "self-determination" model of autonomy, effectiveness, and relatedness. Fifth, leaders and managers need to behave in a manner that earns the trust of employees and engenders employees' beliefs that they are respected as unique individuals and that their managers care about their personal growth and development.

Being this type of learning organization does not mean that managers and leaders have to be soft on quality or accountability. Good business learning organizations are learner-centric and have high standards for performance and personal accountability. I know from my executive education teaching and consulting that many managers and leaders find it easy to think in terms of process and financial metrics, but to succeed as a learning organization, it's necessary to think and to measure performance in terms of behaviors as well. Table 5.1 provides a review of some important behavioral examples that are fundamental for learning to occur.

These behaviors should be measured for every employee through 360-degree reviews and rewarded especially with emotional rewards. Every manager and leader must likewise be measured, and a material amount of their financial compensation should be dependent on those behaviors.

Table 5.1
Behaviors Fundamental to Learning

Foundational Behaviors	Managing Self Behaviors
• Being open minded • Being empathetic and humble • Embracing ambiguity, uncertainty, and new challenges • Being resilient • Being proactive • Treating others with dignity and respect • Being truthful and trustworthy • Knowing what you do not know	• Managing one's fears & other emotions • Managing one's ego defenses • Metacognition • Being mindful • Actively listening • Being sensitive to one's body language, voice tone, and volume • Being positive emotionally
Exploratory Behaviors	**Learning Process Behaviors**
• Being curious and inquisitive • Being willing to explore alternatives • Being willing to go beyond one's comfort zone	• Seeking feedback and stress testing beliefs • Using critical thinking processes • Engaging in critical inquiry and debate • Unpacking underlying assumptions • Actively collaborating with and learning from others

Learning and High Employee Engagement

All of the above behaviors encourage high-engagement learning, which has been a fruitful area for research in the education space. Intriguingly, the attributes that facilitate high-engagement learning are some of the same attributes that are necessary to create high employee engagement. This insight can help clarify how crucial learning is to high performance; let's take a closer look at how all of this is related.

The research-based Gallup Q12® high employee engagement assessment tool is used by thousands of companies to measure the extent of employee engagement in their organizations. Interestingly, at least ten of the twelve Gallup Q12® factors that are used to measure high employee engagement are essentially the same factors that drive high engagement learning. Table 5.2 demonstrates this. The left column indicates the Gallup Q12® assessment statements that, if answered in the affirmative, indicate high employee engagement.[8] In the right column I have provided corresponding, research-based attributes of high-engagement learning.

Although the Gallup Q12® is not a direct measure of employee learning, putting this information side by side demonstrates that an environment

Table 5.2

Congruity Between High Employee Engagement and High Engagement Learning

High Employee Engagement	High Engagement Learning
I have the opportunity to do what I do best.	Learner-centricity, autonomy, effectiveness, self-efficacy
In the last seven days I received recognition or praise for doing good work.	Positive classroom environment, learner-centricity
My supervisor, or someone at work, cares about me as a person.	Respect for individuals, relatedness, learner-centricity
Someone at work encourages my development.	Relatedness, caring teachers interested in individual student's growth
At work, my opinions seem to count.	Autonomy, respect
The mission/purpose of my company makes me feel like my work is important.	Purposeful communities that fill the need for affiliation
My associates are committed to doing quality work.	Same as above
I have a best friend at work.	Meaningful social connections, relatedness
In the last six months, someone gave me feedback.	Caring teachers interested in individual student's growth
In the last year, I have had opportunities to grow and develop.	Opportunities for development and effectiveness

that promotes high employee engagement is very similar to one that promotes high-engagement learning in an educational setting. It would seem, then, that an internal organizational system that produces high employee emotional engagement should also enable and promote high-engagement learning. What's more, research suggests that high employee engagement, along with learning, are major factors in creating consistent high performance in business.

Over the past thirty years, there have been at least eight well-researched studies[9] that have defined the characteristics of consistently high-performing businesses. Although all eight used different research methodologies and terminology, the research findings overlapped substantially, and all eight studies found that consistently high-performing businesses were characterized by:

1. High employee engagement;
2. Relentless, constant improvement (learning);
3. Humble passionate leaders serving as stewards; and
4. Strong purposeful cultures with cultural fit-based hiring practices.

In other words, one can argue that there is a strong correlation between high performance, high employee engagement, and high learning. This kind of connection is not often made in business thinking, so it is worth providing more evidence of this connection by looking at how these four characteristics are intertwined and what their implications are for building a learning organization. Looking at a few specific findings in four of the eight studies can provide further insight.

High Employee Engagement and High Performance

As they detail in their book *Hidden Value: How Great Companies Achieve Extraordinary Results with Ordinary People*, Stanford University professors Charles O'Reilly III and Jeffrey Pfeffer found that high-performing companies treated their people "with dignity, trust, and respect," and engaged them by "the values and culture of the organization."[10] How you behave—how you treat people daily—is very important for both high performance and high learning, and is something that should be codified for managers and leaders.

Teamwork was another key factor in many of the companies they studied. According to Reilly and Pfeffer, high-performing organizations offered to their employees "a sense of community, security, and mutual trust and respect."[11] Each company had a well-articulated and widely-shared set of values that provided the foundation for management practices. Each also had a "remarkable" degree of alignment and consistency among the human resource-related practices that expressed the company's core values.[12]

The *Hidden Value* companies had high employee engagement and a strong culture. They hired for fit and invested in their people. They had widespread information transparency, organized in teams, relied liberally on intrinsic rewards in addition to financial rewards, and encouraged reciprocal trust and mutual accountability among employees, leadership, and the company. Continuous improvement and trial and error learning drove all of them.

Another important study by Jerry Porras and Jim Collins produced the successful book *Built to Last: Successful Habits of Visionary Companies*. Porras and Collins found that consistent long-term high-performance companies: (1) had a purpose beyond making money; (2) had cult-like, strong cultures and hired for cultural fit; (3) engaged in experimentation and learned from trial and error; and (4) relentlessly asked themselves how they could improve themselves to do better tomorrow than they did today.[13] This last finding was evidenced by companies directly creating "mechanisms of discontent" to fight complacency.[14]

Porras and Collins described these high-performance companies as evolutionary in that they relied on Darwinian biological concepts such as adaptation. These companies tried many things, made mistakes, and exploited their successes. The key for them was to experiment, learn, and adapt by making small bets—not betting the ranch.[15] With regard to experimentation and learning from trial and error, Porras and Collins quoted R.W. Johnson, Jr. of Johnson & Johnson: "Failure is our most important product."[16]

Jim Collins's landmark work *Good to Great: Why Some Companies Make the Leap . . . And Others Don't*[17] produced several other interesting findings that illuminate the traits of high-performance organizations. There are a few that are particularly relevant to our discussion: "Level 5 leadership"; a principle Collins names "First Who, Then What"; and finally, confronting the "brutal facts."

Collins defined Level 5 leaders as those who "blend extreme personal humility with intense professional will."[18] Recall that having humble and passionate leaders was found by all eight studies to be a key factor in high organizational performance. Level 5 leaders are those that transfer their ambition and ego needs to the organization and identify themselves by organizational results. They don't think: it's about "me," but rather, it's about "us." Collins said that "good to great" leaders were often described as "quiet, humble, modest, reserved, shy, gracious, mild-mannered, self-effacing, understated."[19]

Why would Level 5 leaders be important for a learning organization? I submit that those types of leaders would more likely be open-minded, good listeners, more collaborative, more Theory Y oriented than Theory X, and better able to manage their egos. All of these qualities would help them to promote learning within the organization and to act as role models in their learning behaviors and leaderships.

"First Who, Then What" refers to Collins's famous pronouncement that managers need to get the right people on the bus and the wrong people off the bus.[20] Collins defined the right people as those who are intrinsically motivated to produce the best results,[21] an idea that's reinforced by the learning science we explored in chapter 4. The other important quality people must have, Collins said, is the desire to be part of building something great. This point relates to Collins's finding that high-performance organizations have a purpose beyond just making money. Wanting to be part of something great, purposeful, or meaningful is an additional motivator that can drive learning, if the organization makes learning a key part of its purposeful mission. Collins emphasized that rigorous hiring for cultural fit was key. Clearly, this means that to be a great learning organization, you need to make hiring as rigorous a scientific process as you can, with the goal of hiring learners (as defined in chapter 4). As we'll see in chapter 9, Bridgewater puts enormous emphasis on and thoughts into hiring.

Collins's third finding, "confront the brutal facts," relates to the learning processes of critical inquiry and logical decision making. He exhorts leaders to "create a climate where the truth is heard and the brutal facts confronted"[22]—a climate, in other words, where employees have "permission to speak freely" without fear of punishment. But speaking freely is only one-half of the equation; managers and leaders also have to be open-minded and actually hear the messages without ego defenses getting in the way. Collins suggests that confronting the brutal facts occurs when leaders begin with questions, not with answers; engage in dialogue and debate, not coercion; conduct "autopsies without blame"; and create mechanisms that illuminate the brutal reality.[23]

Repeatedly now you have read that a culture that provides permission to speak freely and permission to fail is necessary for an organization and its employees to learn and confront brutal facts. Professor Amy Edmondson's work on psychological safety in work teams[24] contributes significantly to our discussion, examining how to create an environment that won't create the kinds of fears that inhibit critical inquiry, debate, and even root cause analysis processes.

Edmondson believes that our fears at work are intensified by our long-held beliefs about the power of hierarchy. As children we often are taught not to speak to elders unless they speak first. Likewise, we are taught to respect our elders, parents, and teachers. Respect effectively meant to do as we were told. This transfers directly to the workplace. In the workplace, Edmondson says people are afraid to speak up because of fear of punishment. In a work context, fear of punishment could be the fear of receiving a bad performance review or of being passed over for a promotion because, for example, one is not being an agreeable team player. It could be the fear of retribution from a superior. In other words, fear of punishment at work is the fear of harm to one's career or the source or amount of one's compensation.

In work environments characterized by Theory X leadership, this fear is probably justified. Likewise, if the organizational mindset frames mistakes as failures instead of learning opportunities, then mistakes are not likely to be voluntarily reported, and people are less likely to take initiative.

Edmondson's research has found that in hierarchical organizations employees do not speak up if they are at a lower level unless they feel like they have psychological safety—that they are in a "safe to speak" environment. Leaders and managers have to "walk the talk" to overcome that fear. Culture, HR policies, measurements, and rewards all have to promote psychological safety. Leaders have to earn the trust of subordinates by inviting them to speak up, heaping praise on the courageous ones that do so, and demonstrating humility by admitting their own failures, mistakes, and ignorance.

This is why leader humility is so important. It's consistent with the research findings we've discussed and is evident in the IDEO and W.L. Gore & Associates, Inc. stories that follow. Humility is also a key part of the Bridgewater, Intuit, and UPS stories that follow.

Edmondson's colleague Professor David Garvin says the litmus test of a learning organization is being receptive to information that goes against the established way and a tolerance for failures and mistakes.[25] Garvin has stated, "Fear does little to encourage learning."[26] Garvin advocates learning by experimentation, the U.S. Army After Action Review process, critical debate in the pursuit of truth, having an open mind, and truly listening to views that are different than yours.

In 2008, Edmondson and Garvin collaborated on an article about learning organizations in the *Harvard Business Review*. They set forth a learning organization diagnostic[27] consistent with what we have discussed in this chapter. Notably, their diagnostic tool asks whether the organization is open to new ideas and gives individuals psychological safety to disagree or dissent. It asks whether the organization promotes critical inquiry, critical debate, and experimentation and whether the behaviors of leaders and managers reinforce learning.

I've also done original research that confirms and enriches some of these findings. In 2004–2005, I conducted a study[28] of twenty-three consistent high-performance companies that grew for long periods of time primarily by "organic growth," which I defined as growth derived from selling more goods and services to more unrelated parties in arms-length transactions on commercially normal terms. My findings were consistent with the finding set forth above and that of other researchers[29]—that high employee engagement is critical for consistent high performance.[30]

My research further suggests that the following employment practices can facilitate high employee engagement:

- Stock ownership
- Promotion-from-within policies
- Humble, passionate, steward-like leaders
- Fairly applied, transparent and stable HR policies[31]
- Mutual accountability
- Devaluation of status, hierarchy and elitism

My research produced findings that were consistent with many of the elements of the Toyota Production System, which until recent years has produced the automobiles most highly ranked for reliability in the world. Toyota's model[32] is to be a great learning organization that seeks relentless and constant improvement from a highly engaged workforce through root cause analysis, team problem solving, and decision making. At Toyota, the root cause analysis process focused on the "5 Whys" not the "5 Who's" (i.e., who's to blame), with the 5 signaling that this is usually the number of "why" questions that need to be asked before a problem can be fully analyzed.[33] Like the companies in *Good to Great*, Toyota wants employees to be open about their mistakes, which requires employees to trust that they won't be punished for reporting them.

In the Toyota system, managers and leaders serve employees as teachers and facilitators, and the company devalues status differentiators and elitist perks. Many of the companies I studied in my own research fought elitism, too. At the time, for example, the CEO of Best Buy and all his direct reports had very small, windowless offices. Best Buy and UPS used no corporate jets. Best Buy, Stryker, TSYS, and UPS were servant leadership companies. The president of Tiffany & Company when asked to describe the Tiffany culture in one word responded: "Humility. There is only one star here, and it is Tiffany."[34]

Overall, the Gallup research and the eight studies on high-performance businesses provide evidence that engaging employees in high performance requires humility, passion, and open-mindedness from managers and leaders. To encourage learning among employees, leaders and managers must engage with employees in an emotionally positive way. They have to build trust by being fair, reliable, consistent, and competent. They must demonstrate that they care about employees as individuals and are investing in their growth and development.

These findings are further buttressed by analogous findings in the field of client-centered therapy by eminent psychologist Carl Rogers. To have an effective, growth-producing therapeutic relationship, Rogers stressed that the following are necessary: transparent honesty between the parties, genuine caring for the client, empathic understanding of the client, mindful presence and listening by the therapist, and mutual trust.[35] You can see that the behaviors and attitudes necessary to create high learner engagement, high employee engagement and an effective client-centered therapeutic relationship are the same.

The research findings in education and clinical psychology and the high performance business research all confirm the power of high emotional engagement. Horst Schulze, who built the Ritz-Carlton Hotel chain, understood this. He built a business around encouraging these behaviors among his employees, and he often visited my classes when I taught at the Goizueta Business School of Emory University. Schulze's mantra was, "We are ladies and gentlemen serving ladies and gentlemen." He gave employees autonomy and showed them his trust of them by giving every one of them the unilateral right to spend up to $2,000 on any guest to make that guest happy. In daily huddles, the employees gathered to engage in learning focused on core values. Schulze's turnover was significantly below industry averages because he provided his employees dignity, meaning, and respect, and made each employee's role important in a best-in-class business.

Another CEO that I had the privilege of getting to know exhibited this same emotional engagement with his company and his employees. Herb Kelleher, one of the founders of Southwest Airlines, arguably built the most successful modern U.S. airline, and did so based on high employee engagement. After a meeting with him in his Dallas office, I witnessed something special while he walked me around the building. He addressed every employee we encountered by first name—and each of them hugged him. Yes, hugged him. The affection was real. The love and respect was deep.

Those two leaders were special people who were able to spread their emotional engagement through their entire companies.

Overall, the research and the science paint a clear picture. A good organizational learning environment is one that promotes high employee engagement and positive emotions. An emotionally positive environment encourages learning by mitigating the big learning inhibitors: fears, ego defenses, complacency, and arrogance. Two critical policies necessary to mitigate those inhibitors are an inviolate permission to speak freely and conditional permission to make mistakes and fail (within acceptable financial risk tolerances). Employee-centricity is also necessary to promote high employee engagement, learning mindsets, and motivation. A specific kind of leadership is required: Theory Y leaders who are employee-centric and whose behaviors are driven by being open-minded, humble, authentic, positive and civil, and who have integrity, trustworthiness, and a passion for learning. High employee engagement and a high learning environment are created by building an internal system that aligns—in a consistent and self-reinforcing manner—the right culture, structures, leadership behaviors, HR policies, measurements, and rewards.

Putting It Into Practice: IDEO and W.L. Gore & Associates

To round out this look at learning environments, let's take a look at two other well-known and well-regarded companies that are admired for their consistent high performance and innovation: IDEO and W.L. Gore & Associates. We will see that they too owe their success to high employee engagement and high learning.

IDEO

IDEO is a world famous, privately owned design firm with ten global offices and approximately 550 employees. Formed in 1991, it is best known for designing Apple's first computer mouse. IDEO is renowned for its innovation—an indication that it must be a great learning organization, because innovation requires discovery and iterative experimentation (i.e., learning).

IDEO's founder David Kelley and his brother Tom Kelley recently wrote a book titled *Creative Confidence: Unleashing the Creative Potential Within Us All* in which they detail the IDEO way.[36] They describe how IDEO has created a culture and processes that enable employees to overcome their fears of failure and their insecurities in order to act creatively. Because acting creatively requires employees to explore many alternatives, have spirited debates, and conduct numerous experiments, IDEO's culture also encourages employees to be open-minded and avoid rushing to judgment.

According to *Creative Confidence*, IDEO believes that failure is part of innovation and that everyone has to learn to face failure directly, learn from it, and try again. Only by truly "owning" failures can anyone build resiliency. Failure is viewed as a good thing at IDEO for another important reason: it builds humility. Humility enables deep empathy, which is needed for employees to put themselves in the shoes of users or customers. At IDEO, employees have permission to fail because innovation and personal learning can result from failure. The Kelley brothers cite Albert Bandura's idea of self-efficacy and Carol Dweck's concept of the growth mindset, discussed in chapter 4, as being part of the IDEO way.

So how does learning at IDEO happen? In teams made up of diverse people. Teams collaborating at every stage of the "Design Thinking" process is one of IDEO's hallmarks, but teams are about more than just work at IDEO. The firm's employees are encouraged to form deep, meaningful friendships at work because caring relationships are part of a positive work environment. A positive work environment with positive relationships enables creativity. IDEO supports Collins's tenet to "confront the brutal facts." IDEO also supports Porras and Collins's argument that iterative learning through experimentation and constant improvement is the underlying corporate adaptive process.

W.L. Gore & Associates, Inc.

Bill Gore was an engineer at DuPont when he became disenchanted with the corporate game.[37] In 1958 he founded what would become a highly successful, global private company revered for its innovation. Today W.L. Gore & Associates, Inc. (Gore) grosses over three billion dollars in revenues and employs over 10,000 employees in thirty different locations. Well known for waterproof, breathable GORE-TEX* fabric, the company's portfolio includes everything from high-performance fabrics and implantable medical devices to industrial manufacturing components and aerospace electronics. Gore is a privately held company owned by members of the Gore family as well as by employees with at least one year of service (referred to as "associates"), who become shareholders through a stock ownership plan. Founder Bill Gore felt it was important for associates to have an equity stake in the company's long-term success and to share in the risks and rewards of the enterprise. This is also a feature of UPS, as we will see in chapter 11.

In creating their company, Bill and Vieve Gore were heavily influenced by the works of Douglas McGregor, developer of the Theory X and Theory

Y management idea, and psychologist Abraham Maslow, a founder of the humanistic psychology movement.[38] The late Mr. Gore disliked bureaucracy and the word "boss." He didn't believe in using traditional management models to build the company. At Gore, someone is a leader only if there are associates willing to follow that person. This is a form of actual authority because such a leader is able to influence the followers through the demonstration of good judgment, unique knowledge, and established trust. Rank, status, and titles minimally impact a person's influence at Gore.

Decisions at Gore are made through collaboration between the associates whose work such decisions impact. Distributed leadership is the model. Manufacturing plants are structured to be small—generally fewer than 250 associates—so that the entrepreneurial spirit isn't snuffed out by corporate bureaucracy. Keeping groups small also allows people to really know each other and talk face-to-face. Gore utilizes tools such as e-mail, voice mail, and video conferencing, but knows that face-to-face communication drives cooperation, collaboration, a high level of associate engagement, and teamwork. There is a willingness to allow associates "face time" to build trust in their relationships, even when this involves international travel.

Bill Gore built a people-centric company because he knew that people are the most valuable resource and that it's only by and through people that things get done. Gore operates under a principle that everyone should be fair in all dealings with each other, with suppliers, with neighbors in the community and with customers. The Gore culture encourages associates to challenge traditional thinking, experiment, and voice differences of opinion openly and directly. They are encouraged to help, support, and encourage one another as they all strive to develop and grow. Asking for help is seen as a positive sign, not as a sign of weakness, and failures are celebrated as learning opportunities and treated as a jumping-off point for the next project.

Gore's hiring process is very rigorous and time consuming, because being hired for cultural fit is key to the candidate's success. The company looks for intrinsically motivated people, and once hired, encourages them to really know themselves—to know their strengths and areas that need further development. Gore continuously focuses on these individual strengths and on minimizing weaknesses, and the company tries to guide associates toward job-related commitments that play to their strengths. You will see this same principle in the Bridgewater story. Gore operationalizes an individual's basic need for autonomy by emphasizing that employees take ownership of their commitments and personal development. All associates are evaluated by teammates and peers according to their contributions to the success of the enterprise.

Gore is committed to supporting every associate's desire to grow and develop. A promotion-from-within practice supports this commitment. Every associate at Gore has a personal development plan and a sponsor. Sponsors are mentors and coaches, not managers. Being a good sponsor is recognized as a contribution; although, associates are ultimately responsible for their commitments and development.

I was very fortunate to learn about Gore's unique culture through interviews with Richard G. Buckingham, a thirty-five-year Gore veteran.[39] Rich's personal Gore story reveals a lot about the company's commitment to associate development. Rich joined Gore in 1978 as an hourly mechanic. Over his long career, he has held many leadership commitments of increasing responsibility. This has included being a part of global teams with activities in the United States, China, Germany, and Scotland. Rich learned a lot on the job, and with Gore's financial help, obtained additional formal education. Today Rich is responsible for a campus of three facilities employing over 300 associates.

Rich explained to me that associates are encouraged to experiment. Everyone is taught the "Waterline Principle." As Rich explained, "You have lots of latitude so long as you don't take any big risks that will sink the ship or sink you."[40] According to Rich, everyone at Gore is taught to evaluate things by asking themselves: "What is the worst thing that could happen if I do this"?[41] Rich told me that key to Gore's culture is an understanding among the associates that if they see a need, and failure isn't going to sink the ship, they should just go do something about it. If it does look to be risky, however, consultation with other associates is required before taking action.

I asked Rich to describe the essence of Gore in one or two words. His response to me was: "Opportunity." He also told me that Gore believes that associates develop a higher level of freedom by developing their capabilities, because by developing their capabilities, they are prepared to take advantage of an opportunity when it presents itself. Gore also believes that in return for these opportunities associates respond with their highest levels of engagement and performance. That implied contract drives mutual accountability and trust. It's the same implied contract that Toyota historically has had with its employees, and chapter 11 shows that it's also the same implied contract that UPS has with its 400,000 employees.

I also asked Rich to explain how Gore fights complacency and arrogance. His quick response was: "Raging curiosity!"

Conclusion

The discussions of high performance organization research projects, the educational learning environment research, research in clinical psychology, along with the IDEO and Gore stories, illustrate some foundational requirements for anyone desiring to build an HPLO. First, high employee engagement is necessary. Second, one needs to create an internal learning system. That internal learning system should consistently align the organization's culture, structure, HR policies, leadership behaviors, measurements, and rewards to (1) enable and promote learning mindsets and behaviors and (2) engender a positive learning environment that supports a high level of emotional engagement that meets employees' needs for autonomy, effectiveness, growth and development, and relatedness. These needs are more likely to be met when individuals feel respected, trusted, and cared for and feel that they can trust the organization and its leaders. One of the indicia of that trust is employees being able to speak freely without punishment. Another is a conditional permission to make mistakes within the limitations we discussed. Third, that system must drive the behaviors set forth in Table 5.1. Fourth, a specific kind of leadership is needed to facilitate learning and high emotional engagement. It should be clear by now that how leaders and managers treat people is critical to high employee engagement and high learning engagement. Good intentions are not enough. Behaviors count.

We are now ready to move to the next element of the HPLO formula—the Right Processes; chapter 6 focuses on processes that support good learning conversations and collaboration, and chapter 7 discusses critical thinking processes and other learning tools.

Reflection Questions

1. What did you read in this chapter that surprised you?
2. What are your top three takeaways that you want to reflect and/or act on?
3. What behaviors do you want to change?

6

Learning Conversations

In chapter 4, we focused on the first part of the High-Performance Learning Organization formula: the Right People. Chapter 5 focused on the second part: the Right Environment for creating a learning system. We now move to the third part of the formula: the Right Processes, and specifically in this chapter, the right kind of communication processes. Here, I talk about having learning conversations and what makes them so difficult.[1] I discuss the other right kind of processes—critical thinking processes—in chapter 7.

First, however, let's review what we have discovered so far. I would guess that before reading chapters 2 and 3, many of you thought of yourselves as good learners and good thinkers. Those chapters probably threw you for a loop. If you read them closely and reflected on the content, you most likely have come to the conclusion that you are not as good a thinker as you thought, and that you are a much more emotional thinker (and learner) than you presumed.

We found out in chapter 2 that learning requires us to change our mental models—our beliefs about the world and how it operates.[2] True learning requires us to process discordant information and make sense of it. This transformation in our thinking requires us to unpack our assumptions, weigh evidence, examine alternatives, and come to a new view of a situation. It also requires us to refrain from defending, denying, or deflecting important new information, and to understand how our emotions and ego defenses are affecting our thinking.

In many learning situations, it's hard for us to do all of this by ourselves. Our mental models are too entrenched and our ego defenses are too strong. Thus, learning, critical thinking, and creative/innovative thinking can best be achieved when facilitated by teachers and others we trust, and in a work environment by mentors, managers, leaders, and teammates. This is especially true when dealing with new situations, uncertainty, or ambiguity. Learning is a team sport. That is why effective learning conversations are so important.

Learning conversations can be difficult in the same way that engaging our System 2 thinking can be difficult. Why? Most of the time we engage in conversations with System 1 type goals, which confirm what we think we know and affirm our self-image. In the same way that ego defenses can sabotage the ability to think logically, they also are active in conversation to protect us from harm, which may include the fear of being wrong, looking bad, or losing. However, those kinds of conversations don't enable much learning. To solidify the connection to System 1 and System 2 thinking, let's call good learning conversations "System 2 conversations." Such conversations are a higher level of talking or conversing called "dialogue."[3]

System 2 Conversations

A System 2 conversation is a deliberate, nonjudgmental, nondefensive, open-minded exchange. It is honestly sharing yourself with another in the hope that he will share himself with you in a similarly honest manner. To engage in this type of conversation, we basically have to agree that our beliefs are not fixed or final and are open to modification. That premise allows us to weigh new information with others and evaluate the underlying strength of support for our own assumptions, beliefs, opinions, and judgments.

The goal of a System 2 conversation is not to confirm what we believe, but to stress test what we believe. A System 2 conversation is not a competition. It is a process in which people come together to learn from each other and to reach the best objective result. We should enter System 2 learning conversations with the mindset that everything we believe is conditional and subject to change based on new information. As my colleague Jeanne Lietdka at the Darden School of Business likes to say: "We all would be better off if we treated everything we think we know as an assumption to be constantly retested with new data."

System 2 conversations require trust, mutual respect, respect for the process, and psychological safety—all of which are also necessary, as discussed in the previous chapter, to achieve the Right Environment for creating a learning system. When all of these features are present, we can practice self-disclosure in our conversations.[4] This is critical; the late professor Sidney Jourard believed that the only way we can really know ourselves is by disclosing ourselves to others.[5] That is why meaningful relationships in an organization are so important.[6] They build trust, which enables self-disclosure, honesty, and learning conversations.

Not just trust and respect, but almost all the concepts discussed in chapter 5 regarding learning environments also apply to System 2 conversations. The quality of learning conversations will be higher if we feel valued and trust the workplace we're in. In many cases, learning conversations require us to admit when we're wrong. To do that takes courage and confidence that we won't be punished or viewed in a negative manner by others. Permission to speak freely and permission to be wrong must exist if we're to have a chance of overcoming our ego defenses and our fears. Employee-centric, positive work environments and high employee engagement enable System 2 conversations.

The earlier one learns that "it is not all about me," the more effective one will be in behaviors that enable System 2 conversations, such as suspending judgment, engaging in active, reflective listening, and considering the views of others. In other words, empathy and humility make for better conversational teammates in a learning organization. Empathy and humility also help negate some major inhibitors of effective learning conversations: personal and intellectual arrogance. Likewise, the devaluation of status and hierarchy makes it easier for people to speak openly, directly, and honestly. This was a factor in the Gore story, and you will see this later in the Bridgewater, Intuit, and UPS stories as well.

A Failure to Communicate

I came from a humble background. I grew up in a two-bedroom, one-bath house with my little brother and my parents in a small town in western Georgia. My mother was from Massachusetts and my father from Germany. We were different from the norm.

From as early as I can remember, my mother told me that good grades were the way to see the world. My parents made that world accessible to me by taking me to bookstores and buying me books that I read voraciously. Books were my transportation to the big "out there." Then the TV brought the big world into my view. After that, I never considered staying put. I was driven to get good grades to move on.

I grew up in a warm, loving environment but one where emotions were frowned upon and leaving things unsaid was the preferred way. We never had really personal conversations. I approached conversations most of my early life the same way I approached thinking—I was a fast thinker, and I was a fast talker and responder. I was a "confirm and affirm" machine. I thought I was a good listener. I thought I was open-minded. I was not. I did not suspend judgment, because my mind was always formulating my response or counterattack while the speaker was still speaking, and I always subconsciously "knew" the right time to interrupt and launch my response.

Looking back on it, I viewed conversations like guerrilla warfare—hit fast and move on. I was an arrogant thinker and conversationalist, but this was masked by a personal and friendly, nonarrogant demeanor. The combination worked for many years. I didn't know how to slow my response system down and listen. In my work environments (law and investment banking), there was pressure to produce as much high-quality work as fast as possible. Speed of thinking and conversing was important.

I was put in my first real big leadership position at age thirty-three. I was a highly effective "boss" in that my teams produced exceptionally well, and I took care of them in both financial and career terms. I viewed learning conversations as a means to teach—not to learn. I was all business and had very little time for personal conversations (or "chit chat," as I called it). I did not relate—I talked. That style worked for me for eight years—or really, for all my life, until 1988.

In that year, in the same week, I suffered my first major failures—three in one week. First, I lost a lot of money in a business deal. Second, and more important, my wife told me she needed time away from me because I was not the person she married—I had become an obsessed work machine and was not "there" even when I was physically present. She said I was emotionally immature and vacuous, not emotionally engaged with her, and a poor listener. I talked, but I did not relate to her as an individual, and I did not share who I was with her. Third, at the same time, I was one of two finalists for a great CEO job, and the senior partner running the CEO search called me in and said: "On paper you are the best person for this job. But I am not going to recommend you because I don't think any job will ever be enough for you. You are too driven and consumed."

Three blows to the ol' ego in a very short period of time. Well, I did what everyone should do in that situation—I sought help, with the goal of figuring out what was wrong with *them*. Yes, that was my mindset. Mental models are hard to change.

I found someone who was highly recommended and specialized in counseling executives—one of the first women to graduate from the College of Physicians and Surgeons at Columbia University. And through conversations with her, I discovered that I was a poor listener and a poor manager of my ego and that I avoided emotional conversations. I was not relating to or emotionally engaging with people. I realized that the problem wasn't with "them"—it was with me.

With her help, I learned how to really listen, how to suspend my automatic response system, and how to be aware of my emotions and be present "in the moment." I learned how to be emotionally more accessible. She transformed my life by helping me understand why I had become such an effective, successful machine that had lost its humanness along the way. She engaged me in exploring how to be effective *and* human.

I am happy to report that my wife and I reconciled shortly thereafter, and we recently celebrated thirty-three years of marriage. She would tell you that I am still a work-in-progress. I would agree and say that I hope to always be one and always continue to improve.

In my work life, I became a Theory Y leader who cared about my employees and colleagues as people. I learned to really listen to them and to clients and to become a trusted and effective adviser, not just a seller of services. The more I truly listened and truly engaged as a person with people, the better my groups' financial results became. The more I related—instead of just talked—the more positive the results were both financially and emotionally.

In other words, what I am talking about in much of this book (although I did not know the science then) worked for me. The research confirms that it can work for you.

Today's business environment is more fast-paced than the environment in which I operated. Many public companies have become so lean that those employees, managers, and leaders who survive are pushed to do more and faster with fewer resources. The pressures are great to increase production, lest you be replaced in the next "reorganization" or "transformation."

(Today the words "termination" and "downsizing" have bad connotations that imply failure, and so corporate speak tries to spin the reality.)

In these environments, the easiest way to grow is through operating efficiencies and productivity matched with acquisitions as needed. This type of strategy rewards machine-like operating systems. Learning in those environments is hard because learning is not an efficient process. Learning requires people to change what they think and how they act. That in turn requires System 2 thinking and System 2 conversations, and they take time. They take emotional engagement. They require the machine to slow down.

While System 2 conversing may not be efficient, this doesn't mean that there aren't best practices when it comes to approaching and institutionalizing this type of dialogue. I next explore a few strategies that can help increase the number and the quality of your System 2 conversations.

Asking Not Telling

Edgar Schein, a professor at MIT and a leading authority on cultures has advocated for "humble inquiry" as a necessary skill and process for learning conversations. He stresses that a learning environment must offer "psychological safety," as discussed in the last chapter. In addition, he believes that the United States has a culture that values "telling" over "asking."[7] If my personal story is any indication, I have to agree with him.

Schein believes that we cannot begin to build trusting relationships unless we engage in humble inquiry.[8] "Telling" assumes the other person does not know. Telling is a hierarchical positioning act that says in effect: "I know more than you, and therefore, I am smarter and better than you." Alternatively, "asking" says: "I care about what you think, and I am ready to invest myself in listening."

Humble inquiry is a process of discovery. It is with open-mindedness and no predetermined or hidden agenda that we seek to learn. This type of seeking cannot happen by asking leading questions or being adversarial. It doesn't work if you're trying to lead someone to your answer. Rather, humble inquiry is "being in the moment" and in a receiving mode. It is being as unbiased, unemotional, and "un-me" as possible. It is also about trusting. Trust enables recognition of our humanness and the fact that we all have weaknesses, make mistakes, and know much less than we think we know. Real learning, in most cases, requires us to change what we believe, and humble inquiry helps us do that.

In most business environments, humble inquiry is hard because it's by getting things done and being good "doers" that people get promoted. The promoted person then thinks her job is to tell people how to do the task just like she did, because clearly that is the way to advance. In most business environments, people are scared to constructively disagree or dissent. They also are scared to ask for help or admit they don't know something.

How many of you who are in leadership positions have frequently admitted to employees that you don't know? Humble inquiry requires that kind of authenticity and humility. Schein believes that we will engage in learning and difficult conversations if and only if we believe that the other person will not take advantage of us, embarrass us, or use what we say against us later, and that he or she will tell us the truth.[9] Basically, we must believe that the person will not hurt us but will have our best interests at heart.

Another good framework to approach difficult conversations comes from the work done by the Harvard Negotiations Project.[10] That framework sees every conversation as three separate conversations: (1) a conversation where the parties each give their own view of what happened or what they believe the facts are; (2) a conversation where the parties each talk about how they felt about what happened; and (3) a personal private conversation that the parties each have with themselves to understand how much of their identities or egos are invested in a particular outcome.[11] Chapter 9 demonstrates the processes that Bridgewater uses in every learning conversation, which recognizes the multilayered nature of these interactions. Every conversation's purpose is declared at the outset and that declared purpose helps set the ground rules for the conversation. Bridgewater also uses a process of "getting in synch" to determine whether people are communicating and reaching an understanding of others' positions in learning conversations. Bridgewater's culture of "Radical Transparency" is intended to drive open, honest, fully transparent conversations.

Being aware of one's feelings, understanding what lies beneath those feelings, and figuring out how much self-image or self-worth one has invested in a particular view or outcome are all necessary in order to move beyond one's ego defense system to truly collaborate. We discussed this same point in chapter 3 when we talked about ways to keep our emotions from hijacking our thinking. We discuss it again in Chapter 7, when we look at the work of Kegan and Lahey with regard to unpacking the beliefs underlying one's feelings, and in chapter 9, when we look at a Bridgewater learning process, called "getting above yourself."

High-Quality Connections at Work

High-quality connections at work[12] help build the kind of relationships that enable System 2 learning conversations. Professor Jane Dutton at the Ross School of Business at the University of Michigan has done some outstanding research in this area, focusing on how respectful personal engagement occurs in workplaces.

Engaging with another person requires us to be present. To be present, we must be emotionally engaged and stay engaged—not be distracted by other thoughts or activities such as our mobile devices.[13] This takes effort and patience, because we can cognitively process up to 600 words a minute while most people only speak at a rate of 100–150 words a minute.[14] In other words, we get bored while listening. Have you ever sat through a conversation and in your head tried to urge the person to talk faster? I have. Fighting that cognitive boredom is key if we are to stay engaged, especially because people can subconsciously sense others' feelings and emotions.

Our emotional systems are triggered not only by the actual words someone speaks to us, but also by the emotional messages they transmit. Those nonspoken emotional messages are what Deborah Tannen called "metamessages."[15] They are evidenced by the speaker's body language, tone, loudness, pitch, and pace of speaking. They are also evidenced by the speaker's feelings that we can sense.[16] People broadcast their feelings both consciously and subconsciously, and metamessages can be received either consciously or subconsciously. We operate emotionally like a giant radar system scanning our environments and picking up others' feelings easily. We can sense whether someone is really present and emotionally engaged with us in the conversation.

Dutton cites research confirming that presence is conveyed by more than just language. Studies have shown that more than 50 percent of the impact of a message is conveyed by body movements, 38 percent is conveyed by tone of voice (e.g., volume, pitch), and only 7 percent of a message is conveyed by the words.[17] In light of this, Dutton suggests that we need to actively send signals to the other person that show we are engaged, and she suggests three ways to do this:

1. At the appropriate time in the conversation, paraphrase back to the speaker what you think they have said and ask whether you understood them correctly;

2. Summarize what the other person said in your own words and ask for clarification; and

3. Ask for further explanation or more details.[18]

It is easy to see that this type of active engagement requires face-to-face interaction. That is why, for example, Gore structures its operations in small units—generally 250 people or less—and explicitly encourages face-to-face conversations rather than conversations through e-mails or voicemail.

High-quality conversations require emotional engagement. Being genuine, being in the moment, being empathetic and acknowledging the other person's feelings and situation in a nonjudgmental way are key. What inhibits this type of active engagement? It's fear, status, hierarchy, and time pressure. As we learned in chapter 5, Gore's abhorrence of hierarchy and status goes all the way back to its founders' beliefs in Theory Y leadership and humanistic psychology. They saw an organization's purpose as helping human beings overcome their weaknesses by joining with others to do meaningful work. Similarly, chapter 9 discusses the immense amount of time spent at Bridgewater in learning conversations.

The power of work connections is really the power of relationships that are built by authentically relating to another person and recognizing their uniqueness, and doing so in a respectful way that builds trust. These types of work connections meet individuals' innate needs for relatedness. John Gabbert, the founder of home-furnishings retailer Room & Board, has built a very successful, privately owned business based on building and maintaining high-quality trusting relationships with employees, customers, and suppliers.[19] It's a relationship business model built by trust, mutual respect, and collaboration—that is, high-quality conversations.

Based in Minneapolis, Room & Board sells high-quality, classically designed home furnishings through thirteen Room & Board stores nationwide and through its website. It has over 800 employees and generates over $375 million in revenue. More than 90 percent of its products are manufactured in the United States by American craftspeople and private family businesses.

Room & Board operationalizes its relationships business model across employees, customers, and suppliers by encouraging transparency and high engagement that engenders mutual respect and trust. For example, every month the employees receive detailed information on the company's strategy and financial results so that everyone knows how their roles contribute to the good of the business. This disclosure says, in effect, "We trust you with this information," and also creates an environment of mutual account-ability among all employees. Room & Board trusts its employees to act pro-fessionally and in accordance with its fundamental *Guiding Principles*—not rules. Room & Board has no employee manual. It doesn't count sick days or personal leave. Managers are taught to make judgments based on a few core principles.

Likewise, annual meetings with suppliers include disclosure of full financial results by both sides to make sure both parties feel they are being treated fairly. Both sides in those annual reviews make commitments to each other, and Room & Board keeps its buying commitments even if the market slows down, because, in return, the family-owned manufacturer commits to interrupting its manufacturing schedules to accommodate and prioritize customized Room & Board orders. The manufacturer can plan its year relying on a base business from Room & Board, and Room & Board can rely on the manufacturer to produce customized orders very quickly—a mutually beneficial relationship.

Room & Board encourages all employees to work only eight hours a day to enable them to have a personal life. Many companies talk about work-life balance, but Room & Board lives it, believing that having good relationships outside of work helps employees come to work with positive attitudes that positively impact their work relationships. When I visit com-panies for research, I typically show up thirty minutes early because I find I can learn so much about a culture by observing people's interactions as they come to work. I did that at Room & Board's home office, and when I arrived at 8 a.m. I found that the front door was locked. After I knocked, a security guard came and invited me to come in. When I asked where everyone was, he answered: "Work starts here at 8:30 A.M., and it gets quite busy around here at 8:25 A.M." He was right. I experienced the same thing at the end of the day; I was interviewing senior management and employees working in the home office and distribution center, and around 4:30 in the afternoon, I informed my host that I was happy to meet with people for a couple more hours. She responded that everyone tries to leave by 5–5:30 P.M.

With respect to customers, Room & Board works to build ongoing, trust-ing relationships by putting customers' long-term interests first and foremost. They accomplish this by allowing customers to customize purchases and receive them in time frames much shorter than industry averages. Room & Board also shuns the practice of paying its store employees on a commission basis, and that puts the Room & Board store employee in the role of being a trusted adviser to customers by delinking how much one is paid to how much the customer buys. Room & Board also focuses on employee retention, knowing that in order to have real long-term customer relationships, it needs to have low employee turnover in each store. If every time a customer were to visit Room & Board, a different Room & Board employee were to assist, building trusting personal relationships would be much harder.

Through its high employee engagement practices, Room & Board achieves very high employee tenure compared to retail industry averages. Room & Board's relationship business model drives its very selective hiring. It works hard to find people who buy into the Room & Board philosophy that personal growth comes from richer experiences and deeper relationships in your current role, not from climbing a corporate ladder.[20] It seeks to hire and retain employees who find meaning in their work. According to Room & Board's *Guiding Principles*: "There is both tremendous productivity for the company and personal fulfillment for each staff member when someone finds their life's work. It's a wonderful circle of success."[21]

Like Gore, UPS, and Bridgewater, Room & Board's model is not for everyone. My MBA students always have a hard time with the Room & Board case because many of them want to climb a corporate ladder as fast as possible.

Sense Making Is Mindfulness

Dutton's work on respectful personal engagement at work ties into landmark work done by University of Michigan professor Karl Weick. In recent years, Weick has focused his studies on how individuals in organizations that require high reliability make sense of their fast-paced, changing environments. He has studied employees engaged in fighting forest fires, controlling air traffic, landing jets on the decks of aircraft carriers, and operating nuclear reactors, focusing on how to mitigate mindlessness or automaticity. In other words, he has focused on what I call System 2 thinking and System 2 conversations in situations where mistakes could cause a lot of harm.[22]

Weick deftly summarizes why learning in successful organizations and by successful employees is so hard: "In effect, success narrows perceptions, changes attitudes, feeds confidence in a single way of doing business, breeds overconfidence in the efficacy of current abilities and practices, and makes leaders and others intolerant of opposing points of view."[23]

He advocates that leaders create cultures and processes to fight this arrogance and complacency by using practices such as permission to speak freely; rewarding the reporting of mistakes; just-in-time, after action reviews; teams checking each other's work; and treating near mistakes as mistakes to be learned from. This research is applicable to every business today because what Weick is advocating is that individuals and organizations must continually learn, sense, and process new information and stress test their mental models.

Weick's work is about how to be mindful. In effect, he is advocating a System 2 approach to perception, because mindfulness is being attentive and noticing what is present and when you are present.[24]

So much of learning requires one to be present—to be sensitive to the need to take our thinking up to a System 2 level; to be sensitive to and manage our emotions and ego; and to be present when engaging with other people to build meaningful trusting relationships that enable emotional engagement and learning. In *The Power of Mindful Learning*, Ellen Langer says that being present also means being alert to differences and novelty, and open to different perspectives.[25]

All of this reminds me of a saying I learned doing business with cattle ranchers in Oklahoma. When you looked someone in the eye and they were clearly "there," they'd say: "someone's home." What they meant was that someone was present and emotionally engaged, authentic and vulnerable.

Maybe Woody Allen was right when he said that showing up is 80 percent of life.[26] Really showing up!

Conclusion

There are three consistent themes running through our discussions of Systems 1 and 2 thinking and conversations:

1. We generally overestimate how good we are at thinking, relating, and learning and how much we know.
2. We are not deeply aware often enough of our thinking, relating, emotions, ego defenses, fears, and the metamessages that we send to others.
3. We generally are not actively present (mindful) enough because we operate too much on autopilot.

We have learned from recent research in neuroscience and positive psychology that emotions have a powerful influence on every stage of cognition and conversation. We have learned that higher level System 2 thinking and conversations are necessary in most cases for learning to occur. To engage at that level takes intentional, deliberate, and mindful hard work. In essence System 2 thinking is aided by engaging in System 2 conversations with others.

We have learned that to enable learning, an environment must be trusting, humanistic, and positive. It must promote high emotional engagement; mutual accountability; open-mindedness; permission to speak freely; reporting of and tolerance for mistakes; a maniacal vigilance against arrogance, elitism, and complacency; and the devaluation of status and hierarchy. All of that enables System 2 thinking and System 2 conversations. If you want to be part of a learning organization, you must engage in effective learning conversations, because as we have discovered, learning is a team sport.

Reflection Questions

1. What did you read in this chapter that surprised you?
2. What are your top three takeaways that you want to reflect and/or act on?
3. What behaviors do you want to change?

7

Critical Thinking Tools

This chapter completes our High-Performance Learning Organization formula by focusing on critical thinking tools as part of the Right Processes.[1] Learning is a process of modifying or completely changing our mental models based on new experiences or evidence. Critical thinking tools are designed to help us identify weaknesses in our mental models and to counteract our human tendencies—cognitive blindness, cognitive dissonance, cognitive biases, and our ego defenses—that make changing our mental models so hard. In their book *Critical Thinking: Tools for Taking Charge of Your Professional and Personal Life*, Richard W. Paul and Linda Elder set forth what I call a "critical thinking creed" that I find helpful to keep in mind when reading about critical thinking tools:

> I will not identify with the content of any belief. I will identify only with the way I come to my beliefs. I am a critical thinker and, as such, am ready to abandon any belief that cannot be supported by evidence and rational considerations. I am ready to follow evidence and reason wherever they lead. My true identity is that of being a critical thinker, a lifelong learner, and a person always looking to improve my thinking by becoming more reasonable in my beliefs.[2]

By detaching our self-image and self-worth from our beliefs, we should be more willing to stress test those beliefs instead of habitually defending them. This means that being who we are won't be tied up in maintaining a particular view, answer, opinion, or conclusion. Rather, we can define our "being" by how we think and converse. Defining everything we know as conditional—subject to change based on new evidence—can help decouple our egos from our beliefs. To be good critical thinkers requires intellectual humility and a healthy respect for the magnitude of what we don't know. I find three simple questions helpful in operationalizing this critical thinking mindset: What do I truly know? What don't I know? What do I need to know?

In this chapter, I focus on some "tools" or processes that address four purposes: (1) slowing down our reflexive, habitual way of thinking so we can appropriately think more deliberately and deeply; (2) increasing the probability that we'll attend to disconfirming data by priming ourselves to be more open to it; (3) helping us unpack the assumptions underlying our beliefs so we can subject them to rigorous testing; and (4) helping us continuously learn from the results of our decisions and actions. I do not address models of "rational decision making" here; you can easily find those in any critical thinking textbook. Instead, I deal with the impact of our humanness on our critical thinking abilities and put forth tools developed and applied in real world situations that mitigate against the usual weaknesses in our thinking.

Klein's Tools

Dr. Gary Klein has developed three tools that can increase the probability that we'll be able to "see" and process new or disconfirming data and mitigate our cognitive blindness and dissonance. Klein is one of the founders of the naturalistic decision-making community of thinkers, whose approach to thinking has been to study how experts make decisions in high-velocity environments where mistakes have high costs, such as with fire fighters and combat soldiers. The three tools I cover in this section are the Recognition-Primed Decision model, the PreMortem tool, and Klein's "insight" process.

Recognition-Primed Decision Model

Klein's Recognition-Primed Decision (RPD) model[3] results from an approach to decision-making research that differs from that generally taken in behavioral economics and traditional judgment and decision-making research. The latter research is valuable because it illuminates a plethora of heuristics and biases that people subconsciously use and that result in sub-optimal decisions. Examples of this include the work of Daniel Kahneman and Max Bazerman on cognitive biases,[4] which we discussed in chapter 2. That research was based primarily on laboratory experiments with students. Klein and others, by contrast, wanted to study how people actually make good decisions in the real world, especially in situations characterized by change, uncertainty, time pressures, and big downsides.[5] Certain cognitive biases, according to Klein, are much less present in the real world situations on which Klein's work has focused. Klein and Kahneman are friends and have debated their different beliefs publicly.[6]

Klein found that people in high-velocity environments, where speed of decision making is important, generally don't take the time to gener-ate alternatives and then weigh the pros and cons of each or engage in a probability evaluation. Instead, they engage in fast pattern matching. They process the environmental cues or conditions generated by the situation, create a pattern of what they think is happening and then match that pat-tern to the patterns "on file" in their minds. They sense, process, interpret, and then pattern match.

According to Klein's research, once decision makers in these high-velocity situations match the existing situation to a pattern on file in their minds, a course of action automatically comes to them based on prior experience and learning. This matching process usually produces only one answer—one response. Obviously, the richer a person's prior experience, the more nuanced and sophisticated will be the patterns on file in her mind. This becomes an expert's competitive advantage.

What happens next, according to Klein, is surprising and critical. These experts don't brainstorm a variety of responses, and they also don't just accept the immediate answer that comes to mind. Instead, they stop and engage their intentional and deliberate System 2 type thinking to simulate and visu-alize the outcome if they were to make that response. They play out in their mind what would likely happen if they made the response. They mentally rehearse the proposed response. They then evaluate what they "see." If they think it will work, they go forward. If they have concerns, they try to modify the response to alleviate them. They adapt their initial response to this situ-ation. If that doesn't satisfy them, only then do they come up with another option. The research has found that this is an effective process.

Here's an example of how this model can work. Let's imagine a fire chief responds with her crew to an industrial fire. Upon arrival, the chief assesses the situation: Are there humans inside the structure? Are there injured people? What is the size and intensity of the fire? What are the materials used to make the structure? What are the contents inside the structure? What are the neighboring structures and their contents? All of this processing happens quickly, as the chief automatically matches this picture to the patterns "on file" in her mind. Similar fires and the subsequent firefighting responses come to mind quickly.

Now here's the key part. The chief doesn't immediately give directions and take action. Rather, she deliberately takes the time to consider what will happen if she handles this situation as the previous ones were handled. She does this by simulating and visualizing what will happen if the course of action that came into her mind is actually implemented. She mentally rehearses or plays out how the action will unfold. As this happens, the chief is sensitive to whether something does not feel right. If the mental simulation feels "off" somehow, then she'll deliberately think about what specifically does not feel right. Is there something in this fire that sticks out as different that should be taken into account? The chief then makes a decision either to go forward, to modify quickly and then go forward, or to take a few minutes and come up with a better response.

This thinking process can be applied in everyday business situations. Every day we make many quick decisions without either deliberately thinking about alternatives or mentally rehearsing the proposed course of action. Some of those decisions are more important than others. We must be aware of our tendency to make quick decisions, and prompt ourselves to slow down when facing important decisions. In those situations, I think the RPD model that Klein has identified can be helpful. The effectiveness of the RPD process tells us that we need to recognize what daily decisions require us to stop and mentally simulate an otherwise quick response. Doing so may cause us to notice something different about the current situation that causes concern. This is key. Is there something meaningfully different about the current fact pattern as compared to the pattern in our mind that we matched? At the same time, we need to be sensitive to our feelings because they can represent our subconscious intuitive knowledge. Does this possible course of action "feel" right? If the answer is "yes," then proceed. If the answer is "not really," then we need to focus on what does not feel right, and why.

This RPD tool is a good one for everyone to use because it applies in any important situation where we tend to act on the first answer that pops into our minds. The RPD tool helps us slow down our quick, initial response to allow us to consider how this response would play out in this fact situation. This may lead us to a different—and better—course of action.

The PreMortem

Klein's RPD works well in situations where you have created patterns in your mind based on previous similar experiences, and when circumstances dictate immediate action. But what about when you're embarking on something new? In a business context, you could be dealing with new initiatives, new processes, innovation, strategy making, expansions, or a major change in any functional area, for instance technology or human resources. In these situations, you may not have patterns on file in your mind based on past experiences because you have either no experience or not enough experience to be meaningful. But you do have mental models about your business and how business is done in your industry. In these situations, the risk is that you could be too attached to your existing mental models. This might lead you to blindly assume that these models apply to the new situation, rather than subjecting those mental models to critical thinking. To help in these kinds of situations, Klein has created a tool called the PreMortem to help stress test decisions involving novel situations.

A PreMortem is a process that should be used after you have preliminarily decided on a course of action but before you take action. It requires everyone involved to assume that the proposed action was implemented—and that it failed miserably.[7] This should put everyone into a different frame of mind, shifting from excitement about a new idea to scrutiny about the reasons for failure. What went wrong? Why did this failure occur? You and each member of your team should individually list all the reasons for this failure. The key here is that by putting yourself into a mindset of actual failure, you should be able to bring new possibilities to mind that you didn't think about during your planning process.

The next step in the PreMortem process is to consolidate the lists of reasons why the action failed, and then go back to the proposed course of action and evaluate whether you have adequately mitigated against those potential pitfalls. You may need to amend the course of action to mitigate the risks of failure, or in some cases, the risks may be so high or numerous that you need to formulate a different plan altogether.

Klein's PreMortem tool has two other potential benefits. Klein's research shows that the PreMortem tool reduces overconfidence. It lessens our certainty, which can make us more open-minded. Also, actually talking about and thinking about what can cause failure can increase the likelihood that, as we move forward, we will attend to data that could be an early warning signal of a failure in process. That is a third benefit of using a PreMortem— it can help prime you to sense and process disconfirming data that you would not ordinarily take heed of. This isn't the only critical thinking tool that uses this approach; the Learning Launch process, which I discuss in the next section, includes an explicit step in which the team is asked to state what specific evidence would call into question or disconfirm an assumption or belief. In both cases, we are required to stop and put ourselves in a different mindset.[8] Doing this creates, in effect, a mental sensitivity to important cues that we may otherwise ignore.

When I discovered Klein's PreMortem tool, it resonated with me because I had used a similar tool with C-Suite executives in three executive education programs. I had asked those executives to write two newspaper articles for a prime business newspaper dated ten years in the future. One article was to be a story of X Corp titled "A Model of Enduring Success." The second article was to be a different story of X Corp—"A Sad Story of Corporate Demise."

The first article was easy for them, and was telling in that it revealed how each executive defined success. The second article, however, was the real purpose of the exercise, and required the executives to think about what could destroy X Corp. In two of the programs, the exercise was productive and resulted in the executives implementing early warning systems at their companies to help detect data that could signal the beginning of demise. In the third case, however, the team of executives thought they were bulletproof; in the story they came up with for the second article, X Corp failed because of government regulation—and X Corp wasn't even in a regulated industry. Clearly, if you're unable to imagine failure at all, these exercises won't be helpful.

This storytelling tool is a lot like scenario planning. Scenario planning tools have been used for a long time in business. They became popular when Shell Oil adopted them in the early 1970s. Their purpose is to help teams create plausible future realities, which requires the people doing the planning to avoid letting their current mental models limit the future alternatives considered. Scenario planning asks: What if this happens or occurs? How does that affect the future? As in my example above, scenario planning is only as good as the underlying team driving the process. Is a diverse team with different viewpoints engaged in the process? Is the team empowered, encouraged, and protected in challenging existing mental models?

The Insight Process

A third process that Klein has created provides yet another way for us to see or consider what we are naturally disinclined to see. Klein describes this important process as gaining "insights,"[9] and advocates that most insights come from two ways of thinking about data: (1) deliberately looking for new ways to combine things (connecting the dots) and (2) noticing differences (contradictions/anomalies/ inconsistencies).

Insights may lead to innovations, new business processes, or new strategies. To look for insights, we have to slow down our thinking and deliberately search. This requires us to suspend judgment and be open-minded. This process is a way to potentially loosen the powerful grip that our mental models have on our thinking. Insight thinking helps us interpret data in novel ways. Insights can be discovered by asking yourself questions like these:

1. Is there any data here that contradicts or is inconsistent with what I believe? If so, what could that mean?
2. Is there something new, unusual, or out of the ordinary present that I should think about? What could that data mean?
3. Can I look at the data differently and produce a different answer?
4. If I define or reframe my question or problem differently, would that open up new alternatives or help me see more data or create a different dot pattern?
5. Have I actively listed what data would be disconfirming, and have I actively searched for disconfirming data? If not, should I?
6. Does my answer feel right and make sense?

Looking for insights requires us to be open to data that does not make sense or fit with what we believe or want to believe. In chapter 10, we will look at Intuit's learning processes and how Intuit looks for surprises (insights) resulting from its learning experiments; those surprises can be the basis for a whole new way of meeting customer needs.

We have talked about how fear inhibits good thinking and learning, but in some cases, fear can be beneficial. For example, fear of missing something that could materially change or negatively impact your business seems to me to be a good fear. I call this "constructive paranoia." I recently spent six hours with a very bright senior management team of a consistently high-performance public company as the guest of the chairman-CEO. The purpose was to discuss how to fight complacency and intellectual arrogance by being paranoid about "what we don't know." My role was to help the team recognize and illuminate their fixed mental models about their business and industry. At the end of the workshop, my host took me aside to thank me and said that he thought the most important thing I'd said all day was, "Treat everything you think you know as hypotheses to be constantly retested by new data."

Let me summarize Klein's contributions this way. The purpose of critical thinking tools is to help us mitigate our natural tendencies to be lazy thinkers, because as lazy thinkers, we generally do not stress test our mental models or our habitual ways of responding to situations. In addition, we usually do not sense or process data that could call into question our mental models and beliefs. We generally operate on autopilot. Klein's tools help us to slow down our thinking because each tool requires us to think critically. Following the RPD framework requires us to stop and mentally simulate and visualize a proposed course of action to assess if it's a good fit for the current situation. A PreMortem requires us to deliberately think about what could cause failure and to assess how the causes of failure impact our proposed course of action. Klein's process of gaining insights helps us discover new ideas.

The next type of tools I want to discuss are tools that help unpack assumptions. Unpacking assumptions is important in testing our beliefs and decisions, changing our mental models and behaviors, and effecting organizational change.

Unpacking Assumptions

Testing our critical thinking requires us to clearly state our beliefs or points of view. The next step is harder—we have to identify the underlying assumptions that we use to justify those beliefs or points of view. To do this, we must unpack—recognize and verbalize—those base assumptions. This unpacking process is similar to conducting a root cause analysis or employing the "Toyota 5 Whys" in a business operations or manufacturing situation. In that case, you have a manufacturing defect and you are trying to figure out what you have to fix to eliminate future defects, and you keep asking "why" until you get to the foundational cause. This process also happens to be similar to the fundamental processes used in cognitive behavioral therapy[10] and clinical psychology consulting[11] to help people change behaviors. In those situations, the client must unpack the feelings, emotional events, and underlying beliefs that drive the behavior they want to change.

The same process needs to occur in an organizational context when we seek to stress test our beliefs and tentative decisions. As a general outline for this process, we need to:

1. State our belief clearly;
2. Unpack the assumptions underlying that belief;
3. Determine what leaps of thought or inferences we're making based on those assumptions;
4. Stress test those assumptions/inferences by evaluating the data that supports and disconfirms them; and
5. Determine whether we have enough quality data to proceed, or whether we need to gather more data.

The kind of "thinking out loud" that this unpacking process requires helps to ensure that the decision-making process will be transparent and deliberate. Think how powerful it would be if in every team meeting to discuss an important issue, the meeting leader followed this five-step process and made "thinking out loud" a norm, especially when making or evaluating alternatives and decisions. Is it a powerful process? Yes. Does it work? Yes. You will read about a very similar process at Bridgewater in chapter 9.

Unpacking assumptions is also a key part of a tool that was developed at Darden in 2007 called a "Learning Launch."[12] It's a low-cost, speedy experiment to test new growth and innovation ideas. Basically, a Learning Launch is the scientific method for a business test or experiment. It involves seven key steps:(1) taking a business idea and restating it as a hypothesis; (2) unpacking the customer value, execution, defensibility and scalability assumptions underlying the idea; (3) prioritizing the key assumptions to test first; (4) designing the experiment to test those key assumptions; (5) doing the experiment; (6) evaluating the results; and (7) deciding next steps.

Since it was first developed, the Learning Launch has morphed into a process to test even business process improvements. Its premise is to test the key assumptions underlying new ideas as fast and as cheaply as possible with customers or internal users. In many ways, it's similar to what entrepreneurs do when using a lean start-up process,[13] except that a Learning Launch does not initially require a prototype to assess customer needs.

The Learning Launch requires us to put ourselves into the customer's shoes and think deeply about what must be true for an idea to be a good one. To do that requires a drilling down to the base-level, "burning" customer need that would be strong enough to overcome customer inertia and drive a change in behavior—that is, buying from us.

Answering the question, "What must be true for this assumption to be true?" is the start. The second step is to continue in the style of "Toyota's 5 Whys" by taking the answer to that first question, asking ourselves what must be true for that answer to be true, and continuing this process until we get to all the underlying foundational facts that must be true for our assumptions about this new product or strategy to be correct. Of course, we must also think critically about our data and decide if it's substantial enough to justify our assumptions, taking into account the seriousness and magnitude of the decision. A good critical thinker knows that all decisions are based on some incomplete data and that we have a tendency to discount or ignore disconfirming data.

Until you unpack your key foundational assumptions, you won't be able to assess the strength of the data that supports or disconfirms your belief. From teaching this process I have learned that most managers and leaders find the unpacking of assumptions to be much harder to do than they think. It is a learnable skill, however, and becomes easier with practice. In their book *Train Your Mind for Peak Performance*, noted research psychologists Lyle Bourne, Jr. and Alice Healy, share their findings that we can learn to think better by engaging in deliberate practice using thinking tools, along with real-time constructive feedback. In other words, unpacking assumptions can be learned, and with practice, practice, and more practice, comes better thinking.

In working on over 200 Learning Launches with managers/leaders in workshops over the past six years, I have found the following step-by-step questionnaire to be helpful in unpacking assumptions and testing underlying data:[14]

1. What is the assumption to be tested?
2. What facts do we already know that confirm the assumption?
3. What facts do we already know that cast doubt on the assumption?
4. What specific facts would confirm the assumption?
5. What specific additional facts would disconfirm the assumption?
6. For each specific additional fact that would confirm the assumption:

> Who knows those facts?
> Where do we find those facts?
> How many different confirming sources do we need?
> How will we mitigate confirmation bias in our search?

7. For each specific fact that would disconfirm or cast doubt on the assumption:

> Who knows those facts?
> Where do we find those facts?
> How many different disconfirming sources do we need?

Gathering data is part science and part art. It's a lot like the discovery process in litigation. In fact, material written for training young litigators to take discovery depositions is a good source of advice on how to frame and ask open-ended discovery questions in a business context. Open-ended questions are different from leading questions; the latter lead the responder to the answer you want from him or her. That is confirmation bias at work. The answer you should want is the truth—just the facts, whatever they may be.

To further mitigate cognitive blindness and confirmation bias in testing assumptions, data discovery should be done by small teams rather than just one person, and the team shouldn't stop questioning when it gets to an answer that everyone likes. Rather, they should keep exploring by asking the question different ways or by getting the responder to elaborate on his or her answers. Again, the point is to get to the truth—not the answer you're hoping for.

An example: Assume you are in charge of creating new growth initiatives at Orange Delicious Corporation. You sell oranges directly to consumers through your own website and Amazon.com. Tasked with coming up with new revenue opportunities, you think it would be a good idea to sell orange juice squeezers, too.

What must be true for your idea to succeed? What assumptions are you making regarding customer needs? What assumptions are you making about your ability to execute on this idea? What assumptions are you making about being able to withstand competitors?

Here are some assumption possibilities. Your first assumption is that many of your customers buy your oranges for squeezing—not just for peeling and eating. Your second assumption is that those customers are using squeezing methods or products that they find inadequate and that they have a need for a different squeezing product. Your third assumption is that good solutions that would resolve the inadequacies aren't already available at a cost customers are willing to pay. Your fourth assumption might be that by selling squeezers you could reach new customers that now buy their oranges from other sources.

What execution assumptions are you making in assuming a customer need exists? First, are you assuming you can create and sell a squeezer at a cost that meets customer needs? Second, are you assuming that customers will buy from you and not another vendor? Why? Third, are you assuming you have the capabilities to manufacture a squeezer directly or indirectly at a cost cheap enough to make a profit? Fourth, are you assuming established competitors will not aggressively respond?

Assumptions underlie our mental models, our ego defenses, and our behaviors. Organizational psychologists Robert Kegan and Lisa Laskow Lahey have written an interesting book, *Immunity to Change*,[15] in which they focused on why it's so difficult for people to change their behaviors even when they are committed to change. They found that even when people want to change, they behave in ways that frustrate or inhibit that change. That's because most people have a strong competing commitment of which they usually are unaware that trumps the motivation to change. To overcome that competing commitment, according to Kegan and Lahey, people first have to uncover it. Then they have to get to the root cause of that inhibiting commitment—what Kegan and Lahey call the "big assumptions."[16]

The big assumptions usually involve a fear or ego defense that arose earlier in our lives. It usually takes the help of others, either a counselor or trusted friends, to uncover that big assumption. Again, we see the power of the unpacking process here. I find it fascinating that across disciplines (business operations, decision making, psychology, behavioral change, and education), human behavior is limited by an individual's mental models and ego defenses. To change behaviors, people must change their mental models. We can't change our mental models unless we unpack the assumptions underlying our beliefs and subject them to rational testing.

In their book *Critical Thinking*[17] Paul and Elder make the same argument when they discuss how irrational emotions inhibit critical thinking. According to them, underlying irrational emotions are irrational beliefs, and the way to tamp down the volume and power of irrational emotions is to challenge the irrational beliefs. To do that, you have to unpack the feelings and then unpack the irrational beliefs underlying the feelings. Paul and Elder then advocate that you try rationally thinking about the irrational beliefs until you can figure out why the irrational beliefs are irrational. Then, when you experience those same feelings in the future, you should be able to retrieve your rational thinking. Again, it's an unpacking process or root cause analysis.

U.S. Army After Action Review

So far, we have focused on tools that can (1) help us slow down our reflexive way of thinking and think more deliberately; (2) mitigate cognitive blindness and help us see disconfirming or new data; and (3) unpack the assumptions underlying our beliefs and our ego defenses in order to critically evaluate our thinking and mitigate against learning inhibitors. The fourth and last type of tool helps us learn from our actions and experiences. That tool is the U.S. Army After Action Review (AAR).[18]

The AAR is a conversation among team members that takes place after an action has happened. A meeting leader leads the team through a discovery conversation with the stated purpose of learning from the action, not finding fault or placing blame. Commonly asked AAR questions are: What happened? Why did it happen? What worked? What did not work? Why did it not work? What should we do differently next time? The objective is to be as factual as possible and to get everyone involved in the discussion regardless of hierarchal position. The Army recommends that people gather in a horseshoe seating arrangement, and if senior officers above the team leader are present, they sit in the back of the room. Regardless of rank, every person is expected to contribute and every person has permission to speak freely.

The process is effective, but like so much of what we have learned so far, the success of it depends on people having the right attitudes and behaviors and trusting each other and the process. To be effective, the process requires confronting the brutal facts, and that can mean discussing failures to perform that could have had dire consequences. Empathy, compassion, and emotional support become critical, because it takes courage for people to admit mistakes before their teammates. The purpose of an AAR is to learn so the team can constantly improve. Improving depends on the quality of the learning conversation, and all of the points we discussed in chapter 6 about learning conversations apply here.

Does it work? Based on my experience with the AAR process while I was in investment banking and strategy consulting, the answer is yes. After each meeting with a client or a target customer, my team and I stopped as soon as we could after leaving the premises and had a fifteen-to-twenty-minute AAR. I asked these questions: What happened in the meeting? What was really being said? What happened that surprised you? Did we accomplish our objective? What could we have done better? Some days we did three or four of these in close proximity to the end of the meeting, while it was still fresh in our minds. It was also a great teaching tool for younger teammates. I suggest that every organization needs some version of the AAR process as a standard learning process.

Conclusion

We have learned that our cognitive sensing and processing system works to confirm our beliefs and to affirm our self-image. Our ego defense system works to protect our self-image and protect us from our fears. Those same fears underlie the big assumptions that restrict our ability to learn and to change our behaviors. Until we unpack and discover those underlying inhibiting assumptions, our learning will be limited.

In a work environment, we will suboptimize thinking and learning unless the environment enables critical thinking. That's only going to happen in a work environment in which people feel safe and trust that the information disclosed publicly will not be used to harm them. We have come full circle and back to chapter 5, in which we discussed in detail the kinds of organizational environments and leadership behaviors that enable personal learning and high-performance organizational learning.

We have learned that becoming an effective learning organization requires high-quality learning by employees. That kind of learning requires high-quality critical thinking and high-quality learning conversations, which in turn require an environment of trust and authenticity, the freedom to speak freely, and the freedom to be "human" and disclose our weaknesses. We overcome our human thinking and learning deficiencies by confronting the brutal facts about our outside world and by confronting the brutal truth about our inside worlds—the fears we have that inhibit our learning and growth. Bridgewater has put in place these processes that enable and promote not only critical thinking but also the confrontation of each individual's ego defenses that inhibit his or her learning and growth. That's why the Bridgewater story in chapter 9 is so important.

Critical thinking tools are important for learning, especially in a business environment characterized by change. Change is hard for individuals and organizations. The purpose of this book is to help facilitate learning that facilitates adaptive change—personally and in business. In researching critical thinking tools for this chapter, one avenue of exploration was the learning research sponsored by the U.S. Army. That is how I found Gary Klein's work. His real-world research approach and findings resonated with me. I reached out to him and asked him to be part of this book. What follows in the next chapter is a fascinating verbatim transcript of my interview with him that I think helps illuminate many topics discussed in the first part of this book.

Reflection Questions

1. What did you read in this chapter that surprised you?
2. What are your top three takeaways that you want to reflect and/or act on?
3. What behaviors do you want to change?

8

A Conversation with Dr. Gary Klein

Gary Klein is a senior scientist with MacroCognition LLC and has spent more than forty years as a research psychologist. He is an expert on how people make decisions in natural settings. Much of his research has occurred in high-velocity environments involving high-reliability occupations and the U.S. military in particular. Gary was one of the founders of the field of naturalistic decision making and is the author of five books; his most recent, *Seeing What Others Don't See: The Remarkable Ways We Gain Insights* (New York: BBS Public Affairs, 2013), is a great read and was named a top ten business book of 2013 by the editors at Amazon.com.

My interview with Gary was fascinating and full of learning opportunities. First, he brings decades of research experience to bear not only on the topic of critical thinking from the last chapter, but on many of the topics we have discussed throughout this first part of the book. He makes important points throughout the interview dealing with: how fixed mindsets limit learning; how important emotions are in making good decisions; how organizational environments inherently inhibit learning; the challenges of operationalizing "permission to speak freely" in a big organization; and the importance of curiosity and open-mindedness. That is just a hint of what is coming in the following interview transcript.

He also shares some interesting stories about Winston Churchill, Intel, the Israeli Defense Force, and two personal stories regarding the role of emotions in making a big personal business decision and how to invite and engage team members in frank, open learning conversations. Last, he discusses how he disagrees with Daniel Kahneman with regard to confirmation biases. As you will read, he does not totally agree with me all the time either.

Without further ado, I welcome Dr. Gary Klein to *Learn or Die*.[1]

Interview Transcript

EH: Gary, Thank you for your generosity of spirit and time in agreeing to do this interview for this book. Gary, I found the title of your book *Street Lights and Shadows: Searching for the Keys to Adaptive Decision Making*, interesting. What do you mean by adaptive decision making?

GK: So much of decision making is taught and treated as if you can predefine the options. And once you can predefine the options and predefine the evaluation criteria, then it's a simple rack 'em, stack 'em type of process. But in the situations that I study, you really don't have evaluation dimensions that apply to all the options. And as you go through the process, you start discovering additional evaluation criteria and additional variations of options. So the belief that we can nicely set up a matrix in advance falls apart because the criteria and the options evolve as you make discoveries. That's the adaptive part.

EH: So really what you're talking about is decision making in environments that are changing or environments that are ambiguous. Decision making where you don't really know the facts. Is that what you're talking about?

GK: Yes I am. So there are two parts of the equation. First, the situation may be ambiguous. Second, the situation will be dynamic so the situation is changing. And a third factor would be the discoveries you make as you go through the process.

EH: I like your Recognition-Primed Decision model as a way to deal with these types of environments. And in your words, can you describe why that model is an adaptive decision-making model?

GK: It is an adaptive decision making model because it really is describing how people handle time, pressure, and uncertainty. It describes how people can rapidly respond to new discoveries or to changes in situations. Research suggests that to set up a decision matrix takes about a half-hour. That's not going to help most of the people that we study who don't have that amount of time for making decisions. And so they're not in a position to be adaptive. Their recognitional strategy shows how people can truly be adaptive by rapidly changing how they size up situations, changing the patterns that are activated. And so, reorienting themselves as they sort out the ambiguity and as they appreciate how the changed situation creates new demands on them.

EH: So to do that well, it seems to me that somebody has got to be very sensitive to their environment and to be able to process that information even though that information is different than what they thought or expected. In other words, they don't have a fixed mindset or they don't want their mental model to inhibit the processing. There's a sensitivity and alertness to new data or different data or conflicting data. This model basically describes how people in these types of environments make better decisions.

GK: I agree with most of that. I think for me the real issue is not whether you have a mental model but whether you're fixated. And so I think to me, that's the gist of what you said—that people who fixate on their initial ideas and try to bend the world (sometimes it's referred to as bending the map to fit your ideas), those people aren't going to be able to handle dynamic situations. And one of the things that you described is really openness to the dynamics so you can have a rapid adaptation.

EH: I want to go down that openness idea. My work in the business world, which is not as dynamic, if you will, as the world that you study. A lot of your studies have been done in dangerous or life-and-death situations. However, the business world is changing at a faster pace, the amount of data is increasing daily, the speed at which decisions have to be made is faster. So the concept of open-mindedness is critical. Based on all your work, how do you train people to be open-minded?

GK: Well, if we had a good answer to this, we'd both be very wealthy. I think part of it is about individual differences that are beyond training. There are some people who are open to new experience and become curious when they see anomalies and there are other people who, they may have risen to high levels because they're determined. You can count on them and that's because once they say something, they're committed to it. And that's sort of the opposite of being open-minded and open to changes in the situation. So part of it is individual differences.

Part of it is the kind of pressures coming from above. Is there a pressure for staying consistent and for not changing your mind? Are people censured when they make those kinds of changes? Or is there appreciation for the importance of rethinking situations? I'm reading a biography of Winston Churchill right now and he had strong opinions. He held them strongly. He tried to push his own way. But he had enough expertise to be aware of the implications of new developments. So I guess where the training would come in is having people build richer mental models so that they can see the implications and nuances of new data and not discard these early warning signs.

EH: Is it basically right-brain people who are better at adapting than left-brain people? Is that a hypothesis that's been tested?

GK: I'm not aware that it's been tested. I've seen many situations where people perform the analyses and they're so committed to the analyses and the results, that they become insensitive to the situation. And there are also people who rely heavily on pattern matching—they can be trapped by the initial patterns that get activated or they can be open to new patterns that get activated when new signals appear. I can see arguing it either way. So I'm not sure. I'm not sure that's the dimension that traps them. I think that it's peoples' reluctance to change their mind or to publicly change their mind, a need to be consistent and to appear consistent, and I think some people are open to experience. I think there's an individual difference there that's beyond training—here it's about openness to experiences. Second, some people have a need to think about implications and others just, once they've made a decision, they're done with it. They don't want to explore any further.

EH: You mentioned the environment you're in and whether it's the pressure from above. Let's talk about the business world for a moment. We've talked before about the difficulty in organizations that are operationally excellent that run on 99 percent defect-free reliability, predictability, and standardization. In that type of environment can people be comfortable in changing their mind and admitting their mistakes? How does the military create that environment versus the business world? What's been your experience? Is it permission to speak freely in the military that gives people permission to change their mind or to express doubt?

GK: I'm going to attack your premise that the military teaches that. I haven't seen that in the military. And even if we say, you know, you have permission to speak freely, if I was a young officer, I might believe it the first time but once I got stomped for speaking my mind, I'd realize that I've got to be very careful and I've got be very cautious in military environments where people believe they have permission to speak freely and they really don't. And the people who give them permission think they mean it. Let me give you an example from my own company.

I ran my own company for twenty-seven years and we used to tell new people who came in, you're a tremendous resource to us because you're seeing everything we do through fresh eyes. And so we want you to tell us what your reactions are because we know you're a way of helping us avoid the blinders we've been building. You don't have those blinders. We said those things. We meant those things. Then I watched in meetings somebody who just joined the company, we were having a discussion and a new person would start to speak out. And senior management, including me, would think, "Wait a second, you shouldn't be speaking. You don't know what's going on here." So there was a feeling of impatience even though we had given them permission to speak freely and we believed we meant it. And so where I've seen it work in the military is a senior commander partners with somebody, say, a young captain, so you have a two-star general finding a captain that he thinks is pretty savvy and they'll have a sidebar type of arrangement between the two of them, where the general will ask for candid responses, and it avoids the entire chain of command. Because in that chain of command, you're going to find somebody who doesn't want certain opinions to be voiced. So the military talks about that arrangement as having a directed telescope where you have a personal relationship and a young officer who's flattered to have a relationship with his senior officer, and comes to trust the senior officer as not betraying confidence. And I had one three-star general tell me that, "yeah, that's the way I like to work with my subordinates. And my, the intermediates, the colonels in between and the one-stars would complain that their authority was being abrogated. And I [the three-star] just told them, 'Get used to it. This is the way I work.'"

EH: Very interesting. You know, I'm just thinking about this concept of open-mindedness. It is related somewhat, if you will, to the work you've done in mindfulness and sense making, the ability of a person to make decisions without the pressure to conform or worry about whether they are going to look bad. Am I just naive? Am I just basically searching for a utopia that just does not exist?

GK: I don't think it's a complete utopia. I don't think it's a complete fantasy. I think that there are organizations where the people in the room have learned to trust each other and learn that they can speak candidly and they won't be punished. I don't think that happens very often but I think it is possible and it can exist as an idea. And I think a stop gap, if you don't have that, is to use this type of directed telescope so that you're not trapped by the official view where folks down at the bottom may have been warning of things but they can't get it up to you because the warnings are getting suppressed. Because it only takes one, one block in the chain of command and all of a sudden those warnings don't appear. So there are ways of working around it or there are ways of moving toward a more open environment. Either way, I think, it gets you what you want. I'd rather have the semi-utopia like view that you have of letting everybody in the room know that it's okay to say what you believe. But that's hard to get to.

EH: Let me go back to mental models. I found in your work some interesting positions about them. I may not be stating it correctly so correct me. You know, a lot has been written about the negative aspects of mental models. You make a point that mental models also serve very positive purposes. How does an individual know what his or her mental model or story is? And then second, how do I know when my mental model is working OK and when it is keeping stuff out and making me rigid or close-minded? How does a person manage that process?

GK: To me it's possible but it's really hard so there are two questions there. One, how do you know your own mental model? The answer to that is easy. You don't. That's what allows you to respond so quickly because you're not consulting your mental model. You're using it so it governs what you see and how you think about it. So it's really a form of tacit knowledge. It's not available to you. That makes it dangerous because if you have flaws in your mental model, you're not going to know it. You're going to be trapped by them. An example of that is, you know the old nine-dot problem that they give people in research environments where you have three rows of three dots and you've got to connect them with four lines.

Let's talk about the nine-dot problem as seeing the invisible. People struggle with it because their mental model traps them. And the mental model includes assumptions and the assumptions are like, I've got to stay within the frame, the nine dots, which is wrong because that was never part of the official instructions. And another assumption is, I can only change directions on a dot and that's wrong. But people don't know that they're making those assumptions. So if you ask people to examine their own mental model, they don't even know they're making those assumptions. If you ask them to list all their assumptions, they won't get anywhere because they're not aware that these are assumptions. People cannot examine their own assumptions.

So the second question is, are we doomed or is there some way around it? And I know, clearly we're not doomed because we're all doing pretty well. So what happens to some people is when the mental model stops working, then some people, sooner than others, start to cast around for reasons and try to examine what's going wrong and so failures, traumatic failures, can cause people to be open, to reexamine their mental models. Early signs of problems are opportunities for people who just aren't so rigid to look at these early signs or problems instead of saying, "I'm going to double down." They start to reexamine, we shouldn't be struggling here, what could the reasons be? It could be that your performance is not as successful as you want. If you're working at an organization in a team it can happen when people who are good disagree with each other. Instead of trying to suppress the disagreement to generate harmony, you can say, "Well, I've got smart people who disagree. Let me understand the nature of the disagreement because this can help me re-examine my mental model and the mental model we've always used." So you can look for confusion, disagreements, and controversy. They create an opportunity to reexamine your mental model.

EH: And what that says to me is that disagreement can be good. It's an early warning signal. But it also says to me, "Okay I've got to be comfortable with disagreement and have rules of engagement where, you know, we're debating what's the right answer not who is right or wrong." I guess people have to basically submerge their ego defenses and openly engage.

GK: Okay, so there are so many facets of that. I'm not sure I can capture all of them but I'll capture a few. First of all, the "rules of engagement" is a wonderful way to put it. And you can state the rules of engagement and maybe that's a starting point. But you have to live the rules of engagement so that people are comfortable. And one set of rules of engagement would be, we want you to speak your mind. If I am in charge of the meeting, I would then say that doesn't mean I'm going to buy into what you say. I pledge that I'm going to listen to what you say. But by the time this meeting is over, I'm going to announce what direction we're going to take. And I want everybody to fall in line, and if you disagree with that, too bad. I need you to fall in line so that we have a coordinated effort. But I don't want you to squash your own disagreement because you can be sensitive to early signs that I may have gotten it wrong. So I'm not asking you to let me brainwash you. I'm just saying for coordinated action, you're going to have to proceed on one interpretation and it's the interpretation that I have set based on what I will hear.

So that's a way of setting up rules of engagement that empower people to disagree and don't try to brainwash them. Once you've done that, what about the people who don't speak up? I mean if you're a leader, you can look at people's faces and you can see if they're on board or, you know, if they have visible looks on their faces and instead of putting them on the spot, you can talk to them afterward and see what's troubling them. And I had that come up yesterday, we had a briefing at a medical school on a new project that we want to start and there was one person who was just really quiet about the plan we put forward. And people said, "Yeah, she's just quiet." Well maybe she's quiet but it's not helping me because I wasn't in a position to go back to her. So I turned to her and I said, "Okay, if you had one suggestion for us about how to improve this plan, what would it be?" And she hesitated for maybe five seconds at most and she said, "Here's what I would look for." So there are ways of, even in a public meeting, of framing it so that you're not having her disagree and make it sound like she's being disrespectful. But you're framing it so that she's helping you by being constructive so that you honestly want to know what she's thinking.

EH: That's very helpful. Let me go to confirmation bias. I've read your great conversation that was published with your friend Danny Kahneman about biases and how you two differ. What are your thoughts on confirmation bias? Is it possible to mitigate it or manage it and how would you recommend doing that?

GK: This is one of the places where Danny and I do not see eye to eye. I don't see confirmation bias as being a big problem. A lot of that research is with college students performing unfamiliar tasks. And so they can be manipulated in certain ways and the phenomenon will appear. I don't see it very often outside of laboratories. Confirmation bias means that once I have a belief I'm only going to look for evidence that supports it and I'm going to actively ignore or suppress evidence that gets in the way. Their research happens in artificial settings but even with college students you can make the task realistic instead of having artificial parts.

The bias pretty much disappears when people have a realistic task. I think what happens in the real world isn't that people suppress anomalous data. That might happen occasionally. But I think generally, the mental models that we have tell us what's important and so the way we search, the way we direct our attention is based on mental models. And so that looks like confirmation bias but it's simply using our mental models to tell us what's relevant and what's not. And if our mental models are weak or flawed, we're not going to look at it in the right way. So it is not that we have a bias to confirm a mental model, it's that our mental models organize the way we pay attention. And if we didn't have that, we would be paying equal attention to everything and then the world would all of a sudden explode and become incomprehensible and bewildering. We would be unable to cope. Having said that, what can somebody do who has strong beliefs and is missing key data? And you know that's why people reasonably worry about experience. That's the downside of experience. As events happen, subordinates can bring it to the leader's attention. They can be alert to the fact that they're not having the success that they expected and start to wonder why.

EH: Well, that feedback, if you will, they've got to really be cognizant and sensitive to their, if you will, personal feedback loops. What feedback are they getting on their actions/behaviors and then have the ability to evaluate that or have teammates, subordinates, or colleagues who are qualified and comfortable to help them evaluate?

GK: Right. It doesn't take much. You know, it just means, "Have you noticed this" or just bringing up the anomalous data. It doesn't always work. In my book, *Seeing What Others Don't*, there's the example of the Israeli Defense Force just before the Yom Kippur War in 1973 where the head of Israeli intelligence was ignoring the feedback from subordinates about what the Egyptians were doing and how that was inconsistent with running a training exercise. He was just impervious. He was captured by his beliefs. And so what you have there is, I'm not sure he was totally ignoring the data, he was explaining it away. And that's the dangerous part: when you get to be skilled, it gets easier to explain away inconvenient data. But yet if you size up the situation incorrectly, those inconsistencies should be increasing rather than decreasing and that's when you should start getting worried that maybe you called it wrong.

EH: Based on all the work you've done, you made me think about the word paranoia, you know, in a positive sense. Worrying about what I'm missing, cognizant of the fact that I don't know everything and things change. I heard Jeff Bezos say in an interview that the difference between good senior leaders and bad senior leaders is that good senior leaders constantly go back and retest the assumptions underlying what they think is true. How do I stay sensitive to the possibility that things change and I may be missing something in my mental model? How do I individually and organizationally institutionalize that type of intellectual decision-making paranoia?

GK: I'm not sure how I feel about the word "paranoia." Paranoia makes it sound like a form of mental illness and I think we're both saying there's something valuable about never wanting to feel smug like they have everything under control. There's a great quote by Colin Powell where he states that if he was 70 percent sure of a decision he'd make it. If he was only 40 percent sure, he would seek more data. For example, if I've done an analysis and my emotions are leading me some place else, I won't say I'm going to go with my emotions but that's sort of a warning sign to me that maybe my analyses aren't sufficient. Maybe there are additional factors or options that I need to take into account. So I try to use my emotions as a sign that maybe I need to broaden my outlook and become more open to the factors that are involved.

Can I tell you a story? Do we have time for that?

EH: Yes

GK: Okay, so about thirty years ago, a little over thirty years ago, my research company had been struggling and I wasn't sure what our future was and I was approached by another company that wanted to buy mine. And it seemed like a perfect solution. They were offering me what my accountant and I thought was a reasonable price and they were going to take over all the things that I was worried about. And everything was looking good and I would meet with them and we would hammer things out. And it all looked good. So it was sort of a go except every time I came back from a meeting with them, I kind of felt stressed and I needed to go for a run. And so I asked myself what's that all about? So I was just about ready to sign but I said, let me sleep on it, something's wrong about this. And I felt, I mean, we had sort of verbally gone so far down the road and I felt sort of trapped— I didn't want to say that I was backing out of the deal. But I felt, emotionally, I'm not comfortable working with the guy who is going to be my new boss. He's saying the right things but I'm not feeling that it's going to be a good working relationship.

And at the last moment, I just backed out of it. I felt badly but I didn't want to trap myself when I had so many concerns. And then I talked to some colleagues, some friends of mine who were in the company and they said, he's terrible, he's a toxic manager. And I asked them, why didn't you tell me that? Why did you let me proceed? And they said we were suffering with him and we were hoping if you got involved, maybe that could help us all out. Well, thanks a lot. That's a case where I was glad that I listened to my emotions because I was talking myself into something and you know, the analyses were working out the way I wanted but I was talking myself into something that frankly would have been a disaster. And a few years later, they closed that office that I would have been working in because this guy was such a toxic manager.

EH: Interesting story. And you know, the point you make, Gary, is so important. And what I keep hearing is almost like balance, managing tensions or balancing a seesaw, and it is rarely all or nothing and you have to somehow be sensitive to, you know, the outside cues and be sensitive to your emotions. You can't let your emotions run rampant, but you also can't, if you will, let the data run rampant. It's not just logic. Yes, it is science but it's also art, the art of trying to be engaged internally and externally.

GK: I don't think I could have put it much better than that. That's exactly the way it is. The science part is the data crunching part, the analytical part. The art part is, I mean, artists are talented. They develop skills and so the art part is the experiential part, the tacit knowledge part that you can't articulate but it's part of what makes you so good and so unique to pay attention to it. And our emotions are one way of noticing that part.

EH: If you got a call tomorrow from the CEO of a Fortune 500 company who called you and said, "Gary, I've read your work. I want to hire you to teach my people to think better." What would you say? One, would you take the work? Two, what would you do? How do you make people think better? I've had CEOs not say those exact words but say to me, "I want you to help my people to think more strategically or to make better decisions." How would you respond to something like that?

GK: With extreme care. I don't think there's a simple answer. I'd try to find out what are the problems. So first I would do some questioning. I would say, all right, you're unhappy with some aspects of the way your company is operating. Give me some examples because otherwise it's so easy to talk past people. And we might believe that we mean the same thing by thinking better or making better decisions and be, you know, pretty far down and find out that we actually meant different things by those terms. So the way to anchor our conversation is by examples, giving me incidents where you were disappointed in the way your people thought and the way they made, not only their decisions and how they turned out but describe the way the decisions were made. And then I could diagnose, to some extent, what was going wrong, and whether I could be of help.

If what was going wrong is that people were sloppy in their reasoning and dispensed with analyses and they need better or more critical thinking, I'm not the answer and I would point them toward people who could provide that kind of training. If they were disappointed that people were falling down with re-gard to being able to anticipate and think strategically and think about long-term consequences, then I think we might have some basis for a discussion. And there it would be about how to help people focus and do a couple of things. One, build richer mental models so that they could do a better job of anticipating what might happen or what they need to pay more attention to. And the second thing I might aim for is whether his people were so bound up by what I call "the down arrow syndrome" and seeing whether they were afraid of creativity, afraid of insights that they were dampening those things and creating environments that suppressed insights; then I would look for ways of undoing that damage and create the right kind of balance.

EH: With the word "insights" you take me to your most recent book *Seeing What Others Don't: The Remarkable Ways to Gain Insights.* I find that book fascinating. What kinds of environments enable insights? What kinds of environments suppress insights?

GK: That was one of the most depressing parts of the book. I thought it might have been one of the most important parts of the book. In writing it, I just came to the conclusion that organizations are inhospitable to insights. Organizations do a better job of managing and eliminating errors, of eliminating, maybe reducing uncertainty, increasing predictability. If every-thing can go as scheduled, my job as a manager is really facili-tated. And insights don't do any of those things. Insights create uncertainty because we're reaching to directions we don't un-derstand. Insights are disruptive. So for a manager, insights are disorganizing. Most of the managerial tools that we give people are about the down arrow. The down arrow is what you want to reduce, errors and uncertainty and so most organizations, most organizational management approaches are emphasizing the down arrow. I think that's a fundamental problem and why organizations struggle even when they have insights.

There's an issue that I raise at the end of the book about organizational willpower. There are so many forces arrayed toward continuing the way they do business now and it's so disruptive to make changes that even when you know the changes need to be made, you fool yourself into thinking "I've got plenty of time and right now things are well, so why, you know, why fix it if it ain't broke?" Not realizing that the pace of change is so fast that you don't have time. Things get unwound in a hurry as we've seen with companies like Kodak, Encyclopedia Britannica, and others like that.

Since I wrote the book, I've been looking for exercises that people can use to try to get themselves out of that mindset and to really stretch their mind and change their perspective. And one that I've written about is a PreMortem, which is: imagine things have gone poorly and try to figure out why they've gone poorly is a way of surfacing problems that you might be denying or ignoring.

A second might be: I can tell you that I'm looking at a crystal ball and things are looming ahead and these are the early signs that we are not paying attention to. What signs should you be watching more carefully now to help give more credence to these weak signals that you might be explaining away?

And a third one that I got from Intel and its leaders is about successors: "If you were replaced right now, what would you hope your successor would do that you're not doing?" And the leaders of Intel when they ran that exercise said, "Gosh, we know it's time to get out of the memory chip business because the profit margins just aren't good enough. We have other parts of the business that are more successful but the memory chip business is central to our identity and there's so much caught up in that. It's too hard, so that's something we'd like to do, but really it's what our successor is going to have to do." And they looked at each other and said, "Wait a second. That's what we think needs to be done. We should be doing it." And so they changed course. So those are a few of those exercises that may help a management team get out of the fixation that things are working well enough, why change before I absolutely have to? By the time you absolutely have to, it might be too late.

EH: Great story. I share your frustration about organizations being naturally antichange. When you think about it, most managers wake up in the morning and have one main job and that is to reduce variance—go find variance and stamp it out. Innovation insights may come from variance, if you will, and they are variance in and of themselves by their nature. If you are really in the innovation game and are testing lots of new ideas, most of them are going to fail and you've got to accept that. Innovation is not 99 percent defect free. And I've gotten frustrated too and I don't have the data to back it up but I have a hypothesis that there is an inverse relationship between the size of an organization and its ability to be innovative. It sounds like you have struggled with the same concept.

GK: Yes. The larger the company, the more links in the chain of command, and it only takes one link, one risk-averse executive, to veto a new idea. It becomes harder to run those gauntlets after a while.

EH: Very interesting. It brought to mind the work that's been done at the Santa Fe Institute by noted physicist Geoffrey West. He's been doing work on analyzing cities and how they operate. And he's hypothesized that when a business organization hits the 150-employee level it crosses that line and it starts in effect on its path to destruction because it begins to lose its ability to be innovative and keep its entrepreneurial spirit. It's something that he was speculating about but it's interesting that, you know, someone from the outside world looking at the world of large organizations is saying there is that crossover point where the law of diminishing returns about getting big is more severe than one thinks.

One area we haven't talked about is your work in mindfulness. As you know, mindfulness is becoming a hot topic in the business environment and world. Now there's contemplative science centers at lots of universities, various corporate CEOs are now freely talking about how meditation helps them be centered and helps them be mindful, helps them to be able to be in the moment, and to better sense and respond. You've done a lot of work in the mindfulness area, what's your bottom line on mindfulness?

GK: Okay, I'm going to disappoint you here. I'm not a big fan of meditative practices or centering activities or things like that.

I just haven't seen enough data that those things are effective but I may be wrong. I'd just like to see more data on that. For me, mindfulness is just having an active mindset—being open to new experiences and open to wondering, actively wondering when you encounter an anomaly or just something that stimulates your curiosity. In *Seeing What Others Don't* I have thirty examples where two different people would have the same data and one person was just doing a job and not really thinking hard, not being mindful. And then the other person would say, "Hmm. I wonder what that means?" or "I wonder what the implications are?" So I think mindfulness, having an active mindset is engaging with the flow of experience rather than just seeing the world through preconceived ideas.

EH: Is it overcoming the natural tendency to operate on autopilot?

GK: It's overcoming that tendency by using the opposite tendency of curiosity. Of wondering what things might be.

EH: Do you think everyone is curious or is it a trait that certain people have and other people don't have? Is curiosity one of those traits that if you want to be an insightful organization, hire curious people?

GK: I think that would be a good idea, yes.

EH: Or some curious people?

GK: At least some curious people, you hire them and listen to them and don't marginalize them if they're telling you things that you're not comfortable with. I think curiosity has a number of facets. I've looked at the literature and I've looked at some tests of curiosity. I think part of it is individual differences. I think some people have a need for cognition in general, just enjoy speculating. I suspect that there are also times when we're kind of brain dead. We just go through the motions and aren't expanding, maybe our mind is elsewhere on something else and we're just mechanically doing our job. And other times when we're on high alert and we're just more open to small, weak signals that might have an implication. But I think it's both. I think it's, you know, individual difference but also a state variable.

EH: Very interesting. What do you think about ignorance?

GK: I have a good friend, Patrick Lambe, who's a knowledge management specialist in Singapore. And he's been working hard on the topic of ignorance, so I'm intrigued by that. And I have a chapter on stupidity in my newest book. Most of the chapter is about my own examples of being stupid. Getting back to ignorance, I don't think people can be aware of what they don't know. I think people become uneasy that they're missing something and I think that creates a kind of openness that we're talking about. Contrast this stance to other people who just become overconfident and smug and therefore not open to weak signals and not open to the early signs that maybe they are ignorant of some important facts about a situation.

EH: Gary, I have really enjoyed our time together and thank you for sharing with my readers. I hope our paths cross again. Good journeys, my friend.

GK: I enjoyed talking with you and thank you for your interest in my work, Ed. I think the work you are doing is very important and I hope it attracts the attention it deserves.

Reflection Questions

1. What did you read in this chapter that surprised you?
2. What are your top three takeaways that you want to reflect and/ or act on?
3. What behaviors do you want to change?

II

Building a Learning Organization

In part I, we focused on the science of learning and asked: How do people learn? What environmental factors enable or inhibit learning? What learning processes promote learning?

In part II, we take an in-depth look at how three very successful companies have operationalized the "science" of learning. These companies range in size from 1,300 to nearly 400,000 employees. Two are public companies and one is private. All are very profitable, consistent market leaders. Their business models range from innovation to operational excellence. Two of the companies are service companies and the other is more of a product company. In two of the companies, the founders are still actively involved; in the third, the late founder's legacy is very much alive.

So, we have these three very different companies all seeking to learn faster and better than the competition. The first company, Bridgewater, is trying to institutionalize its learning culture through learning processes. The second company, Intuit, is trying to change its culture and its leaders' behaviors and make learning by experimentation its business decision model. The third company, UPS, is an operational excellence behemoth. How it maintains its operational excellence edge is the focus of the last chapter.

The purpose of part II is not to suggest that your organization should "copy" these organizations, but rather to illustrate how the science of learning can be implemented in different types of organizations. Chapters 4, 5, and 6 provided "tidbits" about other learning organizations (i.e., Gore, IDEO, Room & Board, and the U.S. Army), but the following chapters look at this question in a much more thorough, detailed way.

As we continue into part II, I hope you'll keep the following questions in mind: As an individual, what can I do to become a better learner? As a team member, manager, or leader, what can I learn to help my organization be a better learner? To help with that analysis, let's first summarize what we've learned so far about individual and organizational learning.

We learned in part I that by their inherent nature, organizations are resistant to change because they are dominated by the drive for predictability, standardization, reliability, and the eradication of variance. Such behavior inhibits learning. People, likewise, are resistant to change. We all have built-in, emotional and cognitive proclivities to seek validation of our existing views of the world (mental models) and our self-worth (egos). These too inhibit learning.

The human mind is a speedy, highly efficient validator that operates on autopilot most of the time. Learning requires deliberate, higher level thinking that challenges and changes an individual's existing views of the world and/or the self. Although we all strive to be rational and logical, we are not rational beings. Emotions impact and influence almost every step in the cognitive and communication processes necessary for learning.

In chapter 1, I stated that one of my objectives was to lay out a blueprint for creating a learning organization. The blueprint starts with a leader—either of a company, a business unit, or even a team—who is not a Theory X leader but rather is a people-centric Theory Y leader who treats people with respect. The next step is defining the learning behaviors necessary for the organization. With these in place, one must then design a "learning system" that seamlessly aligns the culture, structure, leadership behaviors, HR policies, measurements, and rewards to enable and promote those desired learning behaviors. You will read examples of how such a learning system is constructed in the Bridgewater, Intuit, and UPS stories.

An organizational learning system works best if it's based on an understanding of the following principles: better learning results from intrinsic motivation and is a means of meeting our needs for autonomy, effectiveness, relatedness, affiliation, and personal growth; learning occurs best when we feel authentically cared for and trusted; and trust and accountability must be mutual—leaders and the organization must earn the trust of the "learners" and be accountable, too. All of this can result in an implied contract as evidenced by Gore and its employees ("associates") whereby in exchange for high performance, Gore owes its associates the opportunity to grow and develop to their highest potential.

Learning requires people and organizations to change. Change is cognitively and emotionally hard. It's hard for an individual to overcome his mental models and ego defenses by himself. Thus, learning is a team activity. Structuring a learning organization—whether at Gore, IDEO, or the U.S. Army—requires a small team or unit focus. It is through teams that individual needs for autonomy, relatedness, and effectiveness can be met. Bonds of trust can be built that enhance the willingness to learn and the effectiveness of learning. In order to change, people have to overcome their fears and feel safe in admitting mistakes, weaknesses, and ignorance to teammates. Permission to speak freely and honestly can only work in environments where people feel cared for and safe.

The next component is having the right critical thinking and learning conversation processes institutionalized in the organization. A culture of searching for truth facilitates a conditional view of one's beliefs and an acceptance of the limits of what one truly knows. Fundamentally, none of us are as smart as we believe we are, nor are we as good at thinking or communicating as we think we are. That is why processes help. Root cause analysis, unpacking of assumptions, experimentation, PreMortems, visualizations, and After Action Reviews are all basic learning processes. Being mindful, authentic, and humble are important learning behaviors—especially for managers and leaders.

Learning requires three good "meta" self-management skills: metacognition, metacommunicating and metaemotions. We have to be aware (mindful) of when we need to take our thinking and communicating to a higher, more intentional and deliberate level—and by role modeling this behavior, leaders can encourage it in those they manage. We need to be aware of the messages we send through our emotions, body language, and voice. We likewise need to help people manage their fears of failure, punishment, and not being liked that inhibit critical inquiry, debate, collaboration, and learning. Permission to speak freely and permission to fail so long as there is learning (or there is an observed "waterline" like at Gore) are common themes in this book.

Another key conclusion of the research we discussed in part I was the congruity of findings between the field of education regarding the type of environment that fosters high engagement learning and that of a business regarding high employee engagement. Those findings can lead one to conclude that high employee engagement, as defined by the Gallup Q12, is required to be a great learning organization.

The power of positivity also comes through, loud and clear, from the research. An emotionally positive environment enables learning, and positive individual emotions enable personal learning. The U.S. Army's major initiative to bring positive psychology into its training of more than 1,000,000 soldiers is once again a leading indicator of where businesses must look if they want to maximize employee adaptability, learning, and resiliency. High performance, high accountability, and positivity are not mutually exclusive.

Learning basically is the process by which each one of us creates meaningful stories about our world that are more accurate or truthful such that we can act more effectively. That learning process is enhanced by three mindsets. First, we have to accept the magnitude of our ignorance. Second, we need to view everything that we think we know as conditional and subject to change based on new evidence. Third, and most important, we have to define our self-worth not by what we know, but rather by striving to be the best learner we can be.

As you read the following stories, I suggest that you think about how well each leader has addressed the capabilities listed in Figure 9.1.

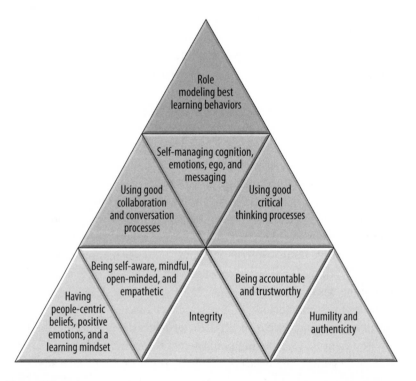

Figure 9.1
Learning Leader Capabilities.

Also keep in mind the checklist for a High-Performance Learning Organization that is provided at the end of this introduction to part II of *Learn or Die.*

Now let's begin our learning journey with Bridgewater, the largest and one of the most successful hedge funds in the world.

High-Performance Learning Organization Checklist

☐ Does the CEO "own" (not unilaterally) the learning culture and "walk the talk"?

☐ Has the organization put in place a culture, structure, leadership behaviors, HR policies, measurements, and rewards to enable and promote learning behaviors?

☐ Are the organization's leaders Theory Y leaders who are mindful, open-minded, accessible, empathetic, trustworthy, authentic, transparent, and humble?

☐ Has the organization created an emotionally positive work environment?

☐ Does the organization have high employee engagement?

☐ Does the organization have a learning culture evidenced by "permission to speak freely"?

☐ Does the organization have a learning culture of "permission to fail so long as you learn from your mistakes"?

☐ Does the organization have processes to promote System 2 critical thinking and learning?

☐ Has the organization established processes for high-quality learning conversations and collaboration?

☐ Does the organization have processes to mitigate individuals' ego defense systems?

☐ Is the organization paranoid about complacency and not knowing?

9

Bridgewater Associates, LP: Building a Learning "Machine"

Bridgewater[1] is the largest hedge fund in the world, and from an investor's return perspective, one of the most successful over the last forty years.[1] Bridgewater has over $150 billion of funds under asset management for approximately 350 clients. Its client base is nearly evenly split among domestic and foreign institutional pension funds, sovereign wealth funds, and corporate clients. Bridgewater is based in Westport, Connecticut and employs over 1,300 employees. Ray Dalio started the firm almost forty years ago and is still the controlling owner.

Ray came into my world after he'd published his *Principles* on the Bridgewater website in 2010. The document is a 123-page compendium of Ray's beliefs and processes that he suggests will lead to a successful life and a successful business if followed. Over the past five years, Ray has been actively taking steps regarding structure, capital base, leadership succession planning, and the institutionalization of Bridgewater's culture, operating model, and learning processes, in order to put Bridgewater in a position to

---

1. Excerpts from *Principles* and all related materials produced and provided by Bridgewater are protected by copyright and are quoted and reprinted here with express permission from Bridgewater Associates, LP and/or Ray Dalio.

endure as a private, financially self-sufficient, employee-controlled organization. Publishing his *Principles* was part of this effort.

The document is segmented into three sections: section 1: "The Importance of Principles"; section 2: "My Most Fundamental Life Principles"; and section 3: "My Management Principles." At the time of publishing, *Principles* was the first public glimpse into the internal workings of Bridgewater. Because of Bridgewater's history of guarding its privacy and its strong penchant for secrecy and staying out of the limelight, the posting of *Principles* created quite a stir, as evidenced by the number of downloads and the ensuing major articles published in 2011 by many of the major New York and financial media outlets.

It was the "Management Principles" section of the piece that really impressed me when I first read it. In that section, Ray confronts, head on, the "humanness" in business by talking about our natural proclivities against thinking logically or deeply and our "automatic" proclivity to seek affirmation of what we think and who we are. The lessons from the piece stayed with me, and I thought of it again, two years later, when planning the syllabus for an Organic Growth course I was teaching at the Darden School of Business. As part of the course, I wanted to explore the culture and experimental processes of Silicon Valley, where failure is not penalized as long as there is learning and where a focus on data drives action learning and the continuous testing of ideas. I decided to add a class session on Bridgewater and Ray's Management Principles. By that point, I had spent two years researching this book, and was convinced that the "science of learning" had advanced significantly since 1991, when Peter Senge published his landmark book, *The Fifth Discipline: The Art and Practice of the Learning Organization*, and that Ray, with his focus on promoting System 2 thinking and mitigating ego defenses, was on the leading edge of using the science of learning in building his organization.

During class in April 2013, I engaged sixty-five smart, second-year MBA students in an exploration of Ray's way of doing business. I thought my students would find Bridgewater interesting, and they did. But not in the way I had expected.

We had a fascinating, probing conversation about Ray's Management Principles. At the end of the class, by a show of hands, I asked how many of the students would like to work at Bridgewater or at a place with similar principles. I expected a lot of hands to be raised because of Bridgewater's stature and because historically the financial industry is a major employer of Darden graduates. Of my sixty-five students, however, only three raised their hands.

I was surprised. We had discussed how Bridgewater is an idea merit-ocracy where learning and self-improvement are cultural pillars. Who wouldn't want that?

The overwhelming reason my students gave had to do with Ray's Princi-ple of transparent, critical review of employees' thinking and personal weak-nesses—a concept Ray calls "Radical Transparency." Employees at Bridgewater are subjected to frequent "drill downs": conversations in which their thinking is challenged and their work and personal weaknesses reviewed. The film-ing or audio recording of all Bridgewater meetings and review conversations operationalizes Radical Transparency. My students found this unusual at the very least, but the clincher for many of them who voted negatively was the fact that the recordings are made available to every Bridgewater employee and are used to teach the "Principles" within *Principles* internally.

My students' overwhelmingly negative responses only increased my curi-osity about Bridgewater. How did Bridgewater overcome people's hesitancy or fear of direct constructive feedback, and how did Bridgewater employees get comfortable with Radical Transparency? What type of person thrived at Bridgewater? Did Bridgewater really behave in accordance with Ray's Prin-ciples? And most crucially, could the Bridgewater model work outside the financial industry and be successfully institutionalized beyond Ray's tenure?

I reached out to Ray to talk further about the Bridgewater culture, and he ended our first phone conversation by inviting me to learn about Bridge-water by spending two days at the Bridgewater office, observing and inter-viewing various people at all levels.

It quickly became clear that this wasn't going to be a usual observation research visit. Ray wanted me not just to observe but also to fully experi-ence the "new hire" learning process before I visited. This meant viewing films of actual meetings and employee conversations that illustrated key Principles. I was sent a Bridgewater iPad loaded with more than ten hours of material, including twelve films illustrating various Principles and drill-downs. They were emotionally gripping and unedited. Ray also assigned two Bridgewater employees to help with my learning and to work with me to come up with a schedule that would meet my learning needs. The visit agenda was thus cocreated; Bridgewater did not dictate it.

The visit occurred in September 2013. It included nearly three hours of personal conversations with Ray and four hours of "shadowing" him in committee meetings, including a two-hour meeting of the Management Committee. It also included interviews with ten other employees of differ-ent tenures and responsibilities.

Under the Principle of Radical Transparency, every meeting and con-versation at Bridgewater, including personal reviews and Management Committee meetings, is filmed or recorded and archived in Bridgewater's library for review by any employee. As such, my interviews and talks during my visit were recorded and filed in the library as well. I was asked if this would be OK and had no hesitation in saying yes.

In this chapter, I want to share with you as much detail as I can about what I learned from Bridgewater. I hope that by doing this, I can prompt some of the same questions for you that this visit did for me: Am I a good learner? Is my organization a learning enabler or a learning inhibitor?

To do justice to this objective, I have divided the Bridgewater story into three sections. Section 1 focuses on Ray, on the Bridgewater business model, and on Ray's Principles. Section 2 focuses on Ray's concept of "The Machine" and what I believe are the key parts of the Bridgewater culture that enable and promote learning. Section 3 focuses on people— the hiring, training, and measuring of employees and the personal trans-formation journey one goes through in adapting to the Bridgewater learning environment.

Section I: Who Is Ray?

I arrived at Bridgewater on a cool fall morning. Bridgewater's headquar-ters, composed of two modern buildings, is located at the end of a winding road in a residential area of Westport, Connecticut, surrounded by trees and set along a small river. The buildings are hidden from the street, and the driveway entrance has no sign. It's a tranquil setting, reminiscent of the historic Japanese temples I once visited in the city of Kyoto.

The interior of the Bridgewater buildings is not luxurious or osten-tatious; fieldstone, wood, and glass dominate, not the marble or lush carpeting so familiar at other investment banking and financial service headquarters. Ray's office is at the end of a corridor, with no waiting area outside or administrative assistants positioned to limit access. There is no private dining room or bathroom.

At exactly 8 A.M., I was taken from the reception area to Ray's office and offered coffee, breakfast, and a seat. Ray's office, like the rest of the Bridgewater headquarters, is very modest—just large enough to accom-modate a wide desk and three small modern chairs for visitors. Instead of the usual CEO office adornments—pictures with politicians, sports stars, and entertainers, and autographed sports memorabilia from Super Bowls or Masters Tournaments—there was an array of family pictures.

I was informed that Ray was running five minutes late. In a few minutes, I observed him coming down the hall. He was bent forward, walking with long strides. He had no entourage. He was wearing dark cotton chinos, a gray Bridgewater long-sleeved polo shirt covered by a dark gray, Bridgewater zippered top, and casual shoes that resembled Dr. Martens. Entering the room, he thrust out his hand and said: "I'm Ray."

"I'm Ed," I said, and thus began two fascinating days.

Ray started the conversation by asking me about my history—where I'd come from and how I had gotten to where I was. He was engaged and curious, and came across as authentic; it didn't feel like he was just going through the motions. As we used to say in my days in rural Oklahoma working with big cattle feedlot barons—when I looked him in the eye, it was clear that there was "someone at home." And I was struck by how Ray phrased his points; he almost always prefaced them with, "I may not be right but . . . " He never said "I think . . . "; instead, he said: "I believe . . . "

As we finished our two-hour talk, Ray asked: "You know why you are here?"

"Yes," I said, "To learn."

"And," Ray added, "To tell me what we are doing wrong and what you think we can improve. I want direct honest feedback—don't worry, you can't offend me. OK?"

"OK!" I answered.

Before sharing what I learned during my visit to Bridgewater, I think it would be helpful for you to know a little about Ray. Understanding his upbringing and education, as well as his early steps both in and out of the financial world, can shed light on his unique approach to the hedge fund business and show how he set himself on the path to build the biggest and most successful hedge fund in the world and become the thirty-first richest American according to Forbes magazine, with a net worth of $12.9 billion in 2013.

Behind Bridgewater's unique and successful learning organization is a successful person who learned how to mitigate his personal weaknesses; how to be very good at what he does; and to learn what he truly valued, which is: "meaningful work and meaningful relationships that are obtained by striving for truth and excellence with great people."[2]

Ray's Story

Ray was born in 1949 and grew up as an only child in a middle-class Long Island family. He was, in his words, "an ordinary kid." His father was a jazz musician and his mother was a stay-at-home mom. Ray was not a good student; he was not good at rote memorization of facts. He had an independent streak, and if he didn't see the relevance or meaningfulness of something, he didn't see the need to learn it.

Ray earned spending money by working odd jobs. He delivered newspapers, mowed lawns, shoveled snow, washed dishes in a restaurant and, at age twelve, became a caddy at a private country club[3]—where he learned about much more than just golf. The players he caddied for were mainly wealthy businessmen who talked a lot about making money in the stock market—and there was good money to be made in that postwar decade, a time of economic growth and confidence. Ray listened to the golfers and thought that investing in stocks could be an easy way to make money, so at age twelve he bought his first stock: Northeast Airlines. He picked that stock because it was cheap and he could buy more shares—and he got lucky, making a lot of money, relatively speaking, on the investment. However, he also quickly learned that these "easy" gains could be just as easily lost. That experience spurred him to learn more about how to pick stocks and how the stock market worked. He realized that he had to get knowledge from other sources. Because he didn't have a lot of money, he needed to find easy, cheap ways to learn and he did. He started ordering the free public annual reports of companies and devouring them. Looking back, it's clear that this was a precursor to what became one of Ray's fundamental ways of looking at the world—as a set of "machines" whose inner workings could be determined and understood through careful observation and research. In this case, Ray had to figure out how he could make a consistent profit buying stocks. And this is what he would devote himself to in his young adult years and, basically, for the rest of his career.

After graduating from high school, Ray attended college at Long Island University and continued his investing. He became interested in trading commodities, as they had low margin requirements. Trading was a humbling experience for Ray. Many times, when he was certain he had picked a winner, it turned out to be a loser. He internalized this experience, and it was the beginning of his wariness of overconfidence.

While in college, inspired by the Beatles' trip to India, Ray also learned about meditation, which is still part of his life. I hypothesize that some of the values that underlie meditation and mindfulness that we discussed in chapter 6 went on to inform and shape Bridgewater's unique culture: Radical Transparency, permission to speak freely, a relentless search for the truth, and having the courage to confront reality by acknowledging and openly discussing personal weaknesses, mistakes, and failures. To excel at Bridgewater and in meditation, one needs the courage to experience reality, humility, discipline, and perseverance. One needs to learn to be in the moment and process reality without allowing one's emotions to "hijack" one's experience.

Unlike in high school, Ray was a good student in college and graduated from Long Island University in 1971. During the summer break, before starting MBA studies at Harvard University, he worked as a clerk on the New York Stock Exchange. A global monetary crisis that occurred that summer piqued Ray's interest in how the currency markets worked, and currency markets and hedging currency risks would go on to become key parts of Ray's investing and advising career.

Ray flourished at Harvard Business School, largely because professors there used the case method of teaching in which students are given complex fact situations—almost like puzzles—that call for a decision. With this method, learning comes from advancing one's ideas and the ensuing critical debate, through which one learns to be open-minded, to think logically, to weigh alternative solutions, to assess probabilities, and to make arguments. The case method is in complete opposition to the rote memorization of facts, and this type of teaching tapped into and honed Ray's strengths: his independence and his drive to make good decisions to win in the stock market.

During Ray's two years at Harvard, world events fueled a high demand for commodities traders that far exceeded the supply of experienced traders on Wall Street. It had created an opportunity for someone young with commodities trading experience like Ray. As a result, upon graduation, Ray became the director of commodities at a small brokerage firm. He soon left that firm to join a big Wall Street firm as director of its institutional hedging business, but he was quickly fired. In his writings, Ray has stated that the firing resulted from "insubordination." Two articles, one in *The New Yorker*[4] and one in *aiCIO*,[5] suggest he was fired for slugging a superior and hiring a stripper to entertain some farming clients in California—two big mistakes. In any case, at nearly age twenty-six, Ray was out of work.

He decided that what he needed to do was work for himself, and he was able to convince a few of his former clients to retain him as an adviser, trader, and risk manager. In 1975, he began what ultimately would become Bridgewater out of his small New York City apartment. From that day on, Ray, the independent kid and thinker, was the independent entrepreneur relying on his abilities to outthink the competition in order to win in a game where winning or losing was a transparent and fast, daily feedback loop.

In trying to understand Bridgewater and how it learns, we need to understand Ray—how he learns, what he values, and what themes seem to have had a big influence in his life. The first step in this exploration is to look at how Bridgewater was built and what caused *aiCIO* to be so bold as to headline a 2011 article: "Is Ray Dalio the Steve Jobs of Investing?"[6]

The Business

When Ray started his business in 1975, he had just a few clients and focused on providing money management and consulting services in the credit and currency markets, including the hedging of currency risks. Early on, he started writing down his reasons for placing a trade, a daily tabulation of the results and why the trade did or did not work. Twenty or so years later, those notebooks became the foundation for the beginning algorithms that drove Bridgewater's global investment platform.

In effect, Ray was trying to understand root causes, and his use of after-trade reviews was his early career way of doing the kind of After Action Reviews that were discussed in chapter 7. His notes and his attempts to understand conceptually how the market worked also formed the beginning of his "machine" theory about the economy and his business. Also, from the beginning of his business, he focused on making lots of small bets and hedging those bets. He was and still is a big believer in reducing the risk of loss to nil.

A big inflection point came in 1985, when the World Bank gave him the opportunity to manage $5,000,000 of its employee retirement fund. That was the start of Bridgewater's institutional asset business. In describing her decision to invest with Bridgewater, Hilda Ochoa-Brillembourg, who was then head of the World Bank Pension Fund, said "Ray was one of the few macroeconomic analysis services that wanted to turn analysis into actionable decisions."[7] Kodak followed the World Bank by investing with Bridgewater in 1989.

In 1991, Bridgewater introduced its Pure Alpha fund. That fund is now reputed to be the most successful hedge fund in history, generating more returns for its investors than any other hedge fund. Bridgewater currently manages two other funds in addition to the Pure Alpha fund and all operate on Bridgewater's fundamental belief of diversification through lots of small, uncorrelated bets. Bridgewater's investment objective is to produce consistent and uncorrelated returns, and today it uses investment algorithms built over a forty-year period to invest in over 100 liquid asset classes globally.

With those investment objectives, Bridgewater focuses on building investment portfolios based on risk allocations rather than capital allocations. And it advises clients to separate strategic investment decisions from tactical investment decisions. In a required form filed annually with the Securities and Exchange Commission, Bridgewater described its investment philosophy this way:

> Bridgewater believes investors can dramatically improve their portfolio's overall results by separately creating a well-diversified beta portfolio (asset allocation) that is balanced against environmental biases and calibrated to one's targeted returns, and by creating a well-diversified alpha portfolio (tactical investments) that reduces systematic biases calibrated to one's targeted returns.[8]

Bridgewater's business is based on a "search for the truth," in a scientific way. The firm's Research Group—composed of professionals with backgrounds in such fields as mathematics, the sciences, and economics—debates how cause-effect linkages in markets should work, and then mines historical data trying to find high probability that their logic actually shows to be true in a "timeless and universal way" (i.e., shown to exist throughout time and across different countries). If a particular rule passes those tests, it goes into the investment machine and its results are constantly reviewed to make sure it performs as expected. Bridgewater was one of the first investment advisers to expand this kind of search globally as well as backward into history.

Fueling this process is Ray's belief that history repeats itself; thus, one can learn what worked and did not work historically and use that data to test forward-looking ideas and make better decisions in similar future situations. Charlie Rose once asked Ray what book he thought all investors should read; Ray answered, *The Lessons of History* by Will and Ariel Durant, a book of only 102 pages published in 1968.

Ray's focus on global and historical data has been a key client value proposition. Ochoa-Brillembourg has stated: "Ray's true innovation is a steadfast attention to the granularity of macroeconomic data. His firm, more than any other, is getting into the nuts and bolts of data analysis. Not data mining, but he does mine the macroeconomic data to a breadth and depth that no other firm mines it."[9] The depth of research and data analysis Bridgewater does is impressive, even to Paul Volcker, former chairman of the Federal Reserve, who described the degree of detail underlying Bridgewater's work as "mind-blowing" and said of Ray, "He has a bigger staff, and produces more relevant statistics and analyses, than the Federal Reserve."[10]

Another Bridgewater differentiator is how it relentlessly engages its clients in conversations about investment ideas and strategies. It publishes the industry-leading *Daily Observations*, which can run up to thirty pages. Bridgewater also publishes monthly updates, quarterly performance reviews, and an annual strategic report. It has frequent calls and meetings with clients. Those engagements are strategic investment discussions, not just a review of results. Over 150 professionals work in Client Services, serving around 350 clients.

What makes Bridgewater successful? Well, it's the right people in the right learning environment using the right learning processes. Underlying that are the fundamental principles and values on which Bridgewater's culture and learning processes were built.

The Principles

As is clear from the way he's approached his investing from the age of twelve on, Ray is a conceptual thinker, and he loves finding patterns, looking for cause-effect rules and synthesizing data. He looks at the world and tries to understand how it works. How does the economy work? How does world class recruiting work? How do people make good decisions? All of us build conceptual models of the world; quite frankly, however, Ray's models are evidenced-based and rigorously reviewed frequently. This constant searching forms the foundation of his Principles.

Just as Ray's investing practices are informed by a rich catalog of historical data, his Principles are, as he puts it, "concepts that can be applied over and over again in similar circumstances as distinct from narrow answers to specific questions."[11] His Principles are ways of thinking, acting, and conversing that have become the common Bridgewater objectives or aspired to processes and behaviors.

Underlying these Principles are Ray's goals and his beliefs. Ray frequently states that his primary goal has never been to make the most money. He explains:

> I have been very lucky because I have had the opportunity to see what it's like to have little or no money and what it is like to have a lot of it. . . . I do know that for me, having a lot more money isn't a lot better than having enough to cover the basics. That's because, for me, the best things in life—meaningful work, meaningful relationships, interesting experiences, good food, sleep, music, ideas, sex, and other basic needs and pleasures—are not, past a certain point, materially improved upon by having a lot of money.[12]

Ray's motivation is to live life fully, which, as he says above, he believes requires meaningful work and meaningful relationships.

As Ray sees it, achieving one's goals is more likely to occur if one strives to be an independent thinker by learning. That, in turn, requires one to be honest about one's strengths and weaknesses and to deal directly with one's weaknesses by accepting them, seeking and being open to feedback, and creating workarounds that mitigate one's weaknesses.

Ray constantly teaches his employees to stress test their thinking by seeking the opinions of smart or smarter people. A key concept in Ray's world is "knowing what you don't know." He once explained it this way: "Our greatest power is that we know that we don't know and we are open to being wrong and learning."[13]

He also encourages his employees to get past their ego barriers and look at their weaknesses objectively, so they can then figure out how to design around their weaknesses and be successful.[14] Because ego barriers also get in the way of people engaging in thoughtful disagreement, Ray urges himself and others to ask themselves: Is it true? Does it make sense?[15] He says his most fundamental Principle is: "Truth—more precisely, an accurate representation of reality—is the essential foundation for producing good outcomes."[16]

Socrates is reputed to have said: "I know one thing, that I know nothing."[17] Stuart Firestein, noted research neuroscientist and chairman of the Department of Biological Sciences at Columbia University, has asserted in his short book *Ignorance: How It Drives Science* that great scientists don't focus on what they know, but rather on what they don't know. In other words, great science focuses on research findings that generally illuminate *more* ignorance not less. Much science occurs in a natural world that is driven by biological and physical laws. Interestingly, biology plays a big role in Ray's conceptual system too, especially with respect to adaptation and system interdependency.

Understanding Ray's beliefs helps us understand Bridgewater, which the rest of this chapter explores. Yes, Bridgewater is more than Ray, but Ray's beliefs underlie its culture and ways of doing business. As you read through some of Ray's Principles, you may find it thought provoking to ask yourself, "Do I believe that?" Not to see whether you agree with Ray, but to help you figure out your own core principles and beliefs.

Beliefs

Here are some representative statements by Ray taken from *Principles*, his writings and talks, and from my interviews.[18]

> *I also believe nothing is certain. I believe that the best we can hope for is highly probable.*
> *I believe that having questions is better than having answers because it leads to more learning.*
> *I believe mistakes are good things because I believe most learning comes via making mistakes and reflecting on them. I fail every day and all over the place.*
> *While most others seem to believe that finding out about one's weaknesses is a bad thing, I believe that it is a good thing because it is the first step toward finding out what to do about them and not letting them stand in your way.*
> *I believe that [psychological] pain is required to become stronger.*
> *I believe that the desire to evolve, i.e., to get better, is probably humanity's most pervasive driving force.*
> *The most important quality that differentiates successful people from unsuccessful people is the capacity to learn and adapt.*
> *The quality of our lives depends on the quality of the decisions we make.*
> *I believe that you can probably get what you want out of life if you can suspend your ego and take a no-excuses approach to achieving your goals with open-mindedness, determination, and courage, especially if you rely on the help of people who are strong in areas that you are weak.*

I learned that failure is by and large due to not accepting and successfully dealing with the realities of life.

I learned that there is nothing to fear from truth.

I learned that I want the people I deal with to say what they really believe and to listen to what others say in reply, in order to find out what is true.

I learned that everyone makes mistakes and has weaknesses and that one of the most important things that differentiates people is their approach to handling them.

I learned that being totally truthful, especially about mistakes and weaknesses, led to a rapid rate of improvement and movement toward what I wanted.

Also, I don't derive satisfaction or angst about how good or bad I am as much as I derive satisfaction and angst about the rate at which I am getting better.

Operate as a meritocracy of ideas not as a bureaucratic hierarchy.

Deal with extreme openness with each other in the pursuit of excellence.

I want Bridgewater to be a company in which people collectively . . .

> *. . . come up with the best independent opinions they can muster.*
>
> *. . . stress-test their opinions by having the smartest people they can find to challenge them so they can find out where they are wrong.*
>
> *. . . are wary about overconfidence and good at not knowing.*
>
> *. . . wrestle with reality, experiencing the results of their decisions, and reflecting on what they did to produce them so that they can improve.*

Treat mistakes as learning opportunities.

Don't worry about looking good—worry about achieving your goals.

Get over "blame" and "credit" and get on with "accurate" and "inaccurate."

Motivation to get better has to be higher than the motivation to be right.

We end this part of the Bridgewater story with a list of Ray's five fundamental personal choices or decisions that he believes every employee must make to flourish at Bridgewater. Ray's Principles force every employee to intentionally or by default make these five key choices. They really determine whether he or she will be successful at and fit into the Bridgewater culture.

RAY'S 5 BIG "FORKS IN THE ROAD"

First: BAD . . . Allow pain to stand in the way of progress
          GOOD . . . Understanding how to manage pain to produce progress
Second: BAD . . . Avoid facing "harsh realities"
          GOOD . . . Face "harsh realities"
Third: BAD . . . Worry about appearing good
          GOOD . . . Worry about achieving the goal
Fourth: BAD . . . Making decisions on the basis of first-order consequences
          GOOD . . . Making decisions on the basis of first-, second-, and third-order consequences
Fifth: BAD . . . Don't hold yourself accountable
          GOOD . . . Hold yourself accountable[19]

Conclusion

In closing section 1 of this chapter, I hope you have an understanding of Ray and the foundational Principles and beliefs that underlie Bridgewater. Now it's time to look at how Ray operationalized those Principles inside Bridgewater. It is an opportune time to consider this, because, as I mentioned, for the last five years Ray has been on a mission to institutionalize his Principles and beliefs to increase the likelihood of Bridgewater enduring as a private, employee-owned business past his lifetime. Already, Ray has stepped down as CEO and now holds the title "Mentor." He also has created a Management Committee charged with managing day-to-day business. Although he is still very engaged in the business, Ray realizes that someday he won't be and that Bridgewater, like everything else in life, will evolve. That's one of Ray's beliefs about how the world works.

Section II: The Machine and the Culture of Bridgewater

In the first section of this chapter, we focused on background material about Bridgewater's business and Ray's codified beliefs, goals, and processes that underlie the firm's spectacular success. Those beliefs include Ray's conceptualization that systems and businesses, just like the human body and the environment, can be thought of as machines. In this section, we explore this idea further and examine how it has shaped the firm's business model, learning processes, and culture.

The Machine

Ray views the Bridgewater business as a machine that, if properly designed to include the right people in the right culture using the right processes, will likely produce outcomes that move the organization toward its goals. "I believe," Ray says, "that to have a great company you have to make two things great—the culture and the people. If these two things are great your organization can navigate the twists and turns to get you where you want to go."[20]

At Bridgewater, the Management Committee manages the "machine." The Committee's job is to determine how well the machine is running by comparing the machine's outcomes with organizational goals. If the performance is not optimal, the problems are diagnosed and addressed to increase positive results. This is what Ray calls the "feedback loop."[21] The rate and quality of an organization's improvement and learning is highly dependent on how effectively and quickly it can process feedback loops. Feedback loops are learning opportunities. Ray's concept of feedback loops as learning opportunities goes back to his early investing days, when he would keep a written log of every stock investment and the reasons why he made that investment. He would then evaluate the investment upon selling and making a gain or loss. He then took the result—the feedback—and tried to learn what worked and what didn't work. For investments that didn't work, he learned lessons to apply going forward. He changed his future behavior based on learning from the feedback of the market.

The feedback loop mechanism relies on what Ray calls his most important Principle: "Truth—more precisely, an accurate understanding of reality—is the essential foundation for producing good outcomes."[22] Ray believes that the difference between bad and great organizations is generally the frequency, quality, and management of these feedback loops. That quality relies directly on being brutally direct, drilling down to the truth—the root causes—and confronting head on the ego defenses and/or emotions that can hijack one's thinking processes. A real diagnosis of the root causes requires acceptance by the responsible party and high-quality decisions on how to improve the outcomes.

Every issue diagnosis meeting I attended or reviewed followed this five-step process:

1. Either someone asked who the person responsible for the meeting was or the responsible person announced herself as such. Bridgewater is not big on "we" or "they." Everything comes down to personal ownership—be it of a meeting, task, problem or result—and because personal accountability is critical, specific names are used.

2. Everyone agreed on what type of meeting was about to occur. Is it a debate? Is it a discussion? Is it teaching? Debates occur among people of roughly equal experience. Discussions are more open-ended and include people of varying experience levels. Teaching moments involve people of different levels.

3. At various times, someone would ask something along the lines of: "Does what I am saying make sense to you? Do you agree that it is true? If not, why not?" Bridgewater cares as much about one's reasoning—one's critical thinking—as it does about the answer. Is the thinking logical? This step is meant to stress test the speaker's thinking. These questions are part of Ray's Principle to "Constantly get in synch"; this Principle is further discussed in section 3 of this chapter.[23] Notice that the questions do not focus on a person being right or wrong; they are designed to encourage people to be independent thinkers who come to their own conclusions. The goal is truth based on the current reality.

4. If the conversation resulted in a "to-do," the group designated a responsible person, who then agreed with the group to a "contract" outlining specifically what that person would do within what time frame. Have you ever left a corporate meeting wondering what was decided or wondering what the next steps were? Bridgewater works hard to eliminate those types of results.

5. At the end of every meeting, the participants evaluated the meeting and put "tidbit comments" into a database regarding any person's performance in the meeting. All of these inputs flow into a massive data system that contains algorithms designed to look for patterns that could help people understand their strengths and weaknesses. These personal reviews are ultimately aggregated and rolled up, along with other employee data, into a real-time scorecard—a "Baseball Card," discussed in more detail in section 3 of this chapter.

This five-step process reminds me of an airplane flight checklist. Even when a pilot has flown thousands of flights, she completes a checklist each time the cockpit is entered. Think of the five steps as Bridgewater's flight checklist. This process is how Bridgewater structures its learning conversations.

In making the diagnoses at meetings like this, Bridgewater tries to understand whether the deviations between actual outcomes (reality) and desired outcomes are a design problem or a people problem. Design problems can be either a structural or a process issue. A structural issue, for example, can be having the wrong group working on the problem or not having the right members of the team. A process issue, for example, could be that the wrong plan was created to do the task or the wrong data was used in making the decision. People problems can be: (1) a mismatch between task needs and people's abilities—a bad fit; (2) a bad performance produced by either lack of experience or training; or (3) a lack of alignment between Bridgewater values and personal values. The first two people problems can likely be solved; the last usually requires exiting the firm.

To determine what the real problem is, a small group of people must engage in high-quality, collaborative, and honest conversations. The diagnostic conversations at Bridgewater that I witnessed or reviewed always contained a directive from Ray or another leader to "take your thinking to a higher level" and "get above yourself and the problem to look down on the machine and yourself objectively." "Getting above yourself" helps one reduce ego defenses and emotional hijacking.

Typically, drilling down to the real root cause of a negative outcome will mean focusing on a responsible party's design or execution. In such cases, there is a natural tendency to want to minimize the discomfort and to end the "painful" part by coming up with a quick solution. Bridgewater understands that quick solutions can lead to bad decisions, which leads to another of Ray's fundamental Principles: Pain + Reflection = Progress.[24]

The diagnosis process should lead to a root cause of the problem. Then the question is whether the problem is a one-off occurrence or part of a bigger problem or a pattern. Just like in any scientific endeavor, Bridgewater is wary of making decisions based on too few occurrences. Sample size is important. Do we have enough data to make a big decision, assuming the root cause is a big issue? Ray's approach to the quantity of data is his concept of triangulation, which means having multiple kinds of data from multiple sources that confirm a pattern.

Bridgewater is also wary of having only one or two people making decisions, especially if one of them is the party responsible for the performance. Small groups of three to five people make better diagnoses, because it is easier for those not directly involved to engage in the process unemotionally and without ego defenses. Once again, we see the power of small teams in learning.

Bridgewater believes that everyone involved in the diagnosis who has a thoughtful point of view should contribute to the conversation; however, not all opinions or thoughts are equal. Some people are more believable than others. One's believability depends on one's experience and track record. Everyone at Bridgewater, including Ray, has an evolving "Believability Index" grade—a number mathematically determined by one's experience, performance reviews, and the composite daily feedback ratings from peers and managers. The opinions of people with a higher Believability Index have more weight in the ultimate decision made in the diagnostic process.

Hundreds of feedback loop conversations take place at Bridgewater every day. These conversations take place in most of Bridgewater's seventeen functional groups:

Account Management—Client Service—Compliance—Core Management—Core Technology—Corporate Counsel—Counterparty and Client Relations—Facilities—Finance—Human Resources—IT—Marketing—Operations—Recruiting—Research—Security—Trading

As stated earlier, one of the goals of this process is to create more logical, independent thinkers who make good decisions based on good data. The root cause diagnosis process is a key step in that process. Likewise, we have seen how Ray uses teams and the Believability Index to further that goal. What is left to look at are Ray's basic decision Principles. One of Ray's Principles is to "Make all decisions logically, as expected value calculations"; another is: "Considering both the probabilities and the payoffs of the consequences, make sure that the probability of the unacceptable (i.e., the risk of ruin) is nil."[25]

Ray is a hyperrealist and not a big risk taker. His approach to decision making is to try to make all decisions small decisions—decisions that do not have big downsides. He believes in making many—fifteen or more—small, uncorrelated bets. He also believes in the 80/20 rule. In his words: "Since 80% of the juice can be gotten with the first 20% of the squeezing, there are relatively few (typically less than five) important things to consider in making a decision."[26] He also says, "Think about the appropriate time to make a decision in light of the marginal gains made by acquiring additional information versus the marginal costs of postponing the decision."[27] Moreover, he says, "Make sure all the 'must do's' are above the bar, before you do anything else," and he adds, "Remember that the best choices are the ones with more pros than cons, not those that don't have any cons."[28]

These rules deal with the reality that in most cases one does not have all the data that exists. They address the issue of whether to proceed and how to proceed. Ray's approach to minimize risk by making small bets is the same one that underlies the experimental learning process called "Learning Launches," discussed in chapter 7.

Ray accepts the reality that there is much more we do not know than we know. As such, people should frequently ask themselves the following four questions before making any important personal or business decision that could impact many people:

1. What do I really know?
2. What don't I know?
3. What do I really need to know that I don't know?
4. How do I learn that?

Culture

It is not surprising that the Bridgewater culture mirrors Ray's Principles and his beliefs and values. This is usually the case when an entrepreneur is able to personally grow as his or her company grows and, thus is able to remain the driving force for decades. This was or has been the case at IDEO, Gore, Room & Board, Southwest Airlines, Intuit, and UPS. The Bridgewater culture is lived out daily in the multitude of meetings that occur where the first act is turning on the tape recorder. It is evidenced by the décor of Bridgewater's buildings, the casual and business casual dress, the modest size of executive offices and the deep friendships among colleagues.

As I like to remind my students, I have lots of "miles on my personal tires." I have been very fortunate in my career journey to experience lots of business environments and leadership styles. I was struck by some consistent themes I experienced at Bridgewater.

TRUTH/HONESTY

Bridgewater people freely volunteered to me (a relative stranger) their personal weaknesses. At Bridgewater, everyone—including Ray—has an announced No. 1 weakness called a "burden," and it was normal to discuss it. It seemed that because they had learned about everyone else's weaknesses, there was nothing to be ashamed of. They had learned that Bridgewater's culture is built on being honest with yourself and others. Some even volunteered to me matter-of-factly—knowing that our conversation was being taped—that they planned to leave Bridgewater in a year. It was refreshing, but it was a new interview experience for me.

Three very experienced people openly told me that they had outgrown their current jobs and were ready for a new one at Bridgewater, but they didn't know if one existed or would be a good fit. If necessary, they said that they would move on. Still, no one appeared or sounded anxious. Their attitudes were that they'd be OK no matter what happened. It seemed to me that being OK was broader than being OK financially; it meant that they were confident entering the unknown. Everything didn't have to be mapped out; it could evolve. As one person stated, "The unknown does not scare me." That is self-efficacy.

Conversations I observed at Bridgewater, even the difficult ones, were calm—no raised voices. In some, you could see the stress on people's faces or in their body language or hear it in their voices, but they remained civil and focused. In one memorable instance, after a personal review, an individual said that he had to leave the meeting and needed some space to process what had been said. But even in that case, tempers didn't flare. Later, the person came back and requested that the meeting continue. It did and everyone agreed progress was made.

Were there disagreements in conversations? Yes. Disagreements are encouraged because it is the process of wrestling through disagreements and stress testing one's thinking and beliefs that one gets to the truth or a better place. One senior manager told me "I don't like conflict. But I deal with it here because it has rational benefits." The search for "truth" is not about being nice or liked or making no mistakes. In one of the prep videos I watched, CEO Greg Jensen stated: "There is a constant pull of people to move away from truth. It is a constant personal and organizational battle to be great at seeking the truth. We want to think better than other companies."[29]

MEANINGFUL RELATIONSHIPS

Searching for the truth and confronting one's personal weaknesses in a radically transparent environment builds personal relationships. Every person I met who had a Bridgewater tenure longer than two years made the point that deep bonds and friendships were made at Bridgewater because of what people endured together. One senior person told me that these close personal relationships were even more important than the generous benefits and compensation at Bridgewater. Like nearly everyone I met at Bridgewater, this person did not wear his feelings on his sleeve, but when he said his colleagues were like family, I remembered Ray's personal goal of "meaningful work and meaningful relationships." I felt the emotions beneath that person's statement and said, "It sounds like you love your close friends here," and he responded, "Yes, I do love them."

TEAM

Bridgewater's team culture does not accommodate arrogance or a "star" self-image or personality. It reminds me of the U.S. Marine Corps and the work I did with the Leadership Faculty at Marine Corps University. The Marine Corps is a values-based organization with a culture of excellence, team focus, and permission to speak freely. The Marine Corps leadership model is one of "servant leadership." A Marine Corps general once told me that what the Corps does is "take lots of ordinary people and transform them into teams that perform at the highest levels under the most difficult circumstances."[30] Maybe what Bridgewater does is take very bright people and transform them into the best thinkers in its industry.

Further support for the military analogy is provided by one of the previsit study videos that Bridgewater sent me. It was a talk given to Bridgewater employees by a Navy SEAL commander about SEAL recruitment and training. The commander described the transformation that occurs with new SEALs as they learn the process of managing their fears and preventing emotions from hijacking their thinking. Clearly, those processes align well with those of Bridgewater.

One of the experienced, new employees that I interviewed at Bridgewater had recently joined the training team that runs Bridgewater's New Hire Boot Camp. Can you guess where he had worked prior to joining Bridgewater? That's right—he was a recently retired Navy SEAL commander. Why in the world, I asked, would a Navy SEAL come to work at Bridgewater? Was the transition hard?

His answers were thought provoking. He told me that he had had several wonderful offers, but had chosen Bridgewater because the culture of the firm and the Navy SEALs "overlapped." He said that both organizations focus on learning, adaptation, recruiting high caliber people, and teaching them to be better thinkers and to relentlessly pursue constant improvement. Both explore action alternatives based on probability and scenario analysis, while being fanatical about mitigating risks. The SEALs, like Bridgewater, have a culture of brutal honesty, transparency that enables frequent hard conversations and confronting one's mistakes. The SEALs view mistakes as learning opportunities and strive not to make the same mistake twice. The SEALs also try to manage emotions (fear) in executing missions.

I am not saying that Bridgewater is just like the Navy SEALs. Making the best investment decisions is not analogous to executing a Navy SEAL mission; however, it's clear that there are common threads between the cultures of these two high-performance but very different organizations. The fact that some of the same learning mindsets, capabilities, and processes apply in high-change environments, both business and nonbusiness, is compelling. It demonstrates that in high-change contexts, the human learning fundamentals are similar. Business leaders can learn from educational and military learning leaders and vice versa.

PERMISSION TO SPEAK FREELY

The Bridgewater culture of Radical Transparency gives all of its people the power to speak openly and honestly. In fact, there is a duty to do so. One accompanying rule is never to speak about someone behind his back. This was illustrated to me in one of the previsit films I studied. Unexpectedly, a conversation in a meeting turned to evaluating someone's performance. Quickly, someone said, "We can't talk about him unless he's here," so they called up the particular person and asked him to join the meeting. In *Principles*, Ray states that next to being dishonest, talking behind someone's back is the worst thing you can do at Bridgewater.[31]

Another rule at Bridgewater is that everyone has the right to ask questions and understand what makes sense, and no one has the right to hold back a critical (thoughtful) opinion.[32]

CONDITIONAL PERMISSION TO MAKE MISTAKES

In the business sphere, especially in larger companies where the prevailing model is scale and efficiency (operational excellence), managers wake up each morning with a mission to eradicate variance. The goal of those "machines" is 99 percent defect-free output. Have you ever worked in a place where management said that mistakes were learning opportunities? I believe that this is the biggest issue every organization that wants to learn better or learn faster faces. Many people were raised and educated in the United States where the dominant culture teaches them to view mistakes as bad and as something to be minimized. This can lead to the mindset that a successful personal strategy is to avoid mistakes at all costs and to take as few risks as possible.

In "knowledge" businesses especially, all companies try to recruit employees with the highest academic test scores. Many of those successful students have made few mistakes in their lives, and their self-worth is dependent on not making them. These are the types of people Bridgewater also recruits. Think of the challenge those types of Bridgewater recruits face coming into a radically transparent, high-accountability culture that focuses on mistakes and personal weaknesses as opportunities for improvement. All of a sudden, the game has changed. If one stays at Bridgewater, one cannot avoid learning that one is not as good or as smart as one thought. These new hires must learn how to thrive in the Bridgewater way and become part of the Bridgewater machine.

It's a big challenge, and it's not for everyone. Mistake-based learning does not occur quickly. It takes effort and a manager's time to go through the learning process with an individual. People are not machines; they have emotions, feelings, and history. It's also a big challenge because learning is not an efficient process—it takes time and lots of conversations and reflection.

The bar at Bridgewater is set high and stays high. Many people leave at various stages of their careers. One senior person who had come from another firm said that working at Bridgewater was a "try-out forever," and that he isn't evaluated on a financial metric—a "financial P&L," but on his thinking—his "idea P&L."

The issue of conditional mistakes is so critical to the Bridgewater learning machine and culture that Ray devotes nine of the Management Principles in *Principles* to explaining the cultural concept of the conditional permission to make mistakes. I have inserted them almost verbatim below because they are so critical to Bridgewater's operating and learning model and because I think Ray says it better than my summary ever could. You'll notice that these Principles strikingly illustrate the concepts discussed in chapters 2, 3, and 4, especially mastery versus performance and approach versus avoidance mindsets, fear of failure, and how one's ego gets in the way of learning.

I say that the permission to make mistakes is "conditional" because, according to Ray, mistakes are acceptable if and only if they are identified and analyzed and learning occurs. Bridgewater's goal is better learning, individually and operationally. In my consulting with companies, I have found this issue to be quite difficult for leaders and managers to accept because of their belief that accountability would be diluted. Bridgewater, Gore, UPS, IDEO, and Intuit demonstrate that dilution is not a given.

Ray's Management Principles on Making Mistakes

The easiest way to read the following excerpts from *Principles* (in Ray's words, except where I added some transitions to make them flow as a narrative) and get the impact is to assume Ray is speaking directly to you:[33]

[At Bridgewater, we created] a culture in which it is OK to make mistakes but unacceptable not to identify, analyze, and learn from them. [Recognize that e]ffective, innovative thinkers are going to make mistakes[2] and learn from them because it is a natural part of the innovation process. For every mistake that you learn from you will save thousands of similar mistakes in the future, so if you treat

---

2. Thomas Edison said about failure: "I have not failed. I've just found 10,000 ways that don't work." "I am not discouraged, because every wrong attempt discarded is another step forward." "Results! Why, man, I have gotten a lot of results. I know several thousand things that won't work." "When I have fully decided that a result is worth getting I go ahead of it and make trial after trial until it comes." "Many of life's failures are men who did not realize how close they were to success when they gave up."

mistakes as learning opportunities that yield rapid improvements you should be excited by them. But if you treat them as bad things, you will make yourself and others miserable, and you won't grow. Your work environment will be marked by petty back-biting and malevolent barbs rather than by a healthy, honest search for truth that leads to evolution and improvement. Because of this, the more mistakes you make and the more quality, honest diagnoses you have, the more rapid your progress will be. That's not B.S. or just talk. That's the reality of learning.[3]

Do not feel bad about your mistakes or those of others. Love them! Remember that (1) they are to be expected, (2) they're the first and most essential part of the learning process, and (3) feeling bad about them will prevent you from getting better. People typically feel bad about mistakes because they think in a short-sighted way that mistakes reflect their badness or because they're worried about being punished (or not being rewarded). People also tend to get angry at those who make mistakes because in a short-sighted way they focus on the bad outcome rather than the educational, evolutionary process they're a part of. That's a real tragedy.

I once had a ski instructor who had taught Michael Jordan, the greatest basketball player of all time, how to ski. He explained that Jordan enjoyed his mistakes and got the most out of them. At the start of high school, Jordan was an unimpressive basketball player; he became a champion because he loved using his mistakes to improve. Yet despite Jordan's example and the example of countless other successful people, it is far more common for people to allow ego to stand in the way of learning. Perhaps it's because school learning overemphasizes the value of having the right answers and punishes wrong answers. Good school learners are often bad mistake-based learners because they are bothered by their mistakes. I particularly see this problem in recent graduates from the best colleges, who frequently shy away from exploring their own weaknesses. Remember that intelligent people who are open to recognizing and learning from their weaknesses substantially outperform people with the same abilities who aren't similarly open.

3. A good book about this is *Einstein's Mistakes: The Human Failings of Genius* by Hans C. Ohanian.

Mistakes serve another useful purpose. One should

[o]bserve the patterns of mistakes to see if they are a product of weaknesses. [I call this connecting t]he dots without ego barriers. If there is a pattern of mistakes, it probably signifies a weakness. Everyone has weaknesses. The fastest path to success is to know what they are and how to deal with them so that they don't stand in your way. Weaknesses are due to deficiencies in learning or deficiencies in abilities. Deficiencies in learning can be rectified over time, though usually not quickly, while deficiencies in abilities are virtually impossible to change. Neither is a meaningful impediment to getting what you want if you accept it as a problem that can be designed around.

Do not feel bad about your weaknesses or those of others. They are opportunities to improve. If you can solve the puzzle of what is causing them, you will get a gem—i.e., the ability to stop making them in the future. Everyone has weaknesses and can benefit from knowing about them. Don't view explorations of weaknesses as attacks. A person who receives criticism—particularly if he tries to objectively consider if it's true—is someone to be admired.

[Likewise, d]on't worry about looking good—worry about achieving your goals. Put your insecurities away and get on with achieving your goals. To test if you are worrying too much about looking good, observe how you feel when you find out you've made a mistake or don't know something. If you find yourself feeling bad, reflect—remind yourself that the most valuable comments are accurate criticisms. Imagine how silly and unproductive it would be if you thought your ski instructor was blaming you when he told you that you fell because you didn't shift your weight properly. If a criticism is accurate, it is a good thing. You should appreciate it and try to learn from it.

Get over "blame" and "credit" and get on with "accurate" and "inaccurate." When people hear, "You did XYZ wrong," they have an instinctual reaction to figure out possible consequences or punishments rather than to try to understand how to improve. Remember that what has happened lies in the past and no longer matters, except as a method for learning how to be better in the future. Create an environment in which people understand that remarks such as "You handled that badly" are meant to be helpful (for the future) rather than punitive (for the past). While people typically feel unhappy about blame and good about credit, that attitude gets everything backwards and can cause major problems. Worrying about "blame" and "credit" or "positive" and "negative" feedback impedes the iterative process essential to learning.

[This is very important: d]on't depersonalize mistakes. Identifying who made mistakes is essential to learning. It is also a test of whether a person will put improvement ahead of ego and whether he [or she] will fit into the Bridgewater culture. A common error is to say, "We didn't handle this well" rather than "Harry didn't handle this well." This occurs when people are uncomfortable connecting specific mistakes to specific people because of ego sensitivities. This creates dysfunctional and dishonest organizations. Since individuals are the most important building blocks of any organization and since individuals are responsible for the ways things are done, the diagnosis must connect the mistake to the specific individual by name. Someone created the procedure that went wrong, or decided we should act according to that procedure, and ignoring that fact will slow our progress toward successfully dealing with the problem.

Write down your weaknesses and the weaknesses of others to help remember and acknowledge them. It's unhealthy to hide them because if you hide them, it will slow your progress towards successfully dealing with them.

When you experience pain, remember to reflect. You can convert the "pain" of seeing your mistakes and weaknesses into pleasure. If there is only one piece of advice I can get you to remember it is this one. Calm yourself down and think about what is causing your psychological pain. Ask other objective, believable parties for their help to figure it out. Find out what is true. Don't let ego barriers stand in your way. Remember that pains that come from seeing mistakes and weaknesses are "growing pains" that you learn from.[4] Don't rush through them. Stay in them and explore them because that will help build the foundation for improvement. It is widely recognized that (1) changing your deep-seated, harmful behavior is very difficult yet necessary for improvement and (2) doing this generally requires

---

4. If you recognize short-term failure as a step toward long-term success, which it really is if you learn from it, you won't be afraid of it or made uncomfortable by it and you will approach all of your experiences as learning experiences, even the most difficult ones.

a deeply felt recognition of the connection between your harmful behavior and the pain it causes. Psychologists call this "hitting bottom." Embracing your failures is the first step toward genuine improvement; it is also why 'confession' precedes forgiveness in many societies.[5] If you keep doing this you will learn to improve and feel the pleasures of it.

Be self-reflective and make sure your people are self-reflective. This quality differentiates those who evolve fast from those who don't. When there is pain, the animal instinct is "fight or flight" (i.e., to either strike back or run away)—reflect instead. When you can calm yourself down, thinking about the dilemma that is causing you pain will bring you to a higher level and enlighten you, leading to progress. That is because the pain you are feeling is due to something being at odds—maybe it's you encountering reality, such as the death of a friend, and not being able to accept it. If when you are calm, you can think clearly about what things are at odds, you will learn more about what reality is like and how to better deal with it. It really will produce progress. If, on the other hand, the pain causes you to tense-up, not think, feel sorry for yourself, and blame others, it will be a very bad experience. So, when you are in pain, try to remember: Pain + Reflection = Progress. It's pretty easy to determine whether a person is reflective or deflective: self-reflective people openly and objectively look at themselves while deflective people don't.

Managers need to "[t]each and reinforce the merits of mistake-based learning":

> We must bring mistakes into the open and analyze them objectively, so managers need to foster a culture that makes this normal and penalizes suppressing or covering up mistakes. Probably the worst mistake anyone can make at Bridgewater is not facing up to mistakes—i.e.,

---

5. Ego often stands in the way of acknowledging your weaknesses (which is the essential first step in overcoming them), like being afraid to ask a question because people might think you're stupid because you don't know something. Yet acknowledging those weaknesses (e.g., "I know I'm a dumb shit, but I'd just like to know . . .") helps you move beyond ego toward learning and improving.

hiding rather than highlighting them. Highlighting them, diagnosing them, thinking about what should be done differently in the future, and then adding that new knowledge to the procedures manual are all essential to our improvement.

Ray's passion about the power of mistakes being learning opportunities comes through loud and clear in these Management Principles. No one can argue with Bridgewater's consistent high performance over decades. I believe that every organization can learn from Bridgewater because the principles underlying its way reflect the best of the science of learning that we know at this point. No matter what business you are in, the principles of learning are the same.

Conclusion

The Bridgewater story is interesting and challenging. I suggest to you that Bridgewater has created its way (not *the* way) to mitigate the fact that we as humans are speedy and efficient processors of information in a way that affirms our stories about our world and ourselves. Bridgewater understands that high-quality thinking and learning requires more deep and critical thinking, which is helped by high-quality conversations with others.

Likewise, Bridgewater understands that working around ego defenses, and modifying our stories about how we see the world and ourselves, is hard to do alone. This type of learning is a team sport. For others to help in this process there must be open, direct, and honest communications. That in turn requires trust that one will not be punished for trying to help. It also requires trust that the system will not punish weaknesses unless they are not improved. Fear of speaking honestly, fear of making mistakes, and fear of looking bad all inhibit learning in organizations. These fears can never be eliminated totally; however, Bridgewater demonstrates that the right culture, the right processes, the right leadership behaviors, and a lot of hard work can reduce them materially.

Bridgewater has confronted the "truth" about how individuals usually think and how their ego defenses and emotions can inhibit learning. It has put in place a culture and critical thinking and learning conversation processes to improve the frequency and quality of Bridgewater's learning. Now let's explore another part of the Bridgewater story: the people part.

Section III: People

Bridgewater is currently involved in a major initiative to make hiring more of a science. Historically, about 25 percent of new hires leave within twelve to eighteen months. In some groups that number approaches 50 percent. Bridgewater's overall turnover rate has averaged 19.6 percent since 2007. Bridgewater is not pleased with those retention numbers. It has always focused on hiring for cultural fit, but now it's looking to make hiring more of a science to increase retention rates. Tenure is close to being evenly split with each of the following tenure groups comprising one-third of the total workforce: 0–2 years, 2–4 years, and over 4 years. Average tenure is 3.5 years. Company turnover rates typically are hard to find, but in a recent article about Amazon.com and its founder Jeff Bezos[34] the average employee tenure rates were listed as 1 year for Amazon, 1.1 years for Google, 4 years for Microsoft, 4.3 years for Intel, and 6.4 years for IBM. This provides perspective on Bridgewater's average tenure.

Ray views turnover as a hiring design problem. As he sees it, Bridgewater's processes are not currently designed well enough to identify people with the highest probability of flourishing at Bridgewater. The process has been good enough for Bridgewater to produce its phenomenal investment results over the last twenty-five years, but the hiring issue has become a bigger focus now that Ray's mission is to create the best, most enduring organization possible.

Ray has stated that the challenge is to find enough smart people who believe in Radical Transparency, and who are able to get through the transformation process that Ray and Bridgewater expect of each hire. Ray calls this process "getting to the other side."[35] It takes about eighteen months on average for people to adapt to Bridgewater's Radical Transparency environment and its constant feedback process, and to go through the personal process of accepting one's weaknesses, mitigating one's ego defenses, and engaging in personal work to make progress in mitigating or managing one's weaknesses. Not everyone makes it through the process. As mentioned, turnover at Bridgewater is higher than Ray wants, which is why he wants to identify the types of people who are most likely to get to the "other side."

Of course, part of the challenge is that those with the best knowledge base for the job often also have traits that can make this transformation difficult. Bridgewater's new hires, both the young and the more experienced, generally fit the following description. They are smart graduates of elite, top-tier schools who:

- Have track records of success;
- Have experienced little failure, if any;
- Have rarely if ever received negative feedback;
- Have strong self-images of being better than most;
- Work hard to avoid looking bad or appearing stupid;
- Have rarely, if ever, had difficult conversations about themselves; and
- Dislike confrontation and work hard to be nice and well liked.

Bridgewater's objective is to transform its people into independent, critical thinkers who:

- Have an open mind;
- Subject their thinking willingly to stress testing;
- Accept and work to improve their weaknesses;
- Accept and work to mitigate and manage their ego defenses;
- Admit freely their weaknesses, being wrong, and not knowing; and
- Believe a career is a journey of learning and self-improvement.

People are complex. Each comes to Bridgewater having been molded by various environmental experiences and genes. They are an amalgamation of "nature and nurture." All have learned how to succeed in their world and thus, have learned how to "play the game." That is the rub: the game at Bridgewater is different. Radical Transparency, acknowledging personal weaknesses, embracing mistakes, and being comfortable in a hyperevaluative organization is challenging. What are the values, attributes, and abilities of the kind of people who will embrace and succeed in the Bridgewater culture?

This question takes us back to chapter 4 and the discussion of motivation and mindsets. In the past few years, Ray has engaged with the Navy SEALs to understand what types of people pass that organization's arduous training process. He has studied the biographies of Albert Einstein, Benjamin Franklin, and Steve Jobs and talked with countless psychologists and consultants. He then has determined that he wants to recruit people with a growth mindset: curious people who want to master their worlds and are not afraid of failure, risk, uncertainty, or the unknown. Their inclination is to approach, not to avoid. Their strongest motivations are intrinsic, not extrinsic. They are more inner-directed than outer-directed. They are more open-minded than close-minded. "Getting to the other side" requires living and behaving in accordance with Bridgewater's values and culture. And it requires engaging in a constant evaluation process that illuminates what must be improved to get to the other side.

Every company I have worked for has had some kind of leadership development program with the obligatory leadership competencies, including standard training or courses for managers to take. Many used a few psychological tests and all engaged in the standard annual review and development plan conversation. In my twenty plus years of business work experience primarily in the financial services industry, however, I never received a critical review or had a discussion about weaknesses that had to be overcome. I never was part of a 360-degree review process. Now, I am not saying that I was *that* good. What I am saying is that no organization even came close to the level of Bridgewater's engagement in each person's development.

What makes Bridgewater so interesting is the frequency and quality of feedback that employees receive (whether they request it or not). When employees join Bridgewater, they are signing up for that level of engagement for the purpose of accelerating their personal growth. What is the organizational objective? To help every employee become the best independent thinker he or she can be, because a company of the best thinkers is Bridgewater's competitive advantage.

To achieve this objective requires a carefully designed process. Bridgewater's process includes multiple kinds of reviews, Radical Transparency, and intensive engagement of management in the development of each individual, which is made possible by a structure that limits direct reports to five to ten people. That limit is intended to make it possible that every manager can know his or her direct reports very well, and vice versa. Out of that eighteen-month transformation process comes meaningful relationships and deep bonding.

The more time I spent studying and talking with people at Bridgewater, the more I was reminded, yet again, of my work with the Leadership Faculty at the Marine Corps University in Quantico, Virginia. The Marine Corps "machine" is designed to create "Maneuver Warriors." That requires leaders who are mentally agile and creative and have the ability to think critically.[36] The Marine Corps believes that to build a cohesive organization requires shared training experiences, shared ways of doing business, and shared values—honor, courage, and commitment. The Marine

Corps learning process is called "The Transformation," which begins at the recruiting stage (i.e., assuring a cultural fit) and continues throughout a recruit's career.

Leadership training in the Marine Corps is designed to be stressful and to test people. That testing is followed by extensive, direct, immediate feedback. The Marine Corps describes its transformation process as taking "raw iron" and turning it into "polished, magnetized steel."[37] As one Marine Corps general stated to me years ago: "We take average people and transform them into cohesive teams that consistently perform exceptionally well in the most difficult of circumstances."[38] This has striking similarities to the type of transformation that is expected of new hires at Bridgewater. In the following sections, I discuss some of the tools Bridgewater uses to guide its employees through this transformation, and help them "get to the other side."

Employee Evaluations

Ray's Principles about employee evaluation, at all levels, can be summarized in one overriding phrase: "Evaluate people accurately, not 'kindly.'"[39]

That is hard work. Evaluating people accurately takes time and deep thinking. It takes time and deep thinking to assess data, come to tentative conclusions, and reflect on those conclusions before talking with an employee. Delivering bad news is hard, and no one wants to be disliked for doing it. Having spent this time getting to the truth, Bridgewater managers have to be careful not to water it down or deliver it in a wishy-washy manner that makes understanding even harder. Also, because rarely does a person see his or her weaknesses the same way as the reviewer does, there are likely to be disagreements that can become emotional. The reviewed employee usually needs time to reflect and to come back for more conversation(s) until the parties agree on the issue.

Then they have to determine whether the issue is part of a pattern or a one-off problem. If the issue is determined to be part of a pattern, then the reviewer and employee must discuss whether it is a design or personal issue. If the former, the party responsible for the relevant part of the machine must be called in to discuss how to fix the design. If it's the latter, then it becomes a question of whether it is a job mismatch or a training issue. Again, a solution has to be agreed upon.

Even in the best of cases, this process is lengthy, and it is obvious that Bridgewater invests significant time in every employee's evaluation and in trying to get everyone in a role where they can succeed. Any company that views people as its most important asset will face similar challenges. Most of the organizations that I have worked in, consulted with, or researched do not, however, pursue this level of engagement or analysis.

Even with the right principles, the right evaluation tools/tests and the right data analytics, it still comes down to human beings taking the time and doing the hard work to analyze, critically think, and come to thoughtful conclusions that are then stress tested with the employee in multiple conversations, all with the goal of personal improvement and fulfillment. Most managers and leaders are not trained in psychology or clinical counseling, and so a big challenge for Bridgewater is that its managers and leaders must execute excellently in these difficult conversations.

In Management Principle 106,[40] Ray urges Bridgewater's employees to provide constant, clear, and honest feedback, and encourages discussion of this feedback. He tells them to put their compliments and criticisms in perspective for the other person. Because people tend to blow negative feedback out of proportion, he stresses the importance of clarifying and drawing attention to people's strengths, too. He also constantly reminds people of why Bridgewater focuses intensely on mistakes and weaknesses— it's not for spite's sake, but because they are growth opportunities and they help Bridgewater get everyone in the right position.[41]

"Personal evolution," Ray states, "occurs first by identifying your strengths and weaknesses, and then by changing your weaknesses (e.g., through training) or changing jobs to play to strengths and preferences."[42]

He says, "Typically it takes six to twelve months to get to know a person in a by-and-large sort of way and about eighteen months to change behavior."[43] He also says that there is a difference between "'I believe you made a bad decision' and 'I believe you are a bad decision maker.'"[44] One of his Management Principles is "Don't believe that being good or bad at some things means that the person is good or bad at everything. Realize that all people have strengths and weaknesses."[45]

In coming to judgments about people, Bridgewater stresses that those judgments need to be based on a large enough sample of high-quality data that is then discussed with the employee in an open-minded, fair manner. Principle No. 111 cautions: "Remember that when it comes to assessing people, the two biggest mistakes are being overconfident in your assessment and failing to get in synch on that assessment."[46]

Employees' Personal Growth Tools

Bridgewater has created a series of tools for use in evaluating employees and for employees to use to manage their personal growth. Bridgewater uses different psychological tests: Myers-Briggs Type Indicator, Team Dimensions Profile, Work Place Personality Inventory, and a values inventory based on Elliott Jaques's Stratified Systems Theory.

These tests are just the beginning. We have already discussed how, after every meeting, participants give evaluations on the responsible person and other participants as they see fit and that anyone at any time can submit feedback on any other person. All of this is transparent and accessible by every employee. Each employee has a computed Believability Index based on experience and feedback evaluations that give "appropriate" weight to different people's feedback. All of this feedback is automatically updated daily and available on each employee's Bridgewater iPad.

Bridgewater uses a number of other tools to frequently give all employees feedback on their strengths and weaknesses and to help them grow and develop. All of these tools are contained on every employee's Bridgewater iPad. To give you a sense of how extensive and detailed this evaluation process is I discuss four tools: the Dot Collector and Dot Connector, Issues Log and Issue Log Diagnosis Card, Pain Button, and Baseball Card.

THE DOT COLLECTOR AND DOT CONNECTOR

The "Dot Collector" is the tool that allows every employee to give any other employee performance feedback based on personal observations, meetings, conversations, or teamwork experiences. The rater can give feedback on any of the seventy-seven behavioral or attitudinal "attributes" that Bridgewater measures. (More detail on and a list of some of those attributes are included in the discussion of the Baseball Card below.) Raters can also give feedback on how well an employee's performance adheres to the Bridgewater Principles. At the end of every meeting of any kind at Bridgewater, participants are given time to use the Dot Collector to input any evaluations or feedback they want on any person involved in the meeting. Sometimes, the meeting's designated leader will also directly ask the participants to give feedback on a particular participant's performance. In addition, it's not unusual for a participant to create a poll on Dot Collector with several questions pertaining to how the meeting was conducted or its effectiveness. All of that feedback is completely transparent to every Bridgewater employee under the Bridgewater Principle of Radical Transparency.

The Dot Connector is the output of the feedback received—basically a database of feedback every employee has received from anyone, excluding formal manager reviews over long periods of time. The data is grouped according to the relevant seventy-seven attributes. The data is then summarized to give every employee a "picture" of his and her feedback, by strengths and weaknesses and by attributes. The Dot Connector not only shows the employee how everyone else rated him or her, but it collects and summarizes all the dots given by the employee to others by recipient and attribute. The Dots are graphically displayed by numerical rating and by the rater's Believability Index so that the evaluated employee and his manager can give appropriate weight to individual ratings and to the overall ratings by attribute.

The Dot Connector is an employee's real-time feedback database that can track feedback trends and the number of attributes needing improvement. The Dot Connector is statistically designed to illuminate a rater's biases because it allows the rated employee to easily access that rater's ratings of any other employee in the firm with respect to that attribute. This way, if an employee receives a low rating on an attribute and can see that the rater also has given everyone but himself a low rating, then the employee has data to interpret the credibility of the rating in addition to the rater's overall Believability Index. The Dot Connector also allows any employee to take his overall ratings on an attribute category and compare that to overall firm statistics and to drill down and see who has the same rating and who has a higher rating. This gives an employee data to identify other employees who best role model the behaviors that he needs to improve.

The Dot Connector also allows an employee to see all the ratings data on any other employee, including those who rate that employee similarly to her. Bridgewater uses algorithms to triangulate employees' Dot Connector ratings with their test scores and their formal performance feedback reviews from their designated managers—everyone has a designated manager. This whole process has three overriding purposes: to provide an accurate picture of a person's strengths and weaknesses, to track performance trends over time, and to use that data to place people into positions that play to their strengths. All employees at Bridgewater, including Ray, know where they stand—there are no surprises come review time.

The Dot Connector data on each employee is the starting point for the other Bridgewater tools. Because every human being has weaknesses, and the Dot Connector will illuminate them. What happens next? It is not surprising that Bridgewater asks each employee and his or her designated manager to go through a root cause analysis process to discover what's causing the problem. That analysis is the purpose of the Issues Log and Issue Log Diagnosis Card.

ISSUES LOG AND ISSUE LOG DIAGNOSIS CARD

As part of correcting or improving the process and people issues that can lead to suboptimal performance of the Bridgewater "machine," the firm uses an Issues Log and a diagnostic process. The Issues Log is just that—a list of all the various personal or process issues related to a specific individual. The company has a centralized Issues Log, which managers use to understand the people and process issues in their area, working with each person to diagnose the root causes of the most important issues. The diagnosis methodology used by Bridgewater is reflected in the Issue Log Diagnosis Card (see figure 9.2).

The diagnostic process determines if a mistake was caused by a "machine" design issue or a personal weakness. If it's the latter, then the process determines whether the weakness represents a pattern for this person and/or is the result of a lack of ability or training. The last step is for the manager and employee to determine what steps (design and/or personal) need to be taken to solve the problem long term and to reduce the probability of it reoccurring. In some cases this means putting a development plan in place for the individual, and in others it can mean that the individual may not be fit for the role and needs to be removed from that position. All of this contributes to the ongoing picture of an employee at Bridgewater and is documented on the Baseball Card—the root cause and the plan to ameliorate the cause or improve the weakness.

These cards are transparent to all employees. Everyone can know everyone else's weaknesses, which has two positive effects. First, it makes transparent that everyone has weaknesses. Second, it makes transparent how the firm deals with weaknesses or problems in a way that can lead to trust in the system, empathy for others, and personal humility.

THE PAIN BUTTON

Do you remember Ray's formula: Pain + Reflection = Progress? "Pain" represents the psychological struggle of confronting and acknowledging one's

ISSUE LOG DIAGNOSIS CARD

BRIDGEWATER

1. Ask the person who logged the issue: "What sub-optimality did you experience?" "What pain did you encounter?"

🔍 Or ask the person who logged the issue: "What pain did you encounter?"

⭐ **What is good?** Being specific about the badness. Clarity around what is sub-optimal.

2. Ask the manager of the area: "From which responsibility did this outcome arise? Who owns this responsibility?"

🗄 Open up the responsibility map and find the right listing(s).

⭐ **What is good?** Both the responsibility and the responsible party are clear.

3. Ask the owner of the responsibility: "How does your machine for achieving this responsibility currently work?"

🔍 Ask the responsibility owner: **"Describe how you achieve this responsibility. Describe who is responsible for doing what at each step."**

🗄 Open up the machine map related to this responsibility; if a written version doesn't exist, document it during the discussion.

⭐ **What is good?** A clear visual image of how the process works and who owns each step. A tight explanation of how the process achieves the goal.

4. Ask the owner of the responsibility: "What, if anything, broke in this situation?"

🔍 First ask: **"Were the various steps of the machine followed? If not, who didn't do what?"**

🔍 If the machine steps were followed, then ask: **"Is the machine designed well? If not, what's wrong with the design?"**

🔍 Otherwise, ask: **"Is this an acceptable outcome of the machine? Why is that? How do you know?"** Find out if others agree. If this is true, then your diagnosis is complete.

⭐ **What is good?** A clear, concise answer as to what went wrong (e.g., this person at this step in the machine did not do their job, the machine is designed poorly) or clear agreement that this outcome is acceptable. This is your proximate cause.

5. Ask the person(s) responsible for the break: "Why did you fail in this way? What does this event tell us about you?"

🔍 Probe why the responsible person failed. Be willing to "hit the nerve."

🔍 Then ask the person and their manager: **"Is this weakness representative of a pattern with this person?"**

🗄 Pull out the person's baseball card to check the answer.

⭐ **What is good?** A clear, concise statement as to why this person made this mistake and whether this is indicative of pattern with this person . The 'why' will generally be an adjective because it will describe the person. This is your root cause.

6. Ask the responsible parties: "How should the people / machines / responsibilities evolve as a result of this issue?"

🔍🔍 Confirm that the short-term resolution of the issue has been addressed (e.g., fix the printer).

🔍🔍 Determine the steps to be taken for long-term solutions and who is responsible for those steps. Specifically:
- Are there responsibilities that need either assigning or greater clarification?
- Are there machine designs that need to be reworked?
- Are there people whose fit for their roles need to be evaluated?

🗄 Update the responsibility map and machine map(s) based on the learnings from this meeting.

🗄 Update people's baseball cards based on the observations from step 5; use accurate levels of confidence to express observations (e.g., a clear pattern is a weakness; a 'one off' is a question).

Figure 9.2

Source: "©2014 Bridgewater Associates, LP." Used with permission.

weaknesses and taking steps to mitigate them. The Pain Button is an app on every employee's Bridgewater iPad. Unlike all of the other tools, the Pain Button has a feature that allows an employee to restrict access to only himself or only to designated employees. The Pain Button can be used like a personal journal. Because pain is a signal that something may be going wrong, the purpose of the app is for one to write down and reflect on the "pains" one is experiencing in order to understand what's causing them and to deal with those causes effectively.

The first step is "Documenting the Pain"—either in accordance with Radical Transparency or privately—by describing the experience that caused the pain and listing the people (up to four employees) that were involved and all the emotions felt during the experience, as well as the relative intensity of each. Examples of emotions that might be listed are anger, sadness, hurt, anxiety, fear, and the urge to fight or flee. It's a personal decision whether to share this information with anyone else.

The second step is "Reflecting on the Pain." This is the process of thinking deeply about what created the pain and what facts or events led to the pain. If the pain was caused by feedback from others, the employee is encouraged to try to understand through reflection how the person giving the feedback came to the conclusions she did. What facts was the feedback based on? What beliefs did the other person espouse? Then, just as in the assumption unpacking process discussed in chapter 7, the employee is encouraged to try to understand why he felt the pain—that is, to understand the underlying beliefs he has that triggered the feelings and emotional responses in that moment. This process usually involves employees confronting their ego defenses and their fears as discussed in several of the earlier chapters. The employee is then encouraged to log in some reflections and thoughts just as if writing in a personal journal. If an employee doesn't log in such reflections, he or she will see a personal reminder of this as long as no reflection input is logged. That reminder is for the specific employee's eyes only.

The reflection part of the Pain Button also has an outcome or solution section where the employee can create a plan to remedy the pain by reflecting on the question: "Who should do what differently?" The employee can then decide whether to implement that change or not and can then track their progress in the "Progress section," where they can see whether their pains reoccur or whether the solutions they are implementing are alleviating these pains effectively over time.

BASEBALL CARD

The last tool we discuss is a card that on one screen contains an employee's overall evaluation summary. Every Bridgewater employee, including Ray, has a "Baseball Card" that includes his or her picture, an overall performance rating based on formal performance reviews, and a "thinking" rating based on psychological tests and assessments of behaving in accordance with Bridgewater's Principles. The card also contains the employee's grades with respect to the seventy-seven attributes, which fall under seven categories. The Bridgewater Baseball Card is proprietary, but Ray has been gracious in allowing me to share some of the key categories of attributes, as well as a number of the attributes under each category:

- The Five Step Process includes six attributes, three of which are:
  - ☐ Problems—perceiving them
  - ☐ Problems—not tolerating them
  - ☐ Diagnosing the root cause

- Values Fundamentals includes four attributes; true to Bridgewater's culture, three of them are:
  - ☐ Living in the truth
  - ☐ Driven to achieve excellence
  - ☐ Integrity

- Management Fundamentals includes fifteen attributes, five of which are:
  - ☐ Matches people to the job design
  - ☐ Probes deeply to know how the machine is working
  - ☐ "Cuts through it"
  - ☐ Is willing to touch the nerve
  - ☐ Holds people accountable

These attributes represent fundamental processes that are necessary for Bridgewater to achieve its desired outcomes. Probably one of the hardest management fundamentals is to execute well the large number of high-quality feedback conversations that are necessary for the Bridgewater machine to work.

- Thinking Qualities includes seventeen attributes, seven of which are:
  - ☐ Knowing what (s)he doesn't know and what to do about it
  - ☐ Linear thinking
  - ☐ Lateral thinking
  - ☐ Logical reasoning
  - ☐ Seeing multiple possibilities
  - ☐ Dealing with ambiguity
  - ☐ Empathy

- Other interesting attributes that Bridgewater measures are:
  - ☐ Manages conflict to get to the truth
  - ☐ Quick to learn from mistakes
  - ☐ Comfortable accepting what (s)he is really like and building on it
  - ☐ Listens well
  - ☐ Takes the bull by the horns
  - ☐ Proactive

The grades on each attribute are derived from evaluations by the employee's manager and people who work closely with the employee, as well as from evaluations by any other employee concerning a specific meeting or work project. The grader's Believability Index weights all feedback. The Baseball Card also includes the employee's self-ratings on all seventy-seven attributes.

Grades are computed daily and thus represent real-time, evolving ratings. The attribute scores also contain two summary charts. One chart, titled "Rely On," designates attributes with respect to which the employee has a strong enough grade that the employee can be placed in positions or on assignments that require those attributes. The other chart, titled "Watch Out For," designates attributes that represent an employee's weaknesses and should be monitored if the employee's assignments or positions rely heavily on those attributes.

The Baseball Card contains the data to be used in determining job or assignment fit. The Card also can be used to identify behavioral trends and track progress on improving weaknesses. Those progress trends are compiled as part of a formal performance review and given to each employee as a "Rate of Change" numerical grade. All of this data is then used to give each employee an overall grade that is a designated "Belt Color." Every employee is also given a grade that designates the level of management for which she is currently qualified. Every employee's Baseball Card is publicly available for viewing inside the firm.

Where does all this data come from? As stated, every meeting ends with participants grading other participants in a process called "Dotting." Those grades go into the Dot Connector database that was discussed above.

An obvious question about these tools is: Do employees feel comfortable enough to give tough grades to their bosses or senior leaders? My data is limited to having viewed a few senior leaders' Baseball Cards, including Ray's, but the answer from that limited data is yes. For example, I reviewed a detailed e-mail written to Ray by a manager who criticized Ray's performance in a client meeting. It was direct and negative. From memory, in substance it said that Ray came across as unprepared and that the points he made were unclear and disorganized. Both this e-mail and Ray's response were public. Ray's response was not defensive. He was accepting and thankful for the feedback, and he talked about what he would do to ensure that such a performance would not occur again. He apologized for letting the team and the firm down.

Have you ever experienced anything like that in any organization where you have worked? I have not. Have you ever experienced a CEO publicly apologizing to employees? I have not. Have you ever worked for a manager or leader who openly talked about weaknesses? I have not.

One may wonder whether there are ever instances of tough grades being given out of self-interest or malice. Yes, it is possible, but Bridgewater has two processes that give every employee the right to "appeal" any rating that he thinks is unfair. Culturally, Bridgewater is an idea meritocracy. Every idea or judgment can be subjected to probing and stress testing. Everyone has the right to question any judgment, probe for the reasons behind the judgment, and determine whether the reasons stand the test of truth. If the probing does not end in the parties being "in synch," then the employee has the right to "escalate" or appeal the judgment to a higher-level third party. Bridgewater calls this automatic right of appeal its judicial system. In discussing this issue with Bridgewater employees, I was reminded that the firm's entire culture is built on the "search for truth." The intentional submission of a non-truthful evaluation would be grounds for dismissal because such behavior is so anticultural.

The Process of Getting to the Other Side

Of course, knowing what weaknesses need to be improved is just half the struggle; the crucial other half is the transformation process—the "getting to the other side." To explain how this happens at Bridgewater, in the following examples I have created scripts and analysis from Bridgewater films I reviewed and interviews I conducted. Because of the personal nature and confidentiality of the data, I have used fictitious names and weaknesses.

NOT KNOWING IS LIBERATING

For Morgan, the transformation process was difficult. She described it as like "running full speed into a wall," and identified it as a turning point in her life. Morgan learned how liberating it was "not to know" and to admit it. Once she accepted the fact that "not knowing" wouldn't make her stupid or appear stupid to others, she could get on with really solving the problem. No one knows everything.

Remember that Bridgewater recruits are generally superstar students who excelled at elite institutions. Their grades depended on knowing. Their status and self-image depended in part on being perceived as smart and, in large part, on what others thought. That required them to constantly manage how they came across. It also meant avoiding conflict and being as agreeable as possible.

By contrast, to succeed at Bridgewater, employees have to admit that they do not know everything and are not as smart as they once thought they were. And they have to do so publicly. As Morgan stated: "This changes your whole way of thinking. That is hard because your 'old' way of thinking produced lots of personal success and recognition."

Morgan has since progressed to being a manager but still gets direct negative feedback all the time. As a manager, Morgan also has to give such feedback and has had to develop the emotional intelligence to do it in a way that helps the employee deal with and evaluate the feedback. Morgan has learned to give such feedback by observing others, by trial and error, and by "deep caring"—in other words, by having the ability to empathize with the person receiving the feedback.

This process is hard. It's hard to deliver negative feedback and it's hard to receive it. One Bridgewater employee stated: "It is much easier to give the truth than to receive the truth." And Morgan described the transformation process as: "Going against human nature and being human at the same time."

GET ABOVE YOURSELF—LOOK DOWN ON YOURSELF

We are wired to perceive conflict or negative feedback as a threat. This threat goes to our core: it challenges our self-image and can be perceived as personal failure. Our response to a threat is both physical and emotional, which affects our ability to think logically. In many cases we have one of two reactions: fight or flee. In many cases, anxiety is high. Those reactions inhibit being open-minded, cognitive processing, and seeking to understand feedback. Instead one's automatic reaction is to defend, deflect, and deny. One can feel frustrated, demoralized, and miserable.

To counter those automatic responses at Bridgewater, there is a lot of talk about "getting above yourself." That means trying to get above the emotions and look down on yourself as if you were a machine. It means listening to the feedback as if it was a description of a malfunctioning part of a machine. "Getting above yourself" is a metaphor for forcing the conscious, logical part of your mind to take control of the unconscious part of your mind that is driving emotional reactions. In other words, it means: Don't let your emotions hijack your thinking. Take a deep breath or two. Remember that you are with good people who care about you.

I heard this kind of discussion frequently. As I reflect on what I saw at Bridgewater, acknowledging that this is based on a limited data set, the common weaknesses addressed involved intellectual arrogance, intellectual stubbornness, the inability to consider other points of view, fear of failure, fear of looking bad, and defining personal success as having to always be the one with the right answer.

Two employees who worked as a team stated: "The real battle was with ourselves. Egos, blind spots and letting our subconscious self control us. We needed other people to help us recognize our weaknesses, get past our egos and see things we cannot see. What we learned is that by holding each other accountable, we are helping each other to be great."

YOU DON'T KNOW WHAT YOU DON'T KNOW

Sometimes the conversations at Bridgewater are adjourned for reflection—a chance to get out of the moment and let emotions subside. Reflection is the process of trying to understand what has been said, why various people gave the feedback they did, and the feelings one felt as well as their relative intensity. Sometimes it takes multiple conversations for people to really hear and consider feedback. In some cases, it takes a "wake-up call"—a direct statement. One such conversation with an employee I'll call Bryan started with a statement like this:

> We have these four instances where you did not perform. We have a pattern. Why did you not perform? We think it's because you are so defensive. You have way too many inaccurate opinions. You have a strong opinion about everything. You don't know what you don't know. You don't have a sound basis for many of those opinions but you fight to the bitter end because you won't consider that you don't know. Everyone has weaknesses. Everyone makes mistakes. You are not a bad person for having weaknesses and making mistakes. You are human. The most successful people are the ones who learn from their mistakes and have a healthy regard for what they don't know and seek to fill in the missing gaps. Every thought you have is not going to be like a well thought-out, good opinion. You are not that smart. No one is. You don't have to know all the answers. You have to just get the answers. You can't even fathom that you don't know. You are opinionated. You are arrogant about your opinions.

Faced with this direct feedback, Bryan struggled, and responded: "My confidence is shattered. It is scary not knowing. I don't know what to do if I don't know." That led to a conversation about how one compensates for not knowing. Learning that there are steps that can reduce "not knowing" was a relief to Bryan. These kinds of conversations are hard, but Ray says that he has seen countless employees "work through them" successfully. This particular conversation ended with Ray saying: "Bryan, you are invaluable. You are so strong in so many, many ways. I truly want to help you work through this."

Bryan and the team, including Ray, met several days later. Bryan began the meeting saying: "I agree I have failed at some of my responsibilities. I am not qualified to do some of them." The group then discussed how to either design around these weaknesses or get Bryan training to learn how to do the troubling parts of the job.

I am happy to report that Bryan is still at Bridgewater and flourishing in an important role. I met Bryan and asked how the transformation experience affected him outside of work. This response from Bryan was interesting: "I am a much better parent. I don't treat every little mistake my child makes as something bad but rather as a learning opportunity. I am trying to teach him that it is ok to try new things and fail and to admit mistakes and not try to hide them."

DO YOU EMBRACE YOUR TRUE SELF?

The Bridgewater transformation process is an inward extension of Radical Transparency. Being honest about strengths and weaknesses allows employees to play to their strengths and surround themselves with trusted cohorts that complement them by covering for their weaknesses. Arguably, this allows employees to operate at a higher level than if they were expending energy playing the traditional success game, which requires them to appear super human, with no weaknesses, and to always be the "go to" person no matter the issue.

I suggest that this inner Radical Transparency is similar in many ways to mindfulness and the meta skills discussed in previous chapters, including metacognition, metaemotions, and metamessaging. These are competencies that help manage one's thinking, emotions, and how one sends messages to others.

ARE WE IN SYNCH?

After a person reflects on feedback conversations at Bridgewater, the "getting in synch" process starts to take place. It takes varying amounts of time for "getting in synch" to finally happen. This is the process of looking as objectively as possible at the issue and coming to agreement on what the truth is.

Agreeing that what another person has said is true is what Ray calls getting in synch with that person. Many times, getting in synch takes time and patience, especially when someone has to confront a weakness or poor performance. (Remember Ray's formula: Pain + Reflection = Progress.) Sometimes a meeting does not end in synch because further reflection is needed.

Here's the story of a representative meeting I witnessed at Bridgewater.[47] The responsible person was a senior technology manager, and the purpose of the meeting was a discussion of the evolution of Bridgewater's iPad tools and a redesign of the user interface.

As the discussion ended, Ray turned to one of the participants[48] and said, "Jane, I would like to talk about why we are not in synch." A difficult conversation ensued before the entire group. At one point, CEO Greg Jensen intervened to try to clarify the conversation, because it was clear that Jane and Ray were talking past each other. Ray agreed with Greg that he was not being effective, and Greg took the lead in trying to clarify what he was hearing. Interestingly, everyone seemed to understand that once "one of those" conversations starts, it will continue until the parties are in synch or it becomes obvious that more reflection is needed. This particular discussion took about forty-five minutes and ended with Jane acknowledging and accepting that a personal weakness was getting in the way of her facing the facts of the situation. Ray praised Jane and encouraged her to keep working through it.

I share this story to point out that Ray and Jane's conversation did not involve anything that occurred in that particular meeting, but rather concerned an unresolved issue. It would have been easy for Ray to let the issue slide; however, Bridgewater's cultural value of Radical Transparency and Ray's Principle that no problem is too small to avoid meant that this personal conversation had to occur. The fact that it occurred in front of others and was being recorded for review by any employee emphasizes the magnitude of Bridgewater's Radical Transparency.

I witnessed three of these difficult, getting-in-synch conversations in just the two meetings I attended the morning of my second visit to Bridgewater. In such situations, Ray facilitated a conversation with the goal of reaching agreement on the facts surrounding a problem. Then the conversation moved to trying to determine the root cause of the problem. In Bridgewater's "machine" paradigm, there can be only three possible root causes: poor design, lack of capabilities, or failure to perform because of a lack of training.

Below is another, more detailed example of how the getting-in-synch process goes. The participants in this scene were Ray and an employee I'll call Sam:

RAY: "We are not in synch. Let's try and figure out why. OK?"

SAM: "OK."

RAY: "Let's discuss the facts." (Ray lays out the facts.) "Do you agree with the facts? If not, why not?"

SAM: "I am not comfortable, but I don't know why."

RAY: "Suspend your point of view and try to understand. Do the facts seem logical? Is there a body of evidence here?"

SAM: "I am struggling with your mechanical way of thinking. I resort to my default way."

RAY: "You have to go to a higher level of thinking. Go above yourself—take Sam out of this conversation. Look at the facts as if they were about someone else. They are not about you. Now, what do you see?"

(A few minutes pass.)

RAY: "Do you agree with the facts?"

SAM: "I agree."

RAY: "Let's talk about what each of us thinks the problem is that is causing these facts."

(A good back and forth conversation takes place.)

RAY: "Let's both think about this. How much of the issue is a design issue—you being in the wrong position? How much of the issue is a Sam issue—things you have to work on? Our goal is to figure out how you can be more successful. We both want that."

SAM: "I agree."

RAY: "We are in a good place. Let's come back to it at a future date."

These types of conversations have occurred at Bridgewater for years, and I suggest that the more often one views the process, the more likely one understands that it happens to everyone, which could reduce the feeling of being singled out. Nonetheless, few of the managers with more than five years at Bridgewater that I interviewed said the conversations became any easier with experience, but they all admitted to getting more comfortable and gaining the confidence to handle them. They also agreed that the potential personal and organizational upside justified the pain.

THE PURPOSE OF THESE DIFFICULT CONVERSATIONS

Having difficult conversations with employees is hard for managers. It doesn't come naturally to most people. Some Bridgewater managers go through another transformation process when they find that they are scared to have these types of conversations. One manager stated: "People are much too chicken." Ray and the other senior leaders mentor managers on this process, but every person will conduct it differently. Staying calm, talking slowly, not raising one's voice, and watching out for body language, facial expressions, and voice modulations provides information about how to proceed and how long the first or second conversation can go. It's important to be caring and to let people know that everyone involved wants to help them work through the issue.

Repeatedly in these types of meetings, Ray says something like: "We can't avoid painful conversations. We are all fighting against our egos, our blind spots and our subconscious selves. We need others to help us recognize our weaknesses, to get past our egos and see things we can't see by ourselves. What we're really doing by holding one another accountable is helping each other be great."

GETTING THE RIGHT PEOPLE IN THE RIGHT SEATS

Ray defines a successful organization as one with both happy people (meaningful relationships) and excellent outcomes (meaningful work). To achieve this, the organization must put the right people in the right roles. Because even if you get the right people and help facilitate their transformation process, all will be for naught if they're put in the wrong roles.

Thus, once the right people are hired, a major Bridgewater initiative is to determine how to place them in a job that best matches their attributes and abilities. This isn't easy to do, and takes a lot of work. In order to do this, Bridgewater exercises continual analysis and builds position profiles to determine the "people requirements" of each job. Then comes the even more challenging task of getting good data that illuminates people's attributes and abilities.

Ray believes that each individual is a unique mix of attributes, abilities, values, and built-in psychological inclinations. How can Bridgewater make the matching of the right people to the right jobs more scientific—more data based—instead of a "gut reaction"? That ultimately comes down to using the best data available to make a judgment, but it also requires that Bridgewater not lose its humanity, that is its "meaningful relationships" objective. People cannot become fungible objects or "widgets" to be fit into the machine.

At Bridgewater, Ray continually emphasizes that people's differences— their unique ways of thinking and seeing the world—are good, because all jobs are not the same. It is those differences that bring together different ideas and the different perspectives necessary to stress test ideas and create the best outcomes for an organization. The challenge is to educate people to embrace each other's uniqueness and independent thinking.

Ray expresses this sentiment in Management Principles Numbers 44 and 45 when he says to "recognize that people are built very differently" and to "think about their very different values, abilities and skills."[49] According to Ray:

> Values are the deep-seated beliefs that motivate behaviors; people will fight for their vales and values determine people's compatibility with others. Abilities are ways of thinking and behaving. Some people are great learners and fast processors; others possess common sense; still others think creatively or some think more logically . . . it is important for you to know what mix of qualities is important to fit each role and, more broadly, with whom you can have successful relationships.[50]

Ray exhorts his management team to "always be on guard against a Bozo implosion." As companies grow and especially when they grow quickly, they should take their time in hiring and hire right. It's best for everyone involved because dealing with hiring mistakes is a difficult process that no one enjoys.

In addition to Bridgewater's initiatives to properly define what is needed for each type of position and to create an accurate profile of each employee through a collaborative, evaluative, radically transparent process, a third project underway is to select multiple exemplar employees currently in each position and create an anonymous composite profile of their values, attributes, abilities, and psychological inclinations that can be used in hiring and matching people to jobs.

This "exemplar employee profile" has two uses. First, it's a quality control check on the job profiling process. If the profiles of exemplar employees for a specific job classification differ from the job profile created by the managers, then there is a design problem. Second, the anonymous exemplar profiles can be used in the hiring process to compare candidates' psychological profiles and interview evaluations against the exemplar profile. In other words, for a particular job the question becomes: Is this particular candidate like "Jane" or "Bob" from the exemplar composite profile?

Some other organizations attempt this scientific type of job recruiting and placement. What is interesting about Bridgewater's approach is the depth and triangulation of the data they collect on each employee. The data on an exemplar employee is high in quantity and quality and can be compared to other exemplar employees in similar positions. I have not seen any other organization make this type of investment in the collection of so much individual employee evaluative data on so many attributes. Nor have I seen any other organization stress test the results through as much triangulation. Bridgewater in effect is trying to create hiring algorithms that increase the probability of hiring the right people for the right position and for placing or promoting existing employees into positions where they can best utilize their strengths.

Conclusion

At the beginning of part II, I encouraged you to keep an open mind, and suggested that you read the company stories with two questions in mind: What can you as an individual learn that helps you be a better learner? As a team member, team leader, manager, or leader of any organization, what can you learn that would help your organization be a better learner and more effective in achieving its mission?

I hope this introduction to Bridgewater has given you some good food for thought in considering these questions. The Bridgewater story is fascinatingly different from most people's work experiences. It challenged my MBA students so much that their visceral, negative reactions seemed to drive their conclusions that they would not want to work at Bridgewater. Many of my students have similar backgrounds as Bridgewater employees. They reacted emotionally with anxiety about how they would perform in the Bridgewater environment. Did you do the same thing?

If you are truly interested in the science of learning, the kind of environment that enables learning, and how to mitigate the inhibitors of learning, Bridgewater provides a great example of an organization that has put this into practice. It is the only business organization that I have found—after a study of over 100 high-performance companies over the past ten years and after reading hundreds of research papers and hundreds of books written by leading researchers and CEOs—that has squarely faced our "humanness."

Understand that Bridgewater is not perfect by any means. It is still a work-in-progress. Quite frankly, it always will be because of its desire to constantly improve. Based on its performance, however, Bridgewater has succeeded in taking organizational and individual learning to a higher level. As two Bridgewater employees said (I am combining their statements): "Bridgewater is a grand experiment of going against human nature and being human at the same time."

Reflection Questions

1. What did you read in this chapter that surprised you?
2. What are your top three takeaways that you want to reflect and/or act on?
3. What behaviors do you want to change?

10

Intuit, Inc.: "It's Time to Bury Caesar"

Frequently, CEOs or directors of successful companies ask me questions like: "How can we change employees' behaviors so all of us can be better thinkers?" Changing behaviors and ways of thinking in a successful company is a challenge because many employees will revert to a mentality of "if it's not broken why change it?" Intuit[1] is a very successful public company that for the last seven years has been engaged in that type of major change initiative. Intuit has created a company-wide innovation culture and made experimentation the key process component of its decision making. To do this has required Intuit to establish new learning processes, change how and at what level decisions are made, and change how its leaders behave. Those were not small steps or easy tasks—especially given that Intuit is a public company and was neither facing a crisis nor in extremis when it decided to push for a transformation. I encourage you to keep this in mind as you evaluate how Intuit implemented its transformation.

Intuit has over $4.2 billion of revenue and over 8,000 employees. It develops and sells financial, tax, and accounting software solutions to consumers, small businesses, accountants, and financial institutions. Its products include Quicken, QuickBooks, and TurboTax. Intuit generates profit margins higher than 30 percent, and for the last ten years, it has been voted one of the best companies to work for in the United States. Intuit is a consistent market leader and a high-performance company. Its current growth initiatives include expanding its SaaS (software as a service) offerings to its customer segments, expanding into mobile solutions, and moving its offerings to the cloud.[2]

Cofounder Scott Cook—a graduate of Harvard Business School who'd previously worked at Procter & Gamble and as a consultant with Bain & Company—came up with the idea for Intuit in 1982. He'd noticed how frustrated his wife, Signe Ostby, was with the time required to pay and track their bills. He and Ostby's sister started talking with others about bill paying, and they found that many people had similar frustrations. That led Cook to hire Tom Proulx, a Stanford University engineering student, to write the software that became Quicken. Cook and Proulx founded Intuit in 1983 and took it public in 1993.[3]

From the beginning, Intuit has been a customer-driven, product development company. This owes in part to Cook's experiences at Procter & Gamble, where he'd been trained to follow the customer home, so to speak—to gather consumer insights from empathetically watching customers and talking to them about how they use products or perform tasks, in order to discover "pain points." Growing from this mindset, Intuit's focus has been to make financial, accounting, and tax processes easy to use by consumers and small businesses, and its stated mission is: "Improving people's financial lives so profoundly that they can't imagine going back to the old way."[4]

Initially, Intuit's key customer value differentiator was "ease of use." In the early 2000s, however, Intuit found that usability was not as strong a product differentiator as it had once been. This insight came from Intuit's Net Promoter Score (NPS)—the metric that represents the probability that a current customer will recommend a product to a friend. Intuit's NPS wasn't increasing as much as executives wanted.[5] This forced Cook and other Intuit executives to step back and reassess. Did Intuit need to take its game to a higher level? If so, how would it accomplish this transformation?

The Intuit leadership team decided that a transformation was indeed necessary and that the company needed to deliver more to its customers in order to maintain its market leading position. Intuit needed a more compelling product differentiator. Ease of use was still necessary, but no longer sufficient. Intuit had to rethink how it approached product development and had to find different processes to drive a new way of thinking and learning.

A few key executives, new to Intuit, became integral to the transformation story—CEO Brad Smith and Vice President of Design Kaaren

Hanson. Smith came to Intuit in 2003 from ADP, where he'd been senior vice president of Marketing and Business Development. Prior to ADP, Smith had held sales, marketing, and general management positions at Pepsi, Seven-Up, and Advo, Inc. Hanson, who has a Ph.D. in experimental psychology from Stanford University, joined Intuit in 2002. By 2007, she was chosen to lead the development and scaling of the new learning processes that Intuit needed to install to undertake the company-wide transformation. Hanson and her team were ultimately responsible for creating Intuit's transformative tools—Design for Delight and its important component of rapid experimentation.

Design for Delight

Design for Delight came out of the first step in Intuit's transformation process. Hanson had been asked to serve on a small team to help define a new product differentiator, and from those small team meetings and subsequent meetings with the executive team, came four big decisions. First, Intuit's new product development goal would be to create products that would "delight" customers emotionally. Second, "design thinking"—a methodology traditionally used by design professionals to explore, discover, and create innovative new products, services, or solutions—would be the learning process Intuit would use to discover delight. Third, they would call this new initiative Design for Delight (D4D) and make it integral to the company's new product development process. Fourth, D4D would be scaled throughout Intuit. Intuit's stated goal was to create customer-driven innovation—to "find an important problem that we and those we enable can solve well with durable advantage."[6] D4D aimed to achieve that goal by "evoking positive emotions throughout the customer journey by going beyond customer expectations in delivering awesome product experiences that people want to tell the world about."[7]

Critical to the success of D4D was the complete buy-in and active engagement of Cook and Smith. Intuit had many different product development and program management processes. Its engineers knew these well, were comfortable with them, and understood them. Getting them to take on a D4D mindset and add design thinking tools to their repertoires wouldn't be easy. Changing processes is hard enough, but changing how people think is even harder. And changing how people behave is even harder than that, especially when the "old way" of behaving has brought them personal success.

Design thinking is different from the widely used product development stage gate or waterfall processes. The goal is to help explore and discover often unstated customer needs and to use design techniques to create innovative solutions. My academic partner in Darden's growth and innovation academic core, Professor Jeanne Liedtka, is one of the leading luminaries in the movement of design thinking into the business world. She has consulted with many companies and authored three leading design thinking books,[8] which are a great place to start if you want to learn more about this process. Design thinking is not a linear, bottom-line analytical thinking process; it requires a different way of thinking that's learned over time by practice. Eventually, design thinking becomes part of one's repertoire and can be tapped in the appropriate situations. However, a full transformation to a design thinking-driven process, as Intuit hoped for, takes years and requires patience, perseverance, and engagement at the senior leadership level to make it successful.

Hanson's Design Innovation Group knew this. Hanson was confident that design thinking could be a "wow," eye opener for many and that using design thinking in itself would create "delight." However, her group also wisely understood that in order to get people to apply the design thinking tools, the tools needed to be easy to use. As a trained psychologist, Hanson also knew that changing people's habitual ways of thinking would be easier if the required learning was chunked into just a few key concepts. The hardest step would be getting people to try it. Design thinking could only be learned and appreciated by actually using the tools.

Hanson was systematic about instituting the process. She began by choosing ten people from the company to serve as design thinking coaches, facilitators, and mentors for other Intuit employees. They were called "Innovation Catalysts." The Innovation Catalysts program was piloted for a year, and then, under the leadership of Suzanne Pellican, it grew to a team of more than 200. In addition, Intuit took a systems approach to ingraining D4D among its employees. First, its senior leadership actually participated in D4D training. Second, it renamed Intuit's culture an "innovation culture," emphasizing the importance of innovation as its core principle. Third, it gave employees unstructured time to pursue innovation ideas. Fourth, it held "Idea Jams" and gave awards for the most promising ideas. Fifth, on the Intuit website, the company created an "innovation network" for capturing innovation stories, interviews, templates, and frequent blogs by Cook and Smith.

The D4D developed into a three-pronged process that included:

1. Gaining deep customer empathy: being open-minded, suspending judgment, and managing individual egos in order to better observe and act on customer needs;
2. Going broad before going narrow: gaining better customer insights and exploring a wide range of alternatives in an open, unbiased manner before settling on an answer; and
3. Rapid experimentation: quickly and cheaply testing new ideas, and pursuing further development of those ideas that proved most successful in early stage experimentation.

Observing, listening, and collaborating are necessary skills at each step of the process. In addition, Hanson's team created a number of customized D4D design thinking tools to help achieve "deep customer empathy" and to go "broad before going narrow." If you are interested in learning more about these processes, I highly recommend Professor Liedtka's books.[9]

What I want to focus on now is the process that Intuit put in place to test new growth ideas—"rapid experimentation"—because it can be easily used in your business even if you do not put in place the design thinking idea creation processes.

Rapid Experimentation

Although D4D generated lots of good ideas, Intuit also needed a process to test those ideas quickly and cheaply. Further, the testing of new ideas had to be designed to promote iterative learning so that the best ideas could rise to the top for further development and ultimately new product rollouts. Intuit called the method it designed for testing ideas "rapid experimentation." The goal was to institutionalize hypotheses testing as Intuit's decision-making tool. As Hanson put it, "Everything is an experiment."[10]

The idea behind rapid experimentation came from Eric Ries's book: *Lean Start-Up: How Today's Entrepreneurs Use Continuous Innovation to Create Radically Successful Businesses* (New York: Crown Business, 2011).[11] Ries is a protégé of Steve Blank, a successful entrepreneur, and himself an author and coauthor, respectively, of two books, whose premises are that successful entrepreneurship is dependent on doing fast and cheap experiments with customers as soon as possible.[12] Hanson and her team took the *Lean Start-Up* concept and, using Intuit's "ease of use" core principle, designed Intuit's version of a customer cocreation experimental process that was simple, easy to use, and easy to scale throughout Intuit. The basic concepts underlying the lean start-up methodology, Intuit's rapid experimentation process and the Learning Launch process discussed in chapter 7 are the same: testing ideas quickly and cheaply with potential customers. Such a process requires the "unpacking of assumptions," also discussed in detail in chapter 7.

In 2012, Cook explained the importance of rapid experimentation this way:

> To flourish in the innovation age, companies must change how decisions are made and change how leaders lead. To do so you must change how decisions are made to what I call leadership by experiment. Moving from politics and PowerPoints to enabling the idea to prove itself. From boss votes with their opinion, to the customers vote with their feet. From the hierarchy sets the agenda, to the innovators set the agenda.[13]
>
> The . . . role of leaders in the information age is to install the systems and the culture to enable anyone, even brand new employees, to be able to run experiments, real experiments, on real customers, fast and easy. Now, this means that companies have to remove the barriers that naturally exist to prevent people from running experiments on real customers. That means large groups across the company have to participate in removing these barriers.[14]

Let's reflect for a moment on Cook's statements. He uses the interesting phrase "leadership by experiment" even though companies, investors, and employees yearn for leaders who bring stability to a business. However, I don't think Cook is saying that stability is not an objective in the business world today; rather, I believe what Cook is saying is that Intuit is going to be a continuous learning company using experiments as a key learning process. And as his statement about moving "from politics and PowerPoints to enabling the idea to prove itself" clearly indicates, Intuit is trying to create an idea meritocracy. Interestingly, remember that Bridgewater prides itself on being exactly that.

The evolution of the language used by Cook and Smith since 2007 to communicate the Intuit transformation is fascinating. In a statement about burying the "modern day Caesar"—the kind of boss who gives thumbs up or down on all decisions—Smith explained Intuit's management changes: "At Intuit we are asking all of our leaders to work to create and embrace systems that empower any employee to run fast, cheap experiments. You make decisions through experimentation. The best ideas can prove themselves."[15]

Cook's push for innovators to set the agenda was particularly relevant to the story of how a team of young employees in India responded to the company's request to generate ideas to improve the financial lives of people in their country. This is one of Cook's favorite examples of the changing Intuit culture. The innovative team came up with an idea to focus on farmers, which make up half of the population in India. The bosses in India were not interested. Under Intuit's new "Caesar is dead" principle, however, the young employees did their research and spent time with farmers to understand their business challenges.

They learned that farmers didn't know which market to take their farm products to in order to get the best price. Instead, they simply guessed, and because of a lack of transportation, once they committed to travel to one market, there was no way to attend another market on the same day. And once they got to market, they had no information about the market price and had no negotiating position.

The team asked if there was a way to get pricing info and send it to farmers by text messages. They still received no positive encouragement from their bosses—only reasons why their idea would not work. The team persevered anyway and began to experiment. They ran more than ten experiments and found that wholesalers would quote prices to a researcher, and farmers could use the information to attend better markets and negotiate higher prices. Higher prices would translate directly into higher family income and opportunity.

Today, Intuit offers this product, called "Intuit Fasal," to farmers for free. Currently over 1.6 million farmers use it. Fasal sends customized information concerning prices and markets for relevant crops to the farmers in their regional language. In addition, Intuit is now creating a free Fasal marketplace where buyers and buyers' agents can match their buying needs directly with farmers' products and lock in product and pricing, thus disintermediating the wholesalers and creating more income for the individual farmers. Intuit continues to offer this free service daily to a growing number of rural farmers by selling advertisers the opportunity to market their products to these rural farmers using the Fasal database network.

In this example, senior management in India told the young innovators they were, in effect, wasting their time, but the young innovators conducted the experiment anyway. Cook and Smith have made this a prime example of how line employees can be innovative and how the D4D process can quickly and cheaply create new ideas that can lead to products that materially improve people's lives. Intuit's new culture empowered these employees to use the D4D processes.

Clearly, rapid experimentation is a good way to immediately start testing good ideas, but how exactly does the rapid experimentation process play out? Intuit's rapid experimentation process differs substantially from the traditional business planning processes used by many companies to determine which ideas are to be funded. A traditional business plan process usually focuses on market analysis and creating a detailed financial projection to justify an allocation of investment dollars. The focus is analysis to justify an investment. The process is usually colored by risk adversity.

In comparison, rapid experimentation is a fast, low-cost experimental process driven by the need to learn from customers quickly. Its focus initially is deep customer engagement, not financial analysis. Detailed financial analysis is deferred until much later in the process. Small teams use Intuit's rapid experimentation process to test new ideas. As illustrated in figure 10.1, the process has four distinct steps: (1) the Idea, (2) Leap of Faith, (3) Experiment, and (4) Learn.

The Idea step seeks to answer three questions: Who is the customer? What is the problem? What is the possible solution?

The Leap of Faith step requires the team to "unpack" and agree on the most important customer behavior that must be true in order for the idea to work. This unpacking process is like the Learning Launch unpacking process, the Toyota 5 Whys, and the Bridgewater root cause analysis processes.

The Experiment step requires designing a quick experiment that is the minimum required to test the leap of faith assumptions. It requires documenting the hypothesis: "If we do X, then Y percentage of customers will behave in way Z." Before conducting the experiment, the team has to set minimum numerical success criteria—what behaviors they expect and in what quantity. Setting a minimum threshold for the numerical success criteria has the good purpose of preventing experimenters from ending data collection too early. But it also has a risk: experimenters may become more

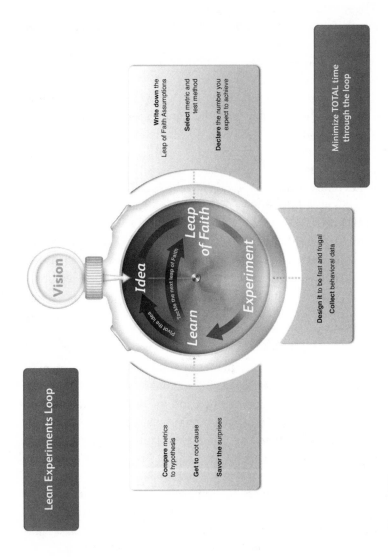

Figure. 10.1

Source: Kaaren Hanson, "Creating a Culture of Experimentation," BRITE Conference Presentation, March 4, 2013, SlideShare, www.slideshare.net/IntuitInc/creating-a-culture-of-experimentation. Used with permission.

focused on hitting the number than on the quality of the data. That risk has to be managed.

Intuit's Learn step refers to reviewing the data gleaned from the experiment with an emphasis on why a hypotheses has been proven, or not; what surprises occurred; and what customer insights can be drawn from any surprises. That's the learning part. Next comes deciding whether to change the idea (pivot) or continue (preserve) it with additional experiments or abandon it.

Intuit not only acknowledges but embraces the fact that many experiments will fail in that they will not prove the original hypotheses. To make this point clear to its employees, Intuit's Field Guide to Rapid Experimentation explains that the purpose of experiments is to facilitate learning that enables better decision making—not simply to validate assumptions.[16] Specifically, the Field Guide lists the following reasons for experimenting: It is a way to change opinions into facts; it will either prove or disprove assumptions; it allows one to discover surprises about customers; it generates data that leads to more informed decisions; and the data can be used to create stories about the idea.[17]

Cook is especially keen on the importance of surprises. An early surprise played a key role in the evolution of Quicken to QuickBooks. Cook and his team "knew" Quicken was a product for consumers. However, they were surprised to discover that many users of Quicken were small businesses. The team had overlooked that fact for years. Finally, they confronted the data and created QuickBooks to better serve that huge customer segment—small businesses. At a recent conference, Cook said, "One of the key benefits of experiments is it allows you to get surprises early. . . . By having small versions where you are testing key hypotheses early, you get surprises . . . and you want those surprises as early as you can get them."[18] I suggest that surprises can come from learning that one's assumptions are wrong.

Intuit has worked to transform the experimental goal of disproving key hypotheses to one of uncovering surprises. Surprises provide unexpected data that may be valuable. Cook embraces the value of surprises and has stated that, "Surprises happen and sometimes that is the market speaking out to you, telling you something you didn't know."[19] Cook's philosophy about surprises is consistent with Klein's "insight" process discussed in chapter 7.

Recognizing the value of surprises requires having a receptive audience. This sometimes requires reeducating leaders and managers who have to learn how to play a key role in maximizing the value of surprises.

It's critical that the disproving of a hypothesis not be treated as a personal failure. That is, leaders must lower the personal costs of suggesting that ideas don't work. At Intuit, the attitude and culture necessary for rapid experimentation is one where there is no failure so long as the company learns something from the experiment. Failures can lead to new insights that can lead to new experiments.

Smith has said he uses the following questions when he explores the results of experiments with employees:

1. What surprised you on the upside, and what did you learn that drove the upside versus expectations?
2. What surprised you on the downside, and what did you learn that caused the downside surprise?
3. What barriers are getting in the way of what you are trying to achieve?[20]

Smith's questions emphasize another key point about experimentation. In most cases we have lots of ideas. Ideas are like sand on a beach—plentiful. Innovation is a giant funneling process, taking the hundreds of ideas to produce lots of experiments that produce a few growth initiatives that may produce one big new S curve, or as one of the CEOs with whom I have worked referred to it, one "needle mover." Because our ideas are just ideas, there's a lot we don't know. In most cases the unknowns exceed what is known. The purpose of doing an experiment is to discover and find data that reduce the number of unknowns. As Smith teases out with his questions, the discovered data can be positive or negative.

In the rollout of rapid experimentation, Hanson said that she realized the only way to really learn the process was by actually doing experiments. "Learn by doing" became the mantra at Intuit.[21] My experience with Learning Launches confirms this. I found that it takes a team doing about three Learning Launches before they're comfortable with the process. If you want your senior management to truly understand your experimentation process, then have them use it to do experiments, too. Intuit did this. Rapid experimentation was the focus of an officer off-site meeting and an off-site meeting of the leadership team. Engaging leadership "in the doing" was critical from several perspectives: culture, language, and buy-in.

Cook has emphasized repeatedly that experimentation has to become Intuit's core decision model, and it appears that Intuit has made progress toward scaling rapid experimentation. Intuit conducted over 1,200 experiments in 2012 and over 2,400 experiments in 2013. Several product groups and other nonproduct departments, such as legal, human resources, and other service functions, also have conducted rapid experiments, demonstrating that customers can be internal as well as external to Intuit.[22]

Learning Starts at the Top

Another important takeaway from the Intuit transformation story is Cook's personal learning journey. Cook is adamant that learning starts at the top and that leaders and managers have to model the behaviors that they ask of employees. In a blog post, Cook stated: "The most important person to be learning and growing in a company is the CEO. . . . If you don't, your company will die."[23] Cook's statement resonates with me, and my experience confirms this: The most successful learning organizations have leaders who are passionately curious and love learning.

In the same blog post, Cook went on to say: "You've got to get somebody who gives you unvarnished truth and consequences."[24] Here Cook was agreeing with Jim Collins's argument in *Good to Great* that great companies have to "confront the brutal facts."[25] It's particularly important for leaders to invite feedback—including uncomfortable feedback—by creating a culture of mutual accountability and permission to speak freely. Cook explained his own journey in getting comfortable with feedback:

> You need to get full Technicolor on your own performance. . . . If you're a CEO, you're not getting that today. . . .Your employees won't do it. That's just not the way employees treat their boss. . . . It could be a Board member. . . . It could be an outsider. . . . It could be an Executive Assistant or someone who has everyone's ears and has the boldness to actually tell you the truth. . . .We had an Executive Coach we were using to help some of our execs grow. . . . Eight years ago now . . . I asked for the same treatment that this outside Executive Coach gives, so he went and did a "360," talked to those that I work with . . . and then talked to me about it. . . . It hit me like a ton of bricks. There was a lot of deferred maintenance. . . . I was screwing up big time. . . . I went out and told the teams I worked with, hey, I am committed to change. . . . I need your help. They weren't of that much help . . . most people cannot say anything negative to a boss. . . . So I've worked with [the Executive Coach] ever since. We meet about once every two months now.[26]

How often have you heard a CEO state that he was floored by his 360-degree feedback and admit to the world that he "had a lot of deferred maintenance"? How many top management teams even subject themselves to a rigorous 360-degree review process? And yet this process strikes me as being so important, because it helps devalue the ridiculous idea that any leader is "all knowing" and has the "right answers." And it should result in some humility, which helps in both System 2 thinking and System 2 conversations.

Like Cook, Smith had to develop his own personal approach to fostering this new learning environment at Intuit. He has described his approach to meetings at Intuit this way: "People need to know reaching out for help is a sign of strength not weakness. . . . Bad news should travel faster than good news."[27] To get that message across to his team, Smith said he asks them these questions in team meetings:

1. This will be a good meeting if _____? (Team members complete the sentence.)
2. Where is the team struggling or having the least amount of confidence?
3. Where can I be most helpful?[28]

In June 2013, Smith wrote a company blog post describing how he tries to allocate his most valuable resource: time. It's revealing. He calls his plan his "40–30–20–10 Plan." It means that he tries to spend 40 percent of his time running the business; 30 percent of his time building organizational capabilities and leaders' development; 20 percent of his time going outside the company to learn from others; and 10 percent of his time on personal growth and development with his personal coach and mentor. To hold himself accountable, Smith measures and grades himself quarterly.[29]

All together, Smith seeks to spend at least 30 percent of his time learning from others and on self-development. That's very interesting. How much time do you spend going out and learning from other companies? How much time do you spend working on your specific leadership weaknesses? There are similarities here to Bridgewater where Ray Dalio—just like everyone else—has an Issue Log Diagnosis Card and a Baseball Card. His issues are as "radically transparent" to everyone in Bridgewater as the issues of the youngest employee. He subjects himself to the same rigorous processes that everyone else engages in.

In their own ways, Cook, Smith, and Dalio understand their limitations and are comfortable enough in their own skins to admit to themselves and the world that they aren't good enough. As important, they talk about that fact and behave differently than a Theory X leader behaves. If you want to be part of a learning organization or a learning team inside an organization, I suggest you look in the mirror and face your reality. Are you a good learner? Do you dedicate time to working on your weaknesses? Have you subjected yourself to review processes by your employees as Cook and Dalio have? If not, why not?

I've spent a lot of time talking about 360-degree reviews with senior management teams. It's a moment of truth. Most are scared of the results. Most don't have the courage to go there. When I interview CEOs before I begin working with them, I ask: What are your objectives? What behaviors are you trying to change or enable? Many answer: "I need help fixing my people." In my experience, CEOs who have that approach are reticent to talk about fixing themselves. We have learned that failure to confront the brutal facts about yourself is an ego defense that inhibits learning.

Conclusion

Intuit has embarked on a mission to learn better and faster throughout its 8,000-person organization. Its leadership is passionate about the necessity for this, and shows this through its engagement in the process. Intuit and its leadership have embraced D4D and rapid experimentation as key learning processes. Intuit's story is instructive for several reasons.

First, it demonstrates that cultural change in successful companies takes time and that such change will only succeed if top management is passionately committed and involved as role models of the desired new behaviors. Cook and Smith themselves seek to personally learn from others. They reject the patina of an "all knowing leader." They don't view lack of knowledge as a weakness. They actively seek feedback from others to learn how they can be better. They, like Ray Dalio, embrace the fact that surprises (failures) are learning opportunities.

Second, the story shows that conducting fast, cheap experiments is a low-risk way to scale learning in an organization. At Intuit, rapid experimentation helps manage financial risks and mitigates employee career risks if experiments do not work.

Third, the story demonstrates that learning is an iterative process that requires the competencies we already have discussed, including high-quality thinking, high-quality learning conversations, being open-minded, and managing one's emotions and ego defenses.

Think about the types of leaders Cook, Smith, and Dalio are. Are they transparent? Authentic? Humble? All-knowing? Theory X or Theory Y? Elitist? Engaged with employees in meaningful ways?

Reflection Questions

1. What did you read in this chapter that surprised you?
2. What are your top three takeaways that you want to reflect and/ or act on?
3. What behaviors do you want to change?

11

United Parcel Service, Inc.:
Being "Constructively Dissatisfied"

You are by nature, a man of inquiring mind and you see much in your job and elsewhere in the company that should be improved. You are impatient to have these defects corrected. You are far more interested in improving what is bad than in crowing about what is good. You are, in a word, constructively dissatisfied.

—JIM CASEY, FOUNDER OF UNITED PARCEL SERVICE, INC. (1956)

Whereas the Intuit case discussed in the last chapter concerned a company's transformation, this chapter on UPS illustrates the development and scaling of a High-Performance Learning Organization (HPLO) from its humble start more than 100 years ago to its current status as a publicly held, global behemoth.[1] I chose UPS for this book because the company is a powerful example of how scale and operational excellence can be achieved through a system that, enabled by employee-centric policies and technology, drives constant learning, improvement, and adaptation. The company's employee-centric culture was built to meet the human need for autonomy and for personal growth. In this regard, UPS is like Gore and Toyota in that all three have made an implied contract with their employees, under which employees earn the opportunity to advance and grow through high performance. Promotion-from-within policies at UPS and Gore implement that potential of upward job mobility.

UPS began as a messenger service in Seattle in 1907 and rose to become the world's largest package delivery company, with $54.1 billion in revenue in 2012. UPS's ability to constantly learn and adapt is unique given the company's massive size and complexity. To give you a sense: UPS has nearly 400,000 employees and has an integrated global network on the ground, in the air, and across the oceans. The company ships packages to more than 220 countries and territories, including every address in North America and Europe. UPS operates the world's ninth-largest airline, handles 16.3 million packages a day to and from 8.8 million customers, and coordinates those operations with the world's largest DB2 relational database and an IT infrastructure consisting of ten mainframes, 18,230 servers, and 194,483 laptops and workstations. The UPS website processes an average of 39.5 million tracking requests daily. It provides supply chain and freight services through 800 facilities in more than 120 countries. Its customer-contact points include 4,741 UPS retail stores, 13,000 UPS authorized outlets, and 40,000 UPS drop boxes.

The foundation of UPS's consistent high performance corresponds directly with the research findings set forth in chapter 5: high employee engagement, relentless constant improvement, and humble, values-based leaders who are stewards of the business. Covering the company's 100 plus years of history in a short chapter has required me to focus on two aspects: (1) UPS's ability to continuously learn, improve, and adapt and (2) its ability to cultivate a highly engaged, massive workforce that produces that constant improvement and adaptation.

The UPS DNA: Learn, Improve and Adapt

Underlying UPS's DNA are four primary strands: (1) mutual accountability implemented through a maniacal focus on measurements; (2) constructive dissatisfaction; (3) a legacy of industrial engineering process improvement; and (4) an employee-centric culture supported by HR policies that result in a highly engaged, loyal, and productive workforce. These levers drive a strict adherence to operational policies and procedures; military-like organizational structure and discipline; and a set of traditional business values bequeathed by late founder Jim Casey, who started the company with little more than $100 and a bicycle. Casey's insatiable demand for operational improvement, personal accountability, and humility among employees at all rungs of the organizational ladder still permeates the company. Casey once said, "For no matter how well conceived our plans may be, they will fail unless administered by people of high motives and honest hearts."[2] Along with this steadfast allegiance to 100-year-old business values is UPS's equally extraordinary ability to transform itself in the face of ever-changing customer demands and global realities.

It's important to understand the company's history in order to grasp how fully learning and adaptation are baked into its DNA. UPS's first area of growth was geographic as it expanded from an intra-city retail package delivery service in 1913 (from department stores to consumers) to, starting in 1919, an intercity one, extending its services to deliveries between cities. Even in the midst of that growth when business was going well, however, the company never settled for the status quo.

For example, during this same period of geographic expansion, UPS also began to build a business of consolidating deliveries (i.e., combining packages for several customers in one delivery vehicle). Unsure about this new process, Casey and his managers wrote to more than 100 delivery companies across the United States to ask how they made a profit. A few years later, they studied and benchmarked against the processes of competitors and other industries to find more efficient ways of doing business, both from a systems engineering perspective and a human resource one.[3] They toured and studied production processes at a Ford plant in Michigan, the steel mills of Pittsburgh and the Armour & Company meatpacking plant in St. Louis. Of this time, Casey once said, "We found no singular idea that was really revolutionary. It seemed a matter of learning as we went along, and that is about all that we have done."[4]

By the postwar era, Casey and his partners foresaw a significant decline in the retail delivery business caused by major changes to the American lifestyle, including the advent of the interstate highway system and the development of the suburban shopping center. They realized that in order to survive, UPS needed to transform itself into a "common carrier"— a delivery service from business to business—with the ability to deliver nationwide. The company faced incredible obstacles both legal and logistical to do so—from state and local regulations that restricted deliveries across borders to the near monopoly held by the U.S. Postal Service.

It took nearly three decades, but through what has become characteristic relentlessness and persistence, the company chipped away at legal and logistical limitations. It created a nationwide network city by city, state by state, and region by region, until 1975 when it became the first package delivery company to achieve the "golden link" (i.e., the ability to provide service to any address in the forty-eight contiguous United States). By 1977 it had added air service to Alaska and Hawaii.

UPS is not a linear growth story, and learning from failures was part of the journey. In fact, while discipline and a constant pursuit of improvement helped the company ensure the efficiency and reliability of its ground-based services, such supreme focus also led to some losses and missed opportunities in the late 1970s and early 1980s. One of the most significant examples of UPS having to learn from failure is with respect to air service.

UPS had experimented with air service on a small scale early in its history, but never with much success. From the 1950s through 1970s, UPS made do with an air business that utilized chartered airline flights that relied on inefficient passenger routes. This allowed several competitors to take preeminence and left a gaping window for an innovative new company called FedEx to blast onto the scene and revolutionize the industry with overnight delivery in the late 1970s and early 1980s.

When the market for expedited air delivery became clear, UPS set about rectifying its ground-based myopia and created a nationwide overnight air delivery network through outsourced carriers by 1985. And when that system proved clunky, UPS launched its own airline in 1988, navigating the complexities of air operations, inculcating a new kind of workforce, and achieving FAA certification faster than any other airline in history.[5] Currently, UPS has a fleet of 235 aircraft, charters another 293 aircraft, and maintains air hubs throughout the United States, Europe, the Asia-Pacific region, Latin America and the Caribbean, and Canada.

What's so crucial here is how well UPS has confronted mistakes and learned from them. The company has made robust course corrections when necessary. As a former UPS COO put it in the case of air delivery: "We discovered that we'd better wake up. Customers clearly wanted international shipping, package tracking and overnight service."[6] At UPS mistakes are admitted and the need for change recognized because the culture is about the *relentless* pursuit of constant, incremental improvement. Dissent, inquiry, questioning, challenging, and critiquing are all valued and encouraged because they help UPS to improve.

Another area in which UPS was forced to combine operational excellence with adaptability and a willingness to fail was in going after international markets. Because of its focus on perfecting ground service nationally, by the 1970s, UPS was way behind competitors in the international delivery market. And when it finally did venture overseas, growing the international business proved a slog that took twenty-eight years to become profitable. UPS learned the hard way that building a global business from scratch and imposing a one-size-fits-all approach was an unsuccessful strategy, and the company's earliest expansions in Canada and Germany became drags to the bottom line. But rather than bowing to internal pressure to stop the losses, UPS held fast to its expansion plan but pulled back on volume to lessen the blow in the short term.[7] Undoubtedly it helped that the company was still privately held at this time.

The company's willingness to learn from failure paid off. Going forward, the company switched from a start-up strategy in international markets to an acquisitions-based one, and to a policy of loosening the reins on global operations and using American expatriates sparingly. In 2012, among full-time management employees, less than half of 1 percent came from outside the country where they work (only 202 expatriates out of 45,527 full-time managers).[8]

By taking the long view and focusing on incremental improvements, UPS found its international footing. It entered the Asia-Pacific Region in 1988 and Latin America in 1989. By 1995, it had entered China. In 2005, UPS launched the first nonstop delivery service between the United States and Guangzhou, China and acquired the interest held by its joint venture business partner, giving UPS access to twenty-three cities that cover more than 80 percent of the country's international trade. In 2012, UPS derived 25 percent of its revenue internationally.

UPS went through a parallel learning process when it realized it had to vastly improve its IT infrastructure. Since 1921, when Jim Casey hired the first industrial engineer to conduct efficiency, time, and motion studies,[9] UPS has been measuring, modeling, and simulating every aspect of the delivery business to optimize the movement of people and packages. This drive for constant improvement has been enabled by exacting standards and a company-wide commitment to the mantra: "In God we trust. Everything else we measure."[10] After having had so much success with the manual delivery processes developed by its much-lauded industrial engineers, however, UPS found itself trailing competitors in information technology. By the mid-1980s, UPS made a decision to catch up fast.

Between 1986 and 1991, UPS spent $1.5 billion on technology improvements, which enabled tracking of all ground packages by 1992. By 1995, UPS offered its customers online tracking of packages in transit from its website. By 2007, UPS had spent more than $10 billion integrating its processes and technology to make the company a real-time, 24/7, 365-day operation.[11] Today, UPS employs 4,292 technology workers and now uses its vast technology infrastructure not only to increase operational efficiencies but also to create customer-focused and user-friendly, shipping, e-commerce, logistics management, and visibility tools.

UPS now has its delivery and logistics operations literally down to a science, from how every delivery driver holds his keys, to the maximum number of inches he should have to move to select the next package (it's 30, incidentally).[12] But the company strives to do ever better. Expressing the purpose of this improve-everything mentality, Vice President of Engineering Jim Holsen said, "We're never satisfied with the way things are, if they can be improved."[13]

As an example, the handheld Delivery Information Acquisition Devices (DIADs) that link every delivery driver (in UPS speak: "driver service provides" or "DSPs") to the UPS network for up-to-the-minute data communication, were revolutionary when developed in the 1990s. Today, math whizzes in the operations research division continue to devise algorithms to shave milliseconds off delivery times, and new DSPs attend a high-tech training program where drivers can practice UPS's "340 methods" for safe and efficient deliveries with a scale-model UPS truck until they can perform them with the automaticity and consistency of a robot.[14]

Recently, the process management experts at UPS began rolling out a new revolutionary tool designed to further optimize DSP efficiency by plotting the shortest delivery routes. The system, called ORION (on-road integrated optimization and navigation), incorporates roughly eighty pages of math formulas to calculate the astronomical number of possible route combinations one driver could make in a day, while also leaving room for drivers to improve upon the computer-suggested plan with additional knowledge gained from accumulated experience.[15] Considering that a simple step, such as decreasing the distance that every UPS driver travels in a day by even one mile, could save the company tens of millions of dollars, UPS's demand for soldier-like precision and constant pushing of its processes and human capital to ever-faster and more efficient standards makes sense.

One of its newest offerings for the retail e-commerce market is "UPS MyChoice," which leverages the ORION tool to allow customers to direct the timing and circumstances of their deliveries. *Fast Company* magazine named UPS to its annual list of the fifty most innovative companies in 2012 due to the success of this feature.

UPS technology efforts also have helped UPS become a recognized leader in innovative corporate sustainability practices. UPS developed proprietary telematics technologies—an integration of telecommunications and informatics—to monitor the behavior and performance of its package delivery trucks and DSPs. The technology uses sensors to gather data, test ideas, and assess performance on the efficiency and fuel usage of deliveries and turns the trucks into "rolling laboratories" for customizing vehicle maintenance, reducing idling times, and optimizing routes.[16] In 2011, this technology—along with proprietary advanced route-planning tools—reduced the number of miles driven by 85 million, which resulted in a savings of 8.4 million gallons of fuel and 83,000 metric tons of CO_2 emissions. These efforts, together with UPS expansion of its fleet of alternative fuel vehicles, earned UPS the highest score on the 2012 Carbon Disclosure Project's Leadership Index of S&P 500 companies.[17]

Another example of the company's continuous learning occurred in the 1990s, when UPS realized that in order to continue to grow it would need to expand beyond the shipping business by selling new, complementary services to an existing customer base and improving the customer experience. As senior management saw it, UPS's expertise in shipping and tracking positioned it well to become an "enabler of global commerce" by facilitating the flow of goods, information, and capital.[18]

In 1995, UPS formed UPS Logistics Group to provide customized supply chain management solutions and consulting services. In 1998 UPS advertised its new strategy as "Synchronized Commerce," and then CEO Mike Eskew declared, "Our new mission is ambitious. It propels us from a $90 billion market into a $3.2 trillion market."[19]

Challenging its longstanding practice of employee ownership, UPS made another transformative move in 1999, by selling 10 percent of its equity in an initial public offering (IPO), in part to fund acquisitions that would support its new business strategy. Raising nearly $5 billion, it was the biggest IPO in the history of the New York Stock Exchange at the time. Since then, UPS has acquired forty companies to effectuate this new business model and expand its capabilities beyond transportation, including provisions of trucking and air freight, retail shipping and business services, customs brokerage, finance, and international trade services.

By 2010, the company was in another transformation mode when it launched a new branding campaign called "The New UPS Logistics" and a new advertising campaign with the tagline "We Love Logistics." Whereas UPS's original strength had been in measuring and perfecting its operating processes to the extent that every customer received the same reliable service (with emphasis on "same"), now, as CEO Scott Davis explained in the company's 2012 Annual Report: "We've been inventing solutions to efficiently deliver customers whatever they need, wherever they need it, whenever they need it." The company now segments its business and pursues revenue growth in six industry verticals: Government, Industrial & Automotive, Professional & Consumer Services, Healthcare, High-Tech, and Retail and reports its financial results in three segments: U.S. Domestic Package, International Package, and Supply Chain & Freight. UPS's business vision is now guided by the following strategies: deploying technology-enabled operations; providing unique, industry-specific customer solutions; expanding the global network; and serving end users' needs around the world.[20]

Over the years, UPS has shown its proclivity for not only finding the best way to do something, but also finding a new way to do it. In similar fashion to the U.S. Army's dual focus on precision and adaptability, UPS's contrasting abilities have everything to do with the paradoxical priority it places on both its intense commitment to cultural traditions and proven business methods as well as continuous learning and improvement (e.g., Casey's standard of being constructively dissatisfied). All of this has been enabled by a loyal, highly productive workforce.

Highly Engaged Employees

Jim Casey built UPS over a fifty-year period with a distinct and well-defined culture that embraced the values of integrity, quality, dignity, respect, stewardship, partnership, equality, and humility. To understand UPS means to understand Casey, a man who went to work at the age of nine when his father fell ill, and started his messenger company at nineteen. Casey was a self-made success who rose above his humble background but never forgot his roots, treating every individual and employee with the dignity and respect he felt each deserved. He built the business on a few core themes: high performance, mutual accountability, constructive dissatisfaction, and employee-centric policies, including a focus on stewardship and the opportunity to be an equity owner of the business. UPS has had employee stock ownership and compensation plans since 1927, and right after its IPO, former and current employees and their families still owned 90 percent of the company. Today that ownership percentage is less than 30 percent due to stock sales by employees, retirees and the foundations formed by the founders to diversify their holdings.

Casey often wrote and spoke about the type of company UPS should be and the values it needed to foster, and he left his imprint on UPS by teaching these values to every new employee. UPS executives are taught that their duty is to make sure those values, those ways of doing business, and those ways of taking care of employees continue. The richness of the UPS culture is evidenced by the policy manual that every employee receives and the compendium of Casey's speeches that the company compiled into a book called *Jim Casey: Our Legacy of Leadership.* These speeches show that Casey wanted to build a business where employees could take pride in working for a company that acts as an outstanding corporate citizen.

Just like the founders of Gore, Casey didn't have a Theory X view of management and employees. Casey knew that to achieve consistent high performance, employees had to be engaged emotionally, which meant that the organization needed to meet human needs of autonomy, effectiveness, relatedness, affiliation, and growth. Casey viewed employees as partners and promoted the opportunity for employees to actually become owners of the business. He viewed leaders and managers as accountable to employees just as employees are accountable to each other and to management, advising managers that "One measure of your success . . . will be the degree to which you build up others who work with you. While building up others, you will build up yourself."[21] He also said: "Good management is not just organization. It is an attitude inspired by the will to do right. Good management is taking a sincere interest in the welfare of the people you work with. It is the ability to make people feel that you and they are the company—not merely employees."[22] Casey took steps to ensure that humility was the rule, not self-promotion or glory-seeking. On the subject of future leaders, Casey said:

Who will those leaders be? They will be people who now, today, are forging ahead—not speculating or with fanfare but modestly and quietly. They are the plain, simple people who are doing their best in their present jobs with us, whatever those jobs may happen to be. Such people will not fail us when called on for bigger things. It is for them, our successors, to remember that all the glamour, romance, and success we have in our business at any stage of its existence must be the product of years of benefiting from the work of many devoted people. And there can be no glamour, no romance, and no truly great success unless it is shared by all.[23]

Maintaining those values over decades has required the company to maintain a high retention rate and build a deep bench of long-tenured employees who have found the UPS way meaningful. UPS has achieved continuity within its workforce and has deeply embedded its fundamental tenets. Many employees have spent their professional careers rising up the ranks from package loaders to district managers and beyond, through

UPS's long-standing promotion-from-within and other employee-centric policies. As compelling evidence of that, the nine members of its management committee have on average spent thirty-three years at UPS, with six of them starting as part-time employees or as drivers. Roughly 56 percent of the firm's full-time drivers were once part-time; nearly 73 percent of full-time managers—including most vice presidents—once held nonmanagement positions; and 40 percent of full-time managers have more than twenty years of service with UPS.[24]

Although UPS's global retention rate for full-time employees has been decreasing in recent years, it still remains relatively high at 90.2 percent in 2012, especially considering the range of positions covered, from front-line package handlers to senior executives, over 294,000 employed under various unions and collective bargaining agreements, and 76,000 employed internationally. In 2012, 27.4 percent of the U.S. management team and nearly 45 percent of the total U.S. workforce came from diverse backgrounds.[25]

The company's approximately 100,000 full- and part-time drivers hold esteemed positions in the company, but outsiders to UPS have often viewed its drivers literally marching to beats dictated by the industrial engineering eggheads at "Big Brown" headquarters and have taken this as evidence that the company is rigid and impersonal. UPS's history of transformations indicates a much different reality. And what becomes clear from looking up and down the organization—from package preloaders to the executive team, and from operations in Indianapolis to those in Istanbul—is that UPS human resource policies are employee-centric and democratic.

UPS executives are fond of reminding the public of their egalitarian polices such as having an "open door" for employee input both literally and figuratively (as Casey always did), of only using first names throughout the organization, and of never eating at their desks (out of respect for field workers without such a luxury). These cultural practices are important, but it's the deeper, long-standing human resource policies that have made the difference. UPS's system of performance measurements and rewards is based on key performance indicators and a long-standing company policy against egoism and favoritism. Compensation plans promote long-term stock ownership for employees, whether full-time or part-time, management or nonmanagement, union or nonunion,[26] and an employee "free agent" program allows any UPS employee to move anywhere in the company and advance.[27] The company provides full-time benefits to part-time employees, including medical and dental coverage and tuition assistance, and leads the industry in salaries and benefits for employees across the organization.[28]

When he was still senior vice president of Sales and Marketing, Kurt Kuehn (now Chief Financial Officer) described the UPS culture to me as one of "mutual accountability" and said, "Everyone is accountable to everyone else for performance—doing what's right and doing it well." And he added, "With our measurement system, we try to take personalities and politics out of judging performance."[29]

Backing up that statement is the relatively egalitarian organization at the UPS headquarters in Atlanta, Georgia. When I visited the headquarters, all of the top twelve executives at UPS had offices on the fourth floor instead of the top floor of the headquarters building. All the executives had offices of the same size, and almost all shared senior administrative assistants. These executives were not provided with limos or drivers. There was no executive dining room. It was rare to see Italian suits, French cuffs, or made-to-order shirts on the fourth floor.[30]

UPS's growth and learning as an organization is also a testament to the significant investments it makes in continually growing and developing its employees. Since early in its history, UPS has cultivated a culture of mentorship to foster leadership development in support of its promotion-from-within policy. In the 1960s, UPS launched formalized, instructor-led training programs. By 2008, however, it was clear that a static approach to training and leadership development was no longer working for an increasingly global workforce—less than 20 percent of whom work in an actual office building.[31] The company embarked on an ambitious plan to consolidate all of its training into an online learning system on a global scale. By 2012, "UPS University" began offering a broad range of content on an electronic platform that enables learning and development to take place anywhere, anytime. It also provides the flexibility for both management-directed training and individual development plans by employees.

"We believe the people we bring on, who learn the business and run the business, understand more about the business than people we could hire fresh off the streets to replace them," Anne Schwartz, vice president of leadership and development at UPS, told *CIO* magazine. "Investing in our employees is a hallmark of our business, and we invest in employees with learning opportunities to reflect that."[32]

Senior managers also realized that UPS's traditional instructor-led, lecture-based training program for new drivers was no longer working for the generation X and generation Y hires who were increasingly comprising the bulk of new drivers. "We realized we needed to make an adjustment when our younger drivers began requiring significantly more time to become proficient, and more of them were leaving the company during their initial training period," said Mary Kay Kopp, global learning network director at UPS.[33]

With a $1.8 million grant from the U.S. Department of Labor and partnerships with leading technical universities and an animation company, UPS developed an interactive, hands-on training program called UPS Integrad, which is located in a $5.5-million, 11,500-square-foot training facility in Landover, Maryland. The program incorporates a mix of computer-based training, simulations, virtual learning, and self-study. Already UPS has experienced a sharp increase in driver proficiency and a reduction in first-year injuries and accidents.[34]

UPS has created a unique organization that's not for everyone. It's an operational excellence behemoth managed through measurements and enabled through technology. Yet it hasn't lost its human essence, which is grounded in its founder's beliefs and values. UPS has created a learning system, aligning culture, leadership behaviors, measurements, and rewards to drive relentless constant improvement and constructive dissatisfaction. So far this has warded off complacency, arrogance, and elitism—common killers of consistent high performance, but two recent developments—the fact that part-time employees make up a large percentage of the ranks (45 percent in 2012), and a 2013 decision to cease providing medical benefits to full-time employees' spouses eligible for coverage under their own employers—raise the question of whether organizational DNA dilution has begun.

UPS also faces several new and continuing challenges to its business model—including increased competition as a result of new e-commerce strategies of major U.S. retailers, such as Amazon with its growing network of distribution warehouses, and Wal-Mart and Best Buy, which are shipping more online orders straight from stores. Also, UPS has staked much of its current model on industry growth in China, but rising fuel costs, increased wages, and intellectual property piracy are making the outsourcing of manufacturing to China less favorable.

In light of these realities, UPS has focused its future growth on (1) emerging markets, particularly in Asia; (2) industry-specific distribution and logistics, particularly health care; and (3) global omni-channel retailing and B2C solutions.[35]

The success of this strategy internally will depend on the company's ability to maintain its commitment to its people, its learning environment, and its processes, which have formed the foundation of its adaptability so far. Considering the demonstrated strength and alignment of the company's culture, leadership behaviors and employee-centric policies—which collectively have enabled the desired learning behaviors crucial for an HPLO—it's likely that the company will continue to recognize the long-held company values and ideals of its founder—ideals such as one stated by Casey almost seventy years ago: "Our company has grown because our people have grown, and our people have grown because our company has grown. And so it will be in the future."[36]

Reflection Questions

1. What did you read in this chapter that surprised you?
2. What are your top three takeaways that you want to reflect and/or act on?
3. What behaviors do you want to change?

Epilogue

In the introduction I stated that one of my objectives in this book was to lay out a blueprint for creating a learning organization. As I conclude, I'd like to revisit some of the foundational points to keep in mind as you strive to build a learning organization.

Learning basically is the process by which each one of us creates meaningful stories about our world—with the aim of making these stories ever more accurate so that we can act ever more effectively. That process is enhanced by three mindsets. First, we have to accept the magnitude of our ignorance. Second, we must realize that everything we think we know is conditional and subject to change based on new evidence. Third, and most important, we have to define our self-worth by striving to be the best learner we can be—not by what we believe or think we know. Utilizing these three mindsets can help us counteract our ego defenses and the automatic 3Ds—denying, defending, and deflecting—and our persistent cognitive and emotional search for confirmation and affirmation that gets in the way of confronting brutal or disconfirming facts. Arrogance and fears of failure, of not being liked, of not being accepted, of looking stupid, and so on, all inhibit learning.

Learning requires three good meta self-management skills: metacognition, metacommunicating and metaemotions. We need to be aware of when to take our thinking and communicating to a higher, more intentional and deliberate level—when, in other words, to move from System 1 to System 2. We need to be aware of the messages we're sending through our emotions, body language, and voices. We also need to adopt the three mindsets mentioned above in order to manage our fears of failure, punishment, and not being liked, all of which inhibit critical inquiry, debate, collaboration, and learning.

All of this applies not only to individual learning, but to organizational learning as well. The most successful learning organizations are those that create an environment that fosters and promotes these learning behaviors and mindsets.

Transforming an existing organization into a learning organization requires the change to start at the top. Intuit is right—"It's time to bury Caesar." Leaders must understand and promote the importance of learning. They must be authentic and humble and wear their humanness on their sleeves. Elitism in leadership's attitudes and behaviors needs to be buried, too. The UPS, Gore, and Bridgewater mutual accountability models should rule—leaders should earn their respect behaviorally everyday rather

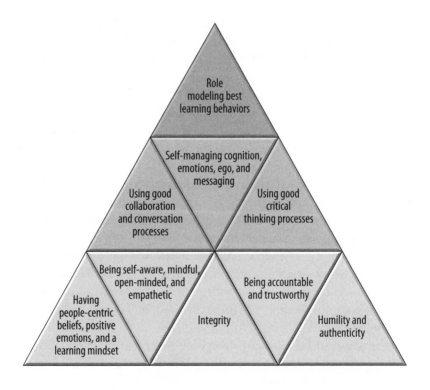

than thinking they're owed respect by positional authority. Mindfulness, reflective listening, being open-minded, being fair-minded, and being an emotionally positive enabler of learning with Learning Leader Capabilities shown in the figure on the previous page are critical behaviors for every leader and manager.

Those behaviors have to be measured by 360-degree feedback and rewarded at the leader/manager levels all the way to the top. Having a leader with these characteristics is the first step to creating a learning organization.

The next step is designing a "learning system" and work environment that seamlessly aligns the organization's culture, structure, leadership behaviors, HR policies, measurements, and rewards to enable and promote those desired learning behaviors. The learning system works best if it encourages employees to be driven by intrinsic motivation and helps them meet their needs for autonomy, effectiveness, relatedness, personal growth, and affiliation.

The meeting of such needs requires that people feel authentically respected, cared for, and trusted, and this trust and accountability must be mutual—leaders and the organization must earn the trust of the "learners" and be accountable, too. A learning system grounded in these principles can result in "meaningful relationships and meaningful work" as the systems do at Bridgewater and at Gore. The learning environment has to consistently send the right messages to employees via culture, leadership behaviors, measurements, and rewards. UPS does this exceptionally well.

Crucial to these systems is the understanding that learning requires change, from both people and organizations. Change is cognitively and emotionally hard. It usually requires help from others. Learning is a team activity, and it's through small teams that individual needs for autonomy, relatedness, affiliation and effectiveness can be met. In order to change, people have to overcome their fears and feel safe in admitting mistakes, weaknesses, and ignorance to teammates. How you treat people and how they feel they are being treated are important aspects to consider, if you truly want an effective learning organization. A people-centric, emotionally positive environment, buttressed by leaders who model learning behaviors, can help negate learning inhibitors. Permission to speak freely and permission to fail as long as there is learning (or, as at Gore, there is an observed "waterline") is key.

The power of positivity comes through loud and clear from the research. A positive emotional work environment enables high employee engagement and learning, and positive individual emotions enable personal learning. The U.S. Army's major initiative to bring positive psychology into its training of over 1,000,000 soldiers is once again a leading indicator of where businesses must look if they want to maximize employee adaptability, learning, and resiliency. Clearly, these types of positive work environments are not necessarily "soft." All of the businesses discussed in this book have a track record of consistent high performance. High performance, high accountability, and positivity are not mutually exclusive.

Another key point coming from the research laid out in this book is the congruity of findings between the field of education regarding what produces high engagement learning and that of business regarding what creates high employee engagement. Upon reflection, that congruity is not that surprising because both areas of study involve figuring out the type of environment and the teacher/manager/leader behaviors that enable people to be more effectively engaged. Those findings can lead us to conclude that high employee engagement, as defined by the Gallup Q12®, is required to be a great learning organization.

After establishing the right learning system and environment, the next component in building a learning organization is to institutionalize critical thinking processes and learning conversations. A culture such as Bridgewater's, which is based on a "search for truth," facilitates this by recognizing that fundamentally, none of us is as smart as we believe we are, nor are we as good at thinking or communicating as we think we are. That is why processes help. Root cause analyses, unpacking and stress-testing beliefs and assumptions, Learning Launches, PreMortems, and After Action Reviews are all core learning processes.

The following four critical thinking questions would make a nice laminated checklist for a desk:

- What do I truly know?
- What don't I know?
- What do I need to know?
- How do I learn what I need to know?

Likewise, the following questions should be institutionalized as part of everyday decision making: What do I believe? What facts support that belief? What facts disconfirm or question that belief? What assumptions am I making? Are those assumptions supported by facts? What inferences am I drawing from my assumptions? Are they reasonable? These questions help illuminate ignorance and doubt. Ignorance and doubt should lead to learning.

Can You Build an HPLO?

Several people in the past year have asked me whether these research findings are scalable in a big company. My answer is: It depends. A private company built by an entrepreneur who aims to create an enduring business (like Gore and Bridgewater) has a good chance if the company executes its model well. Gore has scaled its model to over 10,000 employees globally, because maintaining the "Gore Way" has been a passionate pursuit of the successor leadership teams. Leadership succession coming from inside is critical. McKinsey & Company is another good example of a private business that has scaled and not lost its founder's essence. Is it easier to do this in a private company? Yes, it is. The key is successful leadership succession from within. That is the challenge Bridgewater is tackling now.

Regarding public companies, UPS has scaled its high employee engagement and operational excellence model to over 400,000 employees, because Jim Casey's philosophy is still alive in UPS. If successor leaders grew up in the culture and have lived the values for years, scaling is possible. Other good examples of public companies that have achieved this are Costco, Corning, Inc., Sysco, and Southwest Airlines. Keeping the founder's culture alive is the key, and that is difficult if an organization doesn't build an internal leadership succession pipeline that keeps that culture alive. That is a challenge facing many good learning companies today, for example Starbucks, Amazon, and Google.

I submit that scale, efficiency, and learning are not mutually exclusive. Examples are the U.S. Army, Navy, and Marine Corps, UPS, and Toyota. Are those organizations perfect? No. In today's world, no organization will be perfect, because it's made up of human beings who make mistakes. One can question the examples of the U.S. Army, Navy, and Marine Corps. Aren't they "command and control"? I contend that if you look deeply inside those organizations, you will find strong command, but you will also find high soldier engagement and learning driven by small unit structures. You will find strong, meaningful values of duty, honor, courage, and service that meet individual soldiers' needs for autonomy, relatedness, affiliation, effectiveness, and personal growth. As important, you will find those organizations actively engaged in learning and improvement initiatives based on the science of learning.

How about existing public companies that don't have founders involved that want to create a learning organization? That's harder. The nature of U.S. capital markets, with their nonscientific, one-dimensional focus on short-term shareholder value creation, makes building great public learning companies hard. In my previous book *Smart Growth* I espoused the view that the dominance of short-termism in our public capital markets inhibits growth and innovation. The average public company stock holding period is below twelve months. We no longer have stock ownership; we have stock renting. Likewise, short termism is evidenced by the fact that the average tenure of Fortune 500 public company CEOs is less than 5 years—4.6 years, to be exact. The probability of transforming an existing public company into a great learning organization in 4.6 years is very small, absent a major crisis situation like the one Lou Gerstner inherited at IBM in 1993. Even if a CEO can't transform an existing company into a great learning company in 4.6 years, however, she can begin the journey to create a great learning company and see benefits during her tenure. Likewise, an existing public company can put in place critical thinking, discovery, and experimentation processes and After Action Reviews—but the effectiveness of those processes depends on the adoption and systematization of the key learning enablers discussed above.

If you're a leader, manager, or a teammate and you want to change your organization, the best advice I can give you is to change yourself first. Then, start to work on your sphere of influence, those whom you can influence, or those to whom you look for guidance or leadership. Get to know each person individually and emotionally. Understand their hopes, dreams, fears, and concerns. Then help them learn more so they can be more. Put in place a code of learning conduct for yourself and your team that treats people with respect and dignity and gives them permission to speak freely without fear of punishment. Create a respectful, mutually supportive and accountable, positive team culture.

Role model how to think and communicate better. Admit your ignorance and your mistakes. Be authentic. Act with caring humility. Engage people so they feel like they have some control over their destinies. Be honest, have high standards, and hold everyone, including you, to those standards. Follow a Gore tenet—be the kind of person people want as a leader. Manage your thinking, your emotions, and how you communicate. Be aware and mindful. Strive to be fully engaged in every communication and focus on having a positive impact.

If we sit back together and think critically about the findings set forth in this book, I submit that they challenge the continued viability of the dominant management model and organizational model resulting from the Industrial Revolution—big command and control structures with

Theory X leaders. If we want adaptable learning organizations, we need to humanize our management models, and that requires many companies to fundamentally change attitudes and behaviors toward employees. That ultimately means we would have to humanize the capital markets too. Or we need to form new capital markets to support the building of enduring, value creating, people-centric, learning companies. I find it interesting that many of the businesses that are engaged in the journey of creating an adaptable learning organization are privately owned or are public companies with engaged founders who have significant ownership positions or voting rights.

In addition, management and the capital markets have to accept the fact that the learning process is not efficient. Collaboration takes time. Creating and sustaining high emotional engagement takes hard work and time. Organizations like Bridgewater, Intuit, IDEO, and Gore demonstrate that the time investment and the hard work at learning can create consistent value.

One of the points that this book makes is that the commonly espoused managerial choice between high employee accountability and high employee emotional engagement is a false dichotomy. Consistent high performance requires both high employee accountability and high employee emotional engagement. Likewise, a forced choice between operational excellence and innovation is a false dichotomy, too. Both operational excellence and innovation are dependent upon learning. Both require the HPLO formula with the key difference being the tolerance for failure.

I like to tell my students that business is not "rocket science." Business principles are pretty simple—the difficulty is in the execution, because execution involves people. The same can be said about the principles of creating a high-performance learning organization. The science of learning and learning processes are in many ways the easy part. The hard part is the disciplined daily execution of the principles. I asserted in chapter 1 that learning better and faster was a strategic imperative. Learning can be positively transformative, individually and organizationally, and I believe that institutionalizing and maintaining that positive transformative process can be a sustainable competitive advantage.

A learning journey is a people journey. It is both a continuous "search for the truth" and an emotional journey. One of your roles as a leader or manager or teammate is to "invite, include, and inspire"[1] others to join you in the learning journey.

Good journeys, my friends!

Notes

1. Learn or Die: Building a High-Performance Learning Organization

1. This chapter is based on a synthesis of the following sources: Erik Brynjolfsson and Andrew McAfee, *The Second Machine Age: Work, Progress, and Prosperity in a Time of Brilliant Technologies* (New York: Norton, 2014); Peter H. Diamandis and Steven Kotler, *Abundance: The Future Is Better Than You Think* (New York: Free Press, 2012); Charles H. Fine, *Clockspeed: Winning Industry Control in the Age of Temporary Advantage* (New York: Basic Books, 1998); Innosight LLC, "Creative Destruction Whips Through Corporate America," INNOSIGHT Executive Briefing, Winter 2012, www.innosight.com/innovation-resources/strategy-innovation/upload/creative-destruction-whips-through-corporate-america_final2012.pdf; Ray Kurzweil, *How to Create a Mind: The Secret of Human Thought Revealed* (New York: Penguin, 2013); "The U.S. Army Learning Concept for 2015," TRADOC Pam 525-8-2, January 20, 2011, www.tradoc.army.mil/tpubs/pams/tp525-8-2.pdf, i.

2. Edward D. Hess and Jeanne Liedtka, *The Physics of Business Growth: Mindsets, System, and Processes* (Stanford: Stanford University Press, 2012).

3. Peter Senge, *The Fifth Discipline: The Art & Practice of the Learning Organization* (New York: Currency Doubleday, 1990).

4. Innosight LLC, "Creative Destruction Whips Through Corporate America."

5. Steve Pearlstein, "How the Cult of Shareholder Value Wrecked American Business," *Washington Post*, September 6, 2013, www.washingtonpost.com/blogs/wonkblog/wp/2013/09/09/how-the-cult-of-shareholder-value-wrecked-american-business/.

6. Gary Burnison, "The CEO Pay Circus of 2013," Yahoo Finance/The Exchange, March 21, 2013, http://finance.yahoo.com/blogs/the-exchange/ceo-pay-circus-2013-214028626.html.

7. "The U.S. Army Learning Concept for 2015."

2. Learning: How Our Mind Works

1. This chapter synthesizes the leading work on how we learn from the following sources: Susan A. Ambrose, Michael W. Bridges, Michele DiPietro, Marsha C. Lovett, and Marie K. Norman, *How Learning Works: Seven Research-Based Principles for Smart Teaching* (San Francisco: Wiley, 2010); Dan Ariely, *Predictably Irrational, Revised and Expanded Edition: The Hidden Forces That Shape Our Decisions* (New York: HarperPerennial, 2009); Chris Argyris, *Organizational Traps: Leadership, Culture, Organizational Design* (Oxford University Press, 2010); Chris Argyris, "Teaching Smart People How to Learn," *Harvard Business Review* 69, 3 (1991): 99–109; John A. Bargh and Tanya L. Chartrand, "The Unbearable Automaticity of Being," *American Psychologist* 54, 7 (1999): 462–479; Lyle E. Bourne, Jr. and Alice F. Healy, *Train Your Mind for Peak Performance: A Science-Based Approach for Achieving Your Goals* (Washington, DC: American Psychological Association, 2014); John D. Bransford, Ann L. Brown, and Rodney R. Cocking, eds., *How People Learn: Brain, Mind, Experience, and School* (Washington, DC: National Academy Press, 2000); Arthur W. Combs, "Affective Education Or None at All," *Educational Leadership* 39, 7 (1982): 495–497; Arthur W. Combs, "Humanism, Education, and the Future," *Educational Leadership* 35, 4 (1978): 300–303; Arthur W. Combs, "A Perceptual View of the Adequate Personality," in *Perceiving, Behaving, Becoming: A New Focus for Education: Yearbook 1962* (Alexandria, VA: Association for Supervision and Curriculum Development, 1962), 50–64; Linda Darling-Hammond, "Session 1: How People Learn: Introduction to Learning Theory," The Learning Classroom: Theory Into Practice, Annenberg Learner website, www.learner.org/courses/learningclassroom/session_overviews/intro_home1.html; Alvaro Fernandez and Elkhonon Goldberg, *The SharpBrains Guide to Brain Fitness Second Edition: How to Optimize Brain Health and Performance at Any Age* (San Francisco: SharpBrains, 2013); Kurt W. Fischer, "Mind, Brain, and Education: Building a Scientific Groundwork for Learning and Teaching," *Mind, Brain, and Education* 3, 1 (2009): 3–16; Kurt W. Fischer and Samuel P. Rose, "Growth Cycles of Brain and Mind," *Educational Leadership* 56, 3 (1998): 56–60; John H. Flavell, "Metacognition and Cognitive Monitoring: A New Area of Cognitive-Developmental Inquiry," *American Psychologist* 34, 10 (1979): 906–911; Logan Fletcher and Peter Carruthers, "Metacognition and Reasoning," *Philosophical Transactions of the Royal Society B: Biological Sciences* 367, 1594 (2012): 1366–1378; Michael S. Gazzaniga, "Neuroscience and the Correct Level of Explanation for Understanding Mind," *Trends in Cognitive Sciences* 14, 7 (2010): 291–292; Mariale M. Hardiman, *The Brain-Targeted Teaching Model for 21st-Century Schools* (Thousand Oaks, CA: Corwin, 2012); Alice F. Healey and Lyle E. Bourne, *Training Cognition: Optimizing Efficiency, Durability, and*

Generalizability (New York: Psychology Press, 2012); Daniel Kahneman *Thinking, Fast and Slow* (New York: Farrar, Straus and Giroux, 2011); Daniel Kahneman, Dan Lovallo, and Olivier Sibony, "Before You Make That Big Decision," *Harvard Business Review* 89, 6 (2011): 50–60; Malcolm S. Knowles, Elwood F. Holton III, and Richard A. Swanson, *The Adult Learner: The Definitive Classic in Adult Education and Human Resource Development* (Burlington, MA: Elsevier, 2005); James W. Lussier, Scott B. Shadrick, and Michael I. Prevou, "Think Like a Commander Prototype: Instructor's Guide to Adaptive Thinking," No. ARI-RP-2003-02, Army Research Institute for the Behavioral and Social Sciences, Alexandria, VA, 2003; Michael J. Mauboussin, *Think Twice: Harnessing the Power of Counterintuition* (Boston: Harvard Business Review Press, 2009); Jack Mezirow, "Transformative Learning: Theory to Practice," *New Directions for Adult and Continuing Education* 74 (Summer 1997): 5–12; Michael I. Posner and Gregory J. DiGirolamo, "Cognitive Neuroscience: Origins and Promise," *Psychological Bulletin* 126, 6 (2000): 873–889; Ron Ritchhart and David N. Perkins, "Learning to Think: The Challenges of Teaching Thinking," Keith J. Holyoak and Robert G. Morrison, eds., *The Cambridge Handbook of Thinking and Reasoning* (Cambridge: Cambridge University Press, 2004); Matthew Roser and Michael S. Gazzaniga, "Automatic Brains—Interpretive Minds," *Current Directions in Psychological Science* 13, 2 (2004): 56–59; Daniel L. Schacter, "The Seven Sins of Memory: Insights from Psychology and Cognitive Neuroscience," *American Psychologist* 54, 3 (1999) 182–203; Daniel L. Schacter and Donna Rose Addis, "The Cognitive Neuroscience of Constructive Memory: Remembering the Past and Imagining the Future," *Philosophical Transactions of the Royal Society B: Biological Sciences* 362, 1481 (2007): 773–786; Amos Tversky and Daniel Kahneman, "Judgment Under Uncertainty: Heuristics and Biases," *Science* 185, 4157 (1974): 1124–1131; Daniel T. Willingham, *Why Don't Students Like School? A Cognitive Scientist Answers Questions About How the Mind Works and What It Means for the Classroom* (San Francisco: Jossey-Bass, 2009).

2. Arthur Herman, *The Cave and the Light: Plato Versus Aristotle, and the Struggle for the Soul of Western Civilization* (New York: Random House, 2013).

3. Knowles et al., *The Adult Learner*, 34.

4. Ibid.

5. Ambrose et al., *How Learning Works*; Bourne and Healy, *Train Your Mind for Peak Performance*; Bransford et al., *How People Learn*; Darling-Hammond, "Session 1"; Fernandez and Goldberg, *The Sharp Brains Guide to Brain Fitness*; Hardiman, *The Brain-Targeted Teaching Model for 21st-Century Schools*; Healey and Bourne, *Training Cognition*; Knowles, Elwood and Swanson, *The Adult Learner*; Willingham, *Why Don't Students Like School?*

6. Hardiman, *The Brain-Targeted Teaching Model for 21st-Century Schools*, 17.

7. Kahneman, *Thinking, Fast and Slow*, 35.

8. Ibid., 21.

9. Ibid., 20.

10. Max H. Bazerman and Don A. Moore, *Judgment in Managerial Decision Making*, 7th ed. (Hoboken, NJ: Wiley, 2009), 3.

11. Kahneman, *Thinking Fast and Slow*, 24.

12. Ibid., 28.

13. Knowles et al., *The Adult Learner*, 47.

14. Bourne and Healy, *Train Your Mind for Peak Performance*, x.

15. Schacter, "The Seven Sins of Memory"; Schacter and Addis, "The Cognitive Neuroscience of Constructive Memory."

16. Mezirow, "Transformative Learning: Theory to Practice," 5.

17. Ibid., 7.

18. Jack Mezirow, "Learning to Think Like an Adult: Core Concepts of Transformation Theory," in Jack Mezirow and Associates, *Learning as Transformation: Critical Perspectives on a Theory in Progress* (San Francisco: Jossey-Bass, 2000), 4.

19. I learned this term from Professor Alec Horniman at the Darden Business School.

20. For in-depth coverage of this topic, see Kahneman, *Thinking, Fast and Slow*; Daniel Kahneman, "A Short Course in Thinking About Thinking," Edge Master Class, Rutherford California, July 20–22, 2007, Edge.org, www.edge.org/events/the-edge-master-class-2007-a-short-course-in-thinking-about-thinking; Kahneman, Lovallo and Sibony, "Before You Make That Big Decision"; Daniel Kahneman and Gary Klein, "Conditions for Intuitive Expertise: A Failure to Disagree," *American Psychologist* 64, 6 (2009): 515–526; Bazerman, and Moore, *Judgment in Managerial Decision Making*; Mauboussin, *Think Twice*.

21. Ritchhart and Perkins, "Learning to Think: The Challenges of Teaching Thinking," 780.

22. Flavell, "Metacognition and Cognitive Monitoring: A New Area of Cognitive–Developmental Inquiry."

23. Fletcher and Carruthers, "Metacognition and Reasoning."

24. Knowles, Elwood and Swanson, *The Adult Learner*, 44.

25. Combs, "A Perceptual View of the Adequate Personality."

26. Ibid., 56.

27. Ibid., 57.

28. Argyris, "Teaching Smart People How to Learn," 8.

29. Ibid., 9.

30. Edward de Bono, *Lateral Thinking: Creativity Step by Step* (New York: Harper Colophon, 1990).

31. K. Anders Ericsson, Ralf Th. Krampe, and Clemens Tesch-Romer, "The Role of Deliberate Practice in the Acquisition of Expert Performance," *Psychological Review* 100, 3 (1993): 363–406.

32. Ibid., 366.

33. Ibid.

34. Lussier et al., "Think Like a Commander Prototype."

3. Emotions: The Myth of Rationality

1. This chapter synthesizes research and work on the topic of cognition and emotion from the following sources: Gregory F. Ashby, Alice M. Isen, and U. Turken, "A Neuropsychological Theory of Positive Affect and Its Influence on Cognition," *Psychological Review* 106, 3 (1999): 529–550; Sigal G. Barsade, Lakshmi Ramarajan, and Drew Westen, "Implicit Affect in Organizations," *Research in Organizational Behavior* 29 (2009): 135–162; Gregory Berns, *Iconoclast: A Neuroscientist Reveals How to Think Differently* (Boston: Harvard Business Review Press, 2008); Isabelle Blanchette and Anne Richards, "The Influence of Affect on Higher Level Cognition: A Review of Research on Interpretation, Judgment, Decision Making and Reasoning," *Cognition & Emotion* 24, 4 (2010): 561–595; Gerald L. Clore and Jeffrey R. Huntsinger, "How Emotions Inform Judgment and Regulate Thought," *Trends in Cognitive Science* 11, 9 (2007): 393–399; Gerald L. Clore and Janet Palmer, "Affective Guidance of Intelligent Agents: How Emotion Controls Cognition," *Cognitive Systems Research* 10, 1 (2009): 21–30; Richard J. Davidson and Sharon Begley, *The Emotional Life of Your Brain: How Its Unique Patterns Affect the Way You Think, Feel, and Live—and How You Can Change Them* (New York: Plume, 2013); Jan De Houwer and Dirk Hermans, eds., *Cognition & Emotion: Reviews of Current Research and Theories* (Hove: Psychology Press, 2010); Barbara L. Fredrickson, *Positivity: Groundbreaking Research Reveals How to Embrace the Hidden Strength of Positive Emotions, Overcome Negativity, and Thrive* (New York: Crown, 2009); Barbara L. Fredrickson, "The Role of Positive Emotions in Positive Psychology: The Broaden-and-Build Theory of Positive Emotions," *American Psychologist* 56, 3 (2001): 218–226; Barbara L. Fredrickson and Christine Branigan, "Positive Emotions Broaden the Scope of Attention and Thought-Action Repertoires," *Cognition & Emotion* 19, 3 (2005): 313–332; Karen Gasper, "Do You See What I See? Affect and Visual Information Processing," *Cognition & Emotion* 18, 3 (2004): 405–421; Karen Gasper, "Permission to Seek Freely? The Effect of Happy and Sad Moods on Generating Old and New Ideas," *Creativity Research Journal* 16, 2–3 (2004): 215–229; Karen Gasper and Gerald L. Clore, "Attending to the Big Picture: Mood and Global Versus Local Processing of Visual Information," *Psychological Science* 13, 1 (2002): 34–40; Christina Hinton, Koji Miyamoto, and Bruno Della-Chiesa, "Brain Research, Learning and Emotions: Implications for Education Research, Policy and Practice," *European Journal of Education* 43, 1 (2008): 87–103; Mary Helen Immordino-Yang, "Implications of Affective and Social Neuroscience for Educational Theory," *Educational Philosophy and Theory* 43, 1 (2011): 98–103; Mary Helen Immordino-Yang and Antonio Damasio, "We Feel, Therefore We Learn: The Relevance of Affective and Social Neuroscience to Education," *Mind, Brain and Education* 1, 1 (2007): 3–10; Alice M. Isen, "A Role for Neuropsychology in Understanding the Facilitating Influence of Positive Affect on Social Behavior and Cognitive Processes," in *Handbook of Positive Psychology*, ed. C.R. Snyder and Shane J. Lopez (New York: Oxford University Press, 2002), 528–540; Alice M. Isen, "An Influence of Positive Affect on Decision Making in Complex Situations: Theoretical Issues with Practical Implications," *Journal of Consumer Psychology* 11, 2 (2001): 75–85; Alice M. Isen, Kimberly A. Daubman, and Gary P. Nowicki, "Positive

Affect Facilitates Creative Problem Solving," *Journal of Personality and Social Psychology* 52, 6 (1987): 1122–1131; Alice M. Isen and Johnmarshall Reeve, "The Influence of Positive Affect on Intrinsic and Extrinsic Motivation: Facilitating Enjoyment of Play, Responsible Work Behavior, and Self-Control," *Motivation and Emotion* 29, 4 (2005): 295–323; Bethany E. Kok, Lahnna I. Catalino, and Barbara L. Fredrickson, "The Broadening, Building, Buffering Effects of Positive Emotions," in *Positive Psychology: Exploring The Best in People*, Volume 2, *Capitalizing on Emotional Experiences*, ed. Shane J. Lopez (Westport, CT: Praeger /Greenwood, 2008), 1–19; Lisa Linnenbrink-Garcia, Toni Kempler Rogat, and Kristin L.K. Koskey, "Affect and Engagement During Small Group Instruction," *Contemporary Educational Psychology* 36 (2011): 13–24; Sonja Lyubomirsky, Laura King, and Ed Diener, "The Benefits of Frequent Positive Affect: Does Happiness Lead to Success?" *Psychological Bulletin* 131, 6 (2005): 803–855; Nasir Naqvi, Baba Shiv, and Antoine Bechara, "The Role of Emotion in Decision Making: A Cognitive Neuroscience Perspective," *Current Directions in Psychological Science* 15, 5 (2006): 260–264; Luiz Pessoa, "Emergent Processes in Cognitive-Emotional Interactions," *Dialogues in Clinical Neuroscience* 12, 4 (2010): 433–448; Luiz Pessoa, "On the Relationship between Emotion and Cognition," *Nature Reviews/Neuroscience* 9 (2008): 148–158; Christine L. Porath and Amir Erez, "Overlooked but Not Untouched: How Rudeness Reduces Onlookers' Performance on Routine and Creative Tasks," *Organizational Behavior and Human Decision Processes* 109, 1 (2009): 29–44; Herbert Simon, "What Is an 'Explanation' of Behavior?" *Psychological Science* 3, 3 (1992): 150–161; Justin Storbeck and Gerald L. Clore, "On the Interdependence of Cognition and Emotion," *Cognition & Emotion* 21, 6 (2007): 1212–1237.

2. Antonio Damasio, *Descartes' Error: Emotion, Reason, and the Human Brain* (New York: Penguin, 1994); Immordino-Yang, "Implications of Affective and Social Neuroscience for Educational Theory"; Storbeck and Clore, "On the Interdependence of Cognition and Emotion."

3. Davidson and Begley, *The Emotional Life of Your Brain*, 68, 81, and 89.

4. Storbeck and Clore, "On the Interdependence of Cognition and Emotion," 1235.

5. Pessoa, "Emergent Processes in Cognitive-Emotional Interactions," 439.

6. Immordino-Yang and Damasio, "We Feel, Therefore We Learn," 8.

7. Ibid., 7.

8. Recall that in chapter 2 we established that System 1 and System 2 thinking is a useful, pragmatic way of describing the differences in how we think. Like most dichotomies, this dichotomy probably exists along a continuum.

9. Immordino-Yang and Damasio, "We Feel, Therefore We Learn"; Davidson and Begley, *The Emotional Life of Your Brain*, 113–136.

10. Berns, *Iconoclast*.

11. Clore and Palmer, "Affective Guidance of Intelligent Agents," 2.

12. Ibid.

13. Ibid.

14. Ibid., 1.

15. See, for example, The Center for Positive Organizations at the Ross School of Business, University of Michigan, at http://positiveorgs.bus.umich.edu; Kim S. Cameron,

Practicing Positive Leadership: Tools and Techniques That Create Extraordinary Results (San Francisco: Berrett-Koehler, 2013); Kim S. Cameron, *Positive Leadership: Strategies for Extraordinary Performance* (San Francisco: Berrett-Koehler, 2012); Kim S. Cameron and Gretchen M. Spreitzer, eds., *The Oxford Handbook of Positive Organizational Scholarship* (New York: Oxford University Press, 2012); Martin E.P. Seligman, *Flourish: A Visionary New Understanding of Happiness and Well-being* (New York: Free Press, 2011).

16. Barbara L. Fredrickson, "Updated Thinking on Positivity Ratios," *American Psychologist* 68, 9 (2013): 814–822.

17. Ibid. See also Fredrickson, "The Role of Positive Emotions in Positive Psychology"; Fredrickson and Branigan, "Positive Emotions Broaden the Scope of Attention and Thought-Action Repertoires"; Barbara L. Fredrickson and Marcial F. Losada, "Positive Affect and the Complex Dynamics of Human Flourishing," *American Psychologist* 60, 7 (2005): 678–686; Kok et al., "The Broadening, Building, Buffering Effects of Positive Emotions."

18. Isen, "An Influence of Positive Affect on Decision Making in Complex Situations"; Isen, "A Role for Neuropsychology in Understanding the Facilitating Influence of Positive Affect on Social Behavior and Cognitive Processes"; Isen and Reeve, "The Influence of Positive Affect on Intrinsic and Extrinsic Motivation."

19. Ashby et al., "A Neuropsychological Theory of Positive Affect and Its Influence on Cognition"; Isen, "A Role for Neuropsychology in Understanding the Facilitating Influence of Positive Affect on Social Behavior And Cognitive Processes," 528–540.

20. Michael A. Cohn and Barbara L. Fredrickson, "In Search of Durable Positive Psychology Interventions: Predictors and Consequences of Long-Term Positive Behavior Change," *Journal of Positive Psychology* 5, 5 (2010): 355–366; Robert A. Emmons and Anjali Mishra, "Why Gratitude Enhances Well-Being: What We Know, What We Need to Know," in *Designing Positive Psychology: Taking Stock and Moving Forward,* ed. Kennon M. Sheldon, Todd B. Kashdan, and Michael F. Steger (New York: Oxford University Press, 2011), 248–264; Fredrickson, *Positivity,* 179–224.

21. Ibid.

22. Sara B. Algoe and Barbara L. Fredrickson, "Emotional Fitness and the Movement of Affective Science from Lab to Field," *American Psychologist* 66, 1 (2011): 35–42; Rhonda Cornum, Michael D. Matthews, and Martin E.P. Seligman, "Comprehensive Soldier Fitness: Building Resilience in a Challenging Institutional Context," *American Psychologist* 66, 1 (2011): 4–9.

23. Porath and Erez, "Overlooked but Not Untouched."

24. Blanchette and Richards, "The Influence of Affect on Higher Level Cognition," 563.

25. Ibid.

26. Berns, *Iconoclast,* 61.

27. Ibid., 61–62.

28. Ibid., 104–105.

29. Ibid., 76–81.

30. John D. Mayer and Peter Salovey, "What Is Emotional Intelligence?"; Peter Salovey and David J. Sluyter, eds., *Emotional Development and Emotional Intelligence: Educational Implications* (New York: Basic, 1997).

31. Peter Salovey, John D. Mayer, and David Caruso, "The Positive Psychology of Emotional Intelligence," Lopez and Snyder, *Oxford Handbook of Positive Psychology*, 239.

32. Davidson and Begley, *The Emotional Life of Your Brain*, xiv.

4. Learning: The Right People

1. The basis of this chapter is a synthesis of research and work drawn from the following sources: Millie Abell, "Deepening Distributed Learning: Motivating Soldiers to Learn, Grow, Achieve," Paper presented at the Interservice/Industry Training, Simulation & Education Conference, 2003; Frederik Anseel, Nico W. Van Yperen, Onne Janssen, and Wouter Duyck, "Feedback Type as a Moderator of the Relationship between Achievement Goals and Feedback Reactions," *Journal of Occupational and Organizational Psychology* 84, 4 (2011): 703–722; Albert Bandura, "Personal and Collective Efficacy in Human Adaptation and Change," *Advances in Psychological Science* 1 (1998): 51–71; Albert Bandura, "Perceived Self-Efficacy in Cognitive Development and Functioning," *Educational Psychologist* 28, 2 (1993): 117–148; Paul T. Bartone, "Resilience Under Military Operational Stress: Can Leaders Influence Hardiness?" *Military Psychology* 18, Suppl (2006): S131–S148; Paul T. Bartone, Robert R. Roland, James J. Picanoa, and Thomas J. Williams, "Psychological Hardiness Predicts Success in US Army Special Forces Candidates," *International Journal of Selection and Assessment* 16, 1 (2008): 78–81; Marcus Buckingham and Curt Coffman, *First, Break All the Rules: What the World's Greatest Managers Do Differently* (New York: Simon & Schuster, 1999); Margaret M. Clifford, "Risk Taking: Theoretical, Empirical and Educational Considerations," *Educational Psychologist* 26, 3–4 (1991): 263–297; Margaret M. Clifford, "Students Need Challenge, Not Easy Success," *Educational Leadership* 48, 1 (1990): 22–26; Margaret M. Clifford, "Failure Tolerance and Academic Risk-Taking in Ten-to-Twelve-Year-Old Students," *British Journal of Educational Psychology* 58, 1 (1988): 15–27; Margaret M. Clifford, "The Effects of Ability, Strategy, and Effort Attributions for Educational, Business, and Athletic Failure," *British Journal of Educational Psychology* 56, 2 (1986): 169–179; Margaret M. Clifford, "Thoughts on a Theory of Constructive Failure," *Educational Psychologist* 19, 2 (1984): 108–120; Margaret M. Clifford and Fen-Chang Chou, "Effects of Payoff and Task Context on Academic Risk Taking," *Journal of Educational Psychology* 83, 4 (1991): 499–507; Edward L. Deci, *Why We Do What We Do: Understanding Self-Motivation* (New York: Penguin, 1996); Carol I. Diener and Carol S. Dweck, "An Analysis of Learned Helplessness: Continuous Changes in Performance, Strategy, and Achievement Cognitions Following Failure," *Journal of Personality and Social Psychology* 36, 5 (1978): 451–462; Carol S. Dweck, "Even Geniuses Work Hard," *Educational Leadership* 68, 1 (2010): 16–20; Carol S. Dweck, "Brainology: Transforming Students' Motivation to Learn," *Independent School* 67, 2 (2008): 110–119; Carol S. Dweck, *Mindset: The New Psychology of Success* (New York: Ballantine, 2006); Carol S. Dweck, "Motivational Processes Affecting Learning," *American Psychologist* 41, 10 (1986): 1040–1048; Carol S. Dweck and Ellen L. Leggett, "A Social-Cognitive Approach to Motivation and Personality," *Psychological*

Review 95, 2 (1988): 256–273; Andrew J. Elliot and Marcy A. Church, "A Hierarchical Model of Approach and Avoidance Achievement Motivation," *Journal of Personality and Social Psychology* 72, 1 (1997): 218–232; Andrew J. Elliot and Todd M. Thrash, "Approach and Avoidance Temperament as Basic Dimensions of Personality," *Journal of Personality* 78, 3 (2010): 865–906; Elaine S. Elliott and Carol S. Dweck, "Goals: An Approach to Motivation and Achievement," *Journal of Personality and Social Psychology* 54, 1 (1988): 5–12; Heidi Grant and Carol S. Dweck, "Clarifying Achievement Goals and Their Impact," *Journal of Personality and Social Psychology* 85, 3 (2003): 541–553; E. Tory Higgins, *Beyond Pleasure and Pain: How Motivation Works* (New York: Oxford University Press, 2012); E. Tory Higgins, "Making a Good Decision: Value from Fit," *American Psychologist* 55, 11 (2000): 1217–1230; Onne Janssen and Nico W. Van Yperen, "Employees' Goal Orientations, the Quality of Leader-Member Exchange, and the Outcomes of Job Performance and Job Satisfaction," *Academy of Management Journal* 47, 3 (2004): 368–384; Elizabeth A. Linnenbrink and Paul R. Pintrich, "Achievement Goal Theory and Affect: An Asymmetrical Bidirectional Model," *Educational Psychologist* 37, 2 (2002): 69–78; Jennifer A. Mangels, Brady Butterfield, Justin Lamb, Catherine Good, and Carol S. Dweck, "Why Do Beliefs about Intelligence Influence Learning Success? A Social Cognitive Neuroscience Model," *Social Cognitive and Affective Neuroscience* 1, 2 (2006): 75–86; Douglas McGregor, *The Human Side of the Enterprise-Annotated Edition* (New York: McGraw-Hill, 2006); Rose A. Mueller-Hanson, Susan S. White, David W. Dorsey, and Elaine D. Pulakos, "Training Adaptable Leaders: Lessons from Research and Practice," ARI Research Report 1844, Personnel Decisions Research Institutes, Inc., Arlington, VA, 2005; Kou Murayama and Andrew J. Elliot, "The Joint Influence of Personal Achievement Goals and Classroom Goal Structures on Achievement-Relevant Outcomes," *Journal of Educational Psychology* 101, 2 (2009): 432–447; Reinhard Pekrun, Andrew J. Elliot, and Markus A. Maier, "Achievement Goals and Discrete Achievement Emotions: A Theoretical Model and Prospective Test," *Journal of Educational Psychology* 98, 3 (2006): 583–597; Paul R. Pintrich, "A Motivational Science Perspective on the Role of Student Motivation in Learning and Teaching Contexts," *Journal of Educational Psychology* 95, 4 (2003): 667–686; Richard M. Ryan and Edward L. Deci, "Intrinsic and Extrinsic Motivations: Classic Definitions and New Directions," *Contemporary Educational Psychology* 25, 1 (2000): 54–67; Shari Tishman, Eileen Jay, and David N. Perkins, "Teaching Thinking Dispositions: From Transmission to Enculturation," *Theory into Practice* 32, 3 (1993): 147–153; Nico W. Van Yperen, Andrew J. Elliot, and Frederik Anseel, "The Influence of Mastery-Avoidance Goals on Performance Improvement," *European Journal of Social Psychology* 39, 6 (2009): 932–943; Nico W. Van Yperen and Edward Orehek, "Achievement Goals in the Workplace: Conceptualization, Prevalence, Profiles, and Outcomes," *Journal of Economic Psychology* 39, C (2012): 71–79; Nico W. Van Yperen and Lennart J. Renkema, "Performing Great and the Purpose of Performing Better Than Others: On the Recursiveness of the Achievement Goal Adoption Process," *European Journal of Social Psychology* 38, 2 (2008): 260–271; Susan S. White, Rose A. Mueller-Hanson, David W. Dorsey, Elaine D. Pulakos, Michelle M. Wisecarver, Edwin A. Deagle III, and Kip G. Mendini, "Developing Adaptive Proficiency in Special Forces Officers," Personnel Decisions Research Institutes, Arlington, VA, 2005.

2. Sigmund Freud, *Beyond the Pleasure Principle*, translated by James Strachey (Seattle: Pacific, 2010).

3. For an overview of this line of motivation research, see Higgins, *Beyond Pleasure and Pain*, 3–46.

4. Richard M. Ryan and Edward L. Deci, "Self-Determination Theory and the Facilitation of Intrinsic Motivation, Social Development, and Well-Being," *American Psychologist* 55 (2000): 68–78.

5. Paul P. Baard, Edward L. Deci, and Richard M. Ryan, "Intrinsic Need Satisfaction: A Motivational Basis of Performance and Well-Being in Two Work Settings," *Journal of Applied Social Psychology* 34, 10 (2004): 2046; Edward L. Deci and Richard M. Ryan, "The 'What' and 'Why' of Goal Pursuits: Human Needs and The Self-Determination of Behavior," *Psychological Inquiry* 11, 4 (2000): 227–268.

6. Bandura, "Personal and Collective Efficacy in Human Adaptation and Change," 51.

7. Ibid., 62.

8. Ibid., 61.

9. Ibid., 59.

10. Andrew J. Elliot, "A Conceptual History of the Achievement Goal Construct," in *The Handbook of Competence and Motivation,* ed. Andrew J. Elliot and Carol S. Dweck (New York: Guilford, 2005), 52–72.

11. Norman Doidge, *The Brain That Changes Itself: Stories of Personal Triumph from the Frontiers of Brain Science* (New York: Penguin, 2007); Robert Sternberg, "Intelligence, Competence and Expertise," in *The Handbook of Competence and Motivation*, ed. Andrew J. Elliot and Carol S. Dweck (New York: Guilford, 2005), 15–30.

12. Elliot, "A Conceptual History of the Achievement Goal Construct," 52–72.

13. Dweck, *Mindset*, 16.

14. Ibid.

15. Tishman et al., "Teaching Thinking Dispositions: From Transmission to Enculturation," 148.

16. Ibid.

17. Bartone et al., "Psychological Hardiness Predicts Success in U.S. Army Special Forces Candidates," 78.

18. Ibid.

19. White et al., *Developing Adaptive Proficiency in Special Forces Officers,*" 3, 4, and 7.

20. Douglas McGregor, *The Human Side of the Enterprise-Annotated Edition*.

21. Ibid., 351–352.

22. Ibid., xxiii.

23. Buckingham and Coffman, *First, Break All the Rules*, 28.

5. Creating a Learning Environment

1. This chapter is based on a synthesis of research and work from the following sources: Sara B. Algoe and Barbara L. Fredrickson, "Emotional Fitness and the Movement of Affective Science from Lab to Field," *American Psychologist* 66, 1 (2011): 35–42; Tim Brown, "How Do You Build a Culture of Innovation?" *Yale Insights*, May 2013, http://insights.som.yale.edu/insights/how-do-you-build-culture-innovation;   Kim   S. Cameron, *Positive Leadership: Strategies for Extraordinary Performance* (San Francisco: Berrett-Koehler, 2012); Kim S. Cameron, Jane E. Dutton, and Robert E. Quinn, eds., *Positive Organizational Scholarship: Foundations of a New Discipline* (San Francisco: Berrett-Koehler, 2003); Kim S. Cameron, Carlos Mora, Trevor Leutscher, and Margaret Calarco, "Effects of Positive Practices on Organizational Effectiveness," *Journal of Applied Behavioral Science* 47, 3 (2011): 266–308; Kim S. Cameron and Gretchen M. Spreitzer, eds., *The Oxford Handbook of Positive Organizational Scholarship* (New York: Oxford University Press, 2012); Michael A. Cohn and Barbara L. Fredrickson, "In Search of Durable Positive Psychology Interventions: Predictors and Consequences of Long-Term Positive Behavior Change," *Journal of Positive Psychology* 5, 5 (2010): 355–366; Jim Collins, *Good to Great: Why Some Companies Make the Leap . . . and Others Don't* (New York: HarperBusiness, 2001); Jim Collins and Jerry I. Porras, *Built to Last: Successful Habits of Visionary Companies* (New York: HarperBusiness Essentials, 2002); Rhonda Cornum, Michael D. Matthews, and Martin E.P. Seligman, "Comprehensive Soldier Fitness: Building Resilience in a Challenging Institutional Context," *American Psychologist* 66, 1 (2011): 4–9; Arie de Geus, *The Living Company* (Boston: Harvard Business School Press, 1997); James R. Detert and Amy C. Edmondson, "Implicit Voice Theories: Taken-for-Granted Rules of Self-Censorship at Work," *Academy of Management Journal* 54, 3 (2011): 461–488; Stewart I. Donaldson, Mihaly Csikszentmihalyi and Jeanne Nakamura, eds., *Applied Positive Psychology: Improving Everyday Life, Health, Schools, Work, and Society* (New York: Routledge, 2011); Amy C. Edmonson, *Teaming: How Organizations Learn, Innovate, and Compete in the Knowledge Economy* (San Francisco: Jossey-Bass, 2012); Amy C. Edmonson, "Strategies of Learning from Failure," *Harvard Business Review* 89, 4 (2011): 48–55; Amy C. Edmondson, "The Competitive Imperative of Learning," *Harvard Business Review* 86, 7 & 8 (2008): 60–67; Amy C. Edmondson, "Promoting Experimentation for Organizational Learning: The Mixed Up Effects of Inconsistency," *Rotman Magazine* Winter (2005): 20–23; Amy C. Edmondson, "Speaking Up in the Operating Room: How Team Leaders Promote Learning in Interdisciplinary Action Teams," *Journal of Management Studies* 40, 6 (2003): 1419–1452; Amy C. Edmondson, "Framing for Learning: Lessons in Successful Technology Implementation," *California Management Review* 45, 2 (2003): 34–54; Amy C. Edmondson, "Psychological Safety and Learning Behavior in Work Teams," *Administrative Science Quarterly* 44, 2 (1999): 350–383; Amy C. Edmondson, Richard Bohmer, and Gary Pisano, "Speeding Up Team Learning," *Harvard Business Review* 79, 9 (2001): 125–134; Robert A. Emmons and Anjali Mishra, "Why Gratitude Enhances Well-Being: What We Know, What We Need to Know," in *Designing*

Positive Psychology: Taking Stock and Moving Forward, ed. Kennon Marshall Sheldon, Todd Kashdan and Michael F. Steger (New York: Oxford University Press, 2011), 248–264; Barbara L. Fredrickson, *Positivity: Groundbreaking Research Reveals How to Embrace the Hidden Strength of Positive Emotions, Overcome Negativity, and Thrive* (New York: Crown, 2009); Barbara L. Fredrickson and Marcial F. Losada, "Positive Affect and the Complex Dynamics of Human Flourishing," *American Psychologist* 60, 7 (2005): 678–686; David A. Garvin, *Learning in Action: A Guide to Putting the Learning Organization to Work* (Boston: Harvard Business Review Press, 2000); David A. Garvin, "Building a Learning Organization," *Harvard Business Review* 71, 4 (1993): 78–91; David A. Garvin, Amy C. Edmondson and Francesca Gino, "Is Yours a Learning Organization?" *Harvard Business Review* 86, 3 (2008): 109–116; James K. Harter, Frank L. Schmidt, and Theodore L. Hayes, "Business-Unit-Level Relationship between Employee Satisfaction, Employee Engagement, and Business Outcomes: A Meta-Analysis," *Journal of Applied Psychology* 87, 2 (2002): 268–279; Edward D. Hess, *The Road to Organic Growth: How Great Companies Consistently Grow Marketshare from Within* (New York: McGraw-Hill, 2007); Tom Kelley and David Kelley, *Creative Confidence: Unleashing the Creative Potential Within Us All* (New York: Crown Business, 2013); Jeffrey Liker and Michael Hoseus, *Toyota Culture: The Heart and Soul of the Toyota Way* (New York: McGraw-Hill, 2008); Shane J. Lopez and C.R. Snyder, eds., *The Oxford Handbook of Positive Psychology, Second Edition* (New York: Oxford University Press, 2009); Ingrid M. Nembhard and Amy C. Edmondson, "Making It Safe: The Effects of Leader Inclusiveness and Professional Status on Psychological Safety and Improvement Efforts in Health Care Teams," *Journal of Organizational Behavior* 27, 7 (2006): 941–966; Charles A. O'Reilly III and Jeffrey Pfeffer, *Hidden Value: How Great Companies Achieve Extraordinary Results with Ordinary People* (Boston: Harvard Business School Press, 2000); Jeffrey Pfeffer, *The Human Equation: Building Profits by Putting People First* (Boston: Harvard Business Review Press, 1998); Christine Porath, Gretchen Spreitzer, Cristina Gibson, and Flannery G. Garnett, "Thriving at Work: Toward its Measurement, Construct Validation, and Theoretical Refinement," *Journal of Organizational Behavior* 33, 2 (2012): 250–275; Ivan T. Robertson and Cary L. Cooper, "Full Engagement: The Integration of Employee Engagement and Psychological Well-Being," *Leadership & Organization Development Journal* 31, 4 (2010): 324–336; Carl Rogers, *The Carl Rogers Reader*, Howard Kirschenbaum, and Valerie Land Henderson, eds. (New York: Houghton Mifflin, 1989); Edgar H. Schein, "Taking Culture Seriously in Organization Development: A New Role for OD?" Working Paper 4287-03, 2003, http://dspace.mit.edu/bitstream/handle/1721.1/1834/4287-03.pdf?sequence=1; Leslie E. Sekerka and Barbara L. Fredrickson, "Establishing Positive Emotional Climates to Advance Organizational Transformation," in *Research Companion to Emotion in Organizations*, ed. Neal M. Ashkanasy and Cary Lynn Cooper (Cheltenham, UK: Edward Elgar, 2008), 531–545; Martin E. P. Seligman, *Flourish: A Visionary New Understanding of Happiness and Well-Being* (New York: Free Press, 2012); Kennon Marshall Sheldon, Todd Kashdan and Michael F. Steger, eds., *Designing Positive Psychology: Taking Stock and Moving Forward* (Oxford University Press, 2011); Gretchen Spreitzer and Christine Porath, "Creating Sustainable Performance," *Harvard Business Review* 90, 1 (2012): 92–99; Anita L. Tucker and Amy C. Edmondson, "Why Hospitals Don't Learn From Failures," *California Management Review* 45, 2 (2003): 55–72.

2. Peter M. Senge, *The Fifth Discipline: The Art and Practice of the Learning Organization* (New York: Doubleday, 1990), 12.

3. Edward D. Hess, *Smart Growth: Building an Enduring Business by Managing the Risks of Growth* (New York: Columbia University Press, 2010); Hess, *The Road to Organic Growth*.

4. Hess, *Smart Growth*.

5. Hans Henrik Knoop, "Education in 2025: How Positive Psychology Can Revitalize Education," in *Applied Positive Psychology: Improving Everyday Life, Health, Schools, Work, and Society*, ed. Stewart I. Donaldson, Mihaly Csikszentmihalyi, and Jeanne Nakamura (New York: Routledge, 2011), 97–115.

6. Ibid., 101–102.

7. Susan A. Ambrose, Michael W. Bridges, Michele DiPietro, Marsha C. Lovett, and Marie K. Norman, *How Learning Works: Seven Research-Based Principles for Smart Teaching* (San Francisco, CA: Wiley, 2010); Malcolm S., Knowles, Elwood F. Holton III, and Richard A. Swanson, *The Adult Learner: The Definitive Classic in Adult Education and Human Resource Development* (Burlington, MA: Elsevier, 2005); Mariale M. Hardiman, *The Brain-Targeted Teaching Model for 21st-Century Schools* (Thousand Oaks, CA: Corwin, 2012).

8. Gallup, Inc., "Q12®Meta-Analysis: The Relationship between Engagement at Work and Organizational Outcomes 2012," www.gallup.com/strategicconsulting/126806/q12-meta-analysis.aspx.

9. Collins, *Good to Great*; Collins and Porras, *Built to Last*; de Geus, *The Living Company*; Hess, *The Road to Organic Growth*; William Joyce, Nitin Nohria, and Bruce Roberson, *What Really Works: The 4 + 2 Formula For Sustained Business Success* (New York: HarperBusiness, 2003); O'Reilly and Pfeffer, *Hidden Value*; Thomas J. Peters and Robert H. Waterman Jr., *In Search Of Excellence: Lessons from America's Best-Run Companies* (New York: Warner, 1984); Hermann Simon, *Hidden Champions of the Twenty-First Century: Success Strategies of Unknown World Market Leaders* (New York: Springer, 2009).

10. O'Reilly and Pfeffer, *Hidden Value*, 3.

11. Ibid., 8.

12. Ibid., 232.

13. Collins and Porras, *Built to Last*, 10.

14. Ibid., 186–187.

15. Ibid., 183–184.

16. Ibid., 147.

17. Collins, *Good to Great*, 17–89.

18. Ibid., 21.

19. Ibid., 27.

20. Ibid., 41.

21. Ibid., 42.

22. Ibid., 74.

23. Ibid., 74–79.

24. Edmonson, *Teaming: How Organizations Learn, Innovate, and Compete in the Knowledge Economy*; Edmonson, "Strategies of Learning from Failure"; Edmondson, "The Competitive Imperative of Learning"; Edmondson, "Promoting Experimentation for Organizational Learning: The Mixed Up Effects of Inconsistency"; Edmondson, "Speaking up in the Operating Room: How Team Leaders Promote Learning in Interdisciplinary Action Teams"; Edmondson, "Framing for Learning: Lessons in Successful Technology Implementation"; Edmondson, "Psychological Safety and Learning Behavior in Work Teams"; Edmondson et al., "Speeding Up Team Learning"; Detert and Edmondson, "Implicit Voice Theories"; Nembhard and Edmondson, "Making It Safe"; Tucker and Edmondson, "Why Hospitals Don't Learn From Failures"; Spreitzer and Porath, "Creating Sustainable Performance."

25. Garvin, *Learning in Action*; Garvin, "Building a Learning Organization."

26. Garvin, *Learning in Action*, 41

27. Garvin et al. "Is Yours a Learning Organization?"

28. Hess, *The Road to Organic Growth*.

29. Cameron et al., *Positive Organizational Scholarship*; James L Heskett, W. Earl Sasser Jr., and Leonard A. Schlesinger, *The Value Profit Chain: Treat Employees Like Customers and Customers Like Employees* (New York: Free Press, 2003); James L. Heskett, W. Earl Sasser Jr., and Leonard A. Schlesinger, *The Service Profit Chain: How Leading Companies Link Profit and Growth to Loyalty, Satisfaction, and Value* (New York: Free Press, 1997); Edward D. Hess, "Growth Is the Dynamic Confluence of Strategy, Entrepreneurship, and Values," Case Study UVA-S-0196, University of Virginia Darden School Foundation, Charlottesville, VA, 2011; Hess, *The Road to Organic Growth*; Edward D. Hess and Kim S. Cameron, Eds., *Leading with Values: Positivity, Virtue & High Performance* (Cambridge: Cambridge University Press, 2006); O'Reilly and Pfeffer, *Hidden Value*.

30. These high-performance organizations met the criteria: Best Buy, UPS, Room & Board, Tiffany & Company, U.S. Marine Corps, San Antonio Spurs, Synovus Financial, TSYS, Ritz-Carlton, Southwest Airlines, Outback Steakhouse, Sysco, Chick-fil-A, Starbucks, and Levy Restaurants.

31. Hess, "Growth Is the Dynamic Confluence of Strategy, Entrepreneurship, and Values."

32. Liker and Hoseus, *Toyota Culture*.

33. Ibid., 166.

34. Hess, *The Road to Organic Growth*, 147.

35. Rogers, *The Carl Rogers Reader*, 135–138.

36. Kelley and Kelley, *Creative Confidence*.

37. The facts in this discussion came from the following sources: Richard G. Buckingham, personal interviews with author, October 28 and November 7, 2013; Alan Deutschman, "The Fabric of Creativity: At W.L. Gore, Innovation Is More Than Skin Deep: The Culture Is as Imaginative as the Products," *Fast Company*, December 2004, www.fastcompany.com/51733/fabric-creativity; Alan Deutschman, "Gore's Text for Innovation: W.L. Gore's New Rules of Business Start with Breaking the Old Rules,"

Fast Company, December 2004, www.fastcompany.com/51510/gores-text-innovation; Gary Hamel, "Innovation Democracy: W.L. Gore's Original Management Model," December 29, 2010, Management Innovation eXchange, www.managementexchange.com/ story/innovation-democracy-wl-gores-original-management-model; Gary Hamel, "Lessons from a Management Revolutionary," WSJ Blogs, March 18, 2010, http://blogs. wsj.com/management/2010/03/18/wl-gore-lessons-from-a-management-revolution- ary/; W.L. Gore & Associates, Inc., "What We Believe: Our Beliefs and Principles," www. gore.com/en_xx/careers/whoweare/whatwebelieve/gore-culture.html.

38. Richard G. Buckingham, personal interviews with author, October 28 and November 7, 2013.

39. Ibid.

40. Richard G. Buckingham, personal interview with author, November 7, 2013.

41. Ibid.

6. Learning Conversations

1. This chapter is based on a synthesis of research and work from the following sources: Brigid Barron, "When Smart Groups Fail," *Journal of the Learning Sciences* 12, 3 (2003): 307–359; David Bohm, *On Dialogue* (Abingdon, Oxon: Routledge Classics, 2004); David Bohm, Donald Factor and Peter Garrett, "Dialogue: A Proposal," Infed. org, http://infed.org/archives/e-texts/bohm_dialogue.htm; Kirk Warren Brown, Richard M. Ryan, and J. David Creswell, "Mindfulness: Theoretical Foundations and Evidence for Its Salutary Effects," *Psychological Inquiry* 18, 4 (2007): 211–237; Michael Carroll, *The Mindful Leader: Awakening Your Natural Management Skills through Mindfulness Meditation* (Boston: Trumpeter, 2008); Lahnna I. Catalino and Barbara L. Fredrickson, "A Tuesday in the Life of a Flourisher: The Role of Positive Emotional Reactivity in Optimal Mental Health," *Emotion* 11, 4 (2011): 938–950; Marvin S. Cohen, Leonard Adelman, Terry Bresnick, F. Freeman Marvin, Eduardo Salas, and Sharon L. Riedel, "Dialogue as Medium (and Message) for Training Critical Thinking," in *Expertise Out of Context: Proceedings of the Sixth International Conference on Naturalistic Decision Making*, ed. Robert. F. Hoffman (New York: Taylor & Francis, 2007); Jane E. Dutton, *Energize Your Workplace: How to Create and Sustain High-Quality Connections at Work* (San Francisco: Jossey-Bass, 2003), 219-260; Robyn M. Gillies, "Teachers' and Students' Verbal Behaviours During Cooperative and Small-Group Learning," *British Journal of Educational Psychology* 76, 2 (2006): 271–287; Bhante Gunaratana, *Mindfulness in Plain English* (Boston: Wisdom, 2011); William Isaacs, *Dialogue: The Art of Thinking Together* (New York: Doubleday, 1999); William Isaacs, "Taking Flight: Dialogue, Collective Thinking and Organizational Learning," *Organizational Dynamics* 22, 2 (1993): 24–39; Silvia Jordan, Martin Messner, and Albrecht Becker, "Reflection and Mindfulness in Organizations: Rationales and Possibilities for Integration," *Management Learning* 40, 4 (2009): 465–473; Sydney M. Jourard, *The Transparent Self* (New York: Van Nostrand Reinhold, 1971); Emily R. Lai, "Collaboration: A Literature Overview," Pearson Research Report, 2011,

http://images.pearsonassessments.com/images/tmrs/Collaboration-Review.pdf; Frank J. Lambrechts, Rene Bouwen, Styn Grieten, Jolien P. Huybrechts, and Edgar H. Schein, "Learning to Help through Humble Inquiry and Implications for Management Research, Practice, and Education: An Interview with Edgar H. Schein," *Academy of Management Learning & Education* 10, 1 (2011): 131–147; Ellen J. Langer, *The Power of Mindful Learning* (Cambridge, MA: Perseus, 1997); William R. Marchand, "Mindfulness-Based Stress Reduction, Mindfulness-Based Cognitive Therapy, and Zen Meditation for Depression, Anxiety, Pain, and Psychological Distress," *Journal of Psychiatric Practice* 18, 4 (2012): 233–252; Abraham H. Maslow, *Toward a Psychology of Being* (Princeton, NJ: D. Van Nostrand, 1962); Jack Mezirow, "Learning to Think Like an Adult: Core Concepts of Transformation Theory," in Jack Mezirow and Associates, *Learning as Transformation: Critical Perspectives on a Theory in Progress* (San Francisco: Jossey-Bass, 2000); Kerry Patterson, Joseph Grenny, Ron McMillan, and Al Switzler, *Crucial Conversations: Tools for Talking When Stakes Are High* (New York: McGraw-Hill, 2012); Alex "Sandy" Pentland, "The New Science of Building Great Teams," *Harvard Business Review* 90, 4 (2012): 60–69; Richard M. Ryan and Kirk Warren Brown, "Why We Don't Need Self-Esteem: On Fundamental Needs, Contingent Love, and Mindfulness," *Psychological Inquiry* 14, 1 (2003): 71–76; Edgar H. Schein, *Humble Inquiry: The Gentle Art of Asking Instead of Telling* (San Francisco: Berrett-Koehler, 2013); Edgar H. Schein, *Helping: How to Offer, Give, and Receive Help* (San Francisco: Berrett-Koehler Publishers, 2009); Shauna L. Shapiro, Kirk Warren Brown, and John A. Astin, "Toward the Integration of Meditation into Higher Education: A Review of Research Evidence," *Teachers College Record* 113, 3 (2011): 493–528; Douglas Stone, Bruce Patton, and Sheila Heen, *Difficult Conversations: How to Discuss What Matters Most* (New York: Penguin Books, 1999); Deborah Tannen, *That's Not What I Meant! How Conversational Style Makes or Breaks Your Relations with Others* (New York: HaperCollins, 2011); Deborah Tannen, "Conversational Style," in *Psycholinguistic Models of Production*, ed. Hans W. Dechert and Manfred Raupach (Norwood, NJ: Ablex, 1987), 251-267; Frans H. Van Eemeren and Rob Grootendorst, "Fallacies in Pragma-Dialectical Perspective," *Argumentation* 1 (1987): 283–301; Heidi A. Wayment and Jack J. Bauer, eds., *Transcending Self-Interest: Psychological Explorations of the Quiet Ego* (Washington, DC: American Psychological Association, 2008); Karl Weick and Katherine Sutcliffe, *Managing the Unexpected: Assuring High Performance in an Age of Complexity* (San Francisco: Jossey-Bass, 2001); Netta Weinstein, Kirk W. Brown, and Richard M. Ryan, "A Multi-Method Examination of the Effects of Mindfulness on Stress Attribution, Coping, and Emotional Well-Being," *Journal of Research in Personality* 43, 3 (2009): 374–385; Daniel Yankelovich, "The Magic of Dialogue," *Nonprofit Quarterly*, Fall 2001, www.gobarton.com/administration/aqip/documents/strategyforum/Yankelovich%20article.pdf.

2. Mezirow, "Learning to Think Like an Adult," 3–33.

3. Isaacs, *Dialogue*.

4. Jourard, *The Transparent Self*, 5.

5. Ibid., 6.

6. Barron, "When Smart Groups Fail," 350.

7. Schein, *Humble Inquiry*, 3.

8. Ibid., 5.

9. Ibid., 79.

10. Stone et al., *Difficult Conversations.*

11. Ibid., 7–16.

12. Dutton, *Energize Your Workplace.*

13. Ibid., 27.

14. Ibid., 37.

15. Tannen, *That's Not What I Meant!* 29.

16. Ibid., 45–46.

17. Dutton, *Energize Your Workplace,* 28.

18. Ibid., 39.

19. Edward D. Hess, "Room & Board," Case Study UVA-S-0150, University of Virginia Darden School Foundation, Charlottesville, VA, 2008 (revised 2010).

20. Ibid.

21. Ibid.

22. Weick and Sutcliffe, *Managing the Unexpected.*

23. Ibid., 55.

24. Brown et al., "Mindfulness," 214.

25. Langer, *The Power of Mindful Learning,* 23.

26. Susan Braudy, "He's Woody Allen's Not-So-Silent Partner," *New York Times,* August 21, 1977.

7. Critical Thinking Tools

1. This chapter is based on a synthesis of research and work from the following sources: Max H. Bazerman and Don A. Moore, *Judgment in Managerial Decision Making,* Seventh Edition (Hoboken, NJ: John Wiley & Sons, 2009); Judith S. Beck, *Cognitive Behavior Therapy,* 2nd ed. (New York: Guilford Press, 2011); Lyle E. Bourne Jr. and Alice F. Healy, *Train Your Mind for Peak Performance: A Science-Based Approach for Achieving Your Goals* (Washington, DC: American Psychological Association, 2014); Stephen D. Brookfield, *Teaching for Critical Thinking: Tools and Techniques to Help Students Question Their Assumptions* (San Francisco: Jossey-Bass, 2012); Paul B. Brown, "Analyzing Failure Beforehand," *New York Times,* September 22, 2007, www.nytimes.com/2007/09/22/business/media/22offline.html?fta=y&_r=0; Marvin S. Cohen, Bryan B. Thompson, Leonard Adelman, Terry A. Bresnick, Lokendra Shastri, and Sharon L. Riedel, "Training Critical Thinking for the Battlefield: Volume I: Basis in Cognitive Theory and Research," Army Research Institute Technical Report 00-2, Cognitive Technologies, Inc., Arlington, VA, June 2000; Dolly Chugh and Max H. Bazerman, "Bounded Awareness: What You Fail to See Can Hurt You," *Mind & Society* 6, 1 (2007): 1–18; Marilyn J. Darling and Charles S. Parry, "After-Action Reviews: Linking Reflection and Planning in a Learning Practice," *Reflections* 3, 2 (2001): 64–72; Edward de Bono, *Lateral Thinking: Creativity Step by Step* (New York: HarperPerennial, 1970); Arnoud De

Meyer, Christoph H. Loch, and Michael T. Pich, "Managing Project Uncertainty: From Variation to Chaos," *MIT Sloan Management Review* 43 (2002): 60–67; Kathleen M. Eisenhardt, "Making Fast Decisions in High-Velocity Environments," *Academy of Management Journal* 32, 3 (1989): 543–576; Peter A. Facione, "Critical Thinking: A Statement of Expert Consensus for Purposes of Educational Assessment and Instruction," Research Findings and Recommendations, 1990, http://eric.ed.gov/?id=ED315423; Waldo D. Freeman and William R. Burns, Jr., "Developing an Adaptability Training Strategy and Policy for the Department of Defense (DoD)," IDA Paper P-4591, Institute for Defense Analyses, Alexandria, VA, August 2010; David A. Garvin, *Learning in Action: A Guide to Putting the Learning Organization to Work* (Boston: Harvard Business Review Press, 2000); Mark P. Healey and Gerard P. Hodgkinson, "Troubling Futures: Scenarios and Scenario Planning for Organizational Decision Making," in *The Oxford Handbook of Organizational Decision Making*, ed. Gerard P. Hodgkinson and William H. Starbuck (New York: Oxford University Press, 2008); Edward D. Hess and Jeanne Liedtka, *The Physics of Business Growth: Mindsets, System, and Processes* (Stanford: Stanford University Press, 2012); Keith J. Holyoak and Robert G. Morrison, eds., *The Oxford Handbook of Thinking and Reasoning* (New York: Oxford University Press, 2012); Mary Helen Immordino Yang, "The Smoke around Mirror Neurons: Goals as Sociocultural and Emotional Organizers of Perception and Action in Learning," *Mind, Brain, and Education* 2, 2 (2008): 67–73; Daniel Kahneman, "Bias, Blindness and How We Truly Think (Part 1)," Bloomberg.com, October 24, 2011, www.bloomberg.com/news/2011-10-24/bias-blindness-and-how-we-truly-think-part-1-daniel-kahneman.html; Daniel Kahneman and Gary Klein, "Conditions for Intuitive Expertise: A Failure to Disagree," *American Psychologist* 64, 6 (2009): 515–526; Daniel Kahneman, Dan Lovallo, and Olivier Sibony, "Before You Make That Big Decision," *Harvard Business Review* 89, 6 (2011): 50–60; Robert Kegan and Lisa Laskow Lahey, *Immunity to Change: Immunity to Change: How to Overcome It and Unlock the Potential in Yourself and Your Organization* (Boston: Harvard Business Review Press, 2009); Patricia Margaret Brown King and Karen Strohm Kitchener, *Developing Reflective Judgment: Understanding and Promoting Intellectual Growth and Critical Thinking in Adolescents and Adults* (San Francisco: Jossey-Bass, 2004); Gary Klein, *Seeing What Others Don't: The Remarkable Ways We Gain Insights* (New York: PublicAffairs, 2013): Gary Klein, *Streetlights and Shadows: Searching for the Keys to Adaptive Decision Making* (Cambridge: MIT Press, 2011); Gary Klein "Naturalistic Decision-Making," *Human Factors* 50, 3 (2008): 456–460; Gary Klein, "Performing a Project PreMortem," *Harvard Business Review* 85, 9 (2007): 18–19; Gary Klein, Roberta Calderwood and Donald Macgregor," Critical Decision Method for Eliciting Knowledge," *Systems, Man and Cybernetics* 19, 3 (1989): 462–472; Gary Klein, Neil Hintze, and David Saab, "Thinking Inside the Box: The ShadowBox Method for Cognitive Skill Development," in *Proceedings of the 11th International Conference on Naturalistic Decision Making*, ed. H. Chaudet, L. Pellegrin, and N. Bonnardel, 2013, www.ndm11.org/proceedings/papers/ndm11.pdf; Gary Klein, Brian Moon, and Robert R. Hoffman, "Making Sense of Sensemaking 2: A Macrocognitive Model," *Intelligent Systems* 21, 5 (2006): 88–92; D.Q. McInerny, *Being Logical: A Guide to Good Thinking* (New York: Random House Trade Paperbacks, 2005); Katherine L. Milkman, Dolly Chugh, and Max H. Bazerman, "How Can Decision Making Be Improved?" *Perspectives* on *Psychological Science* 4, 4 (2009): 379–383; John E. Morrison and Larry L. Meliza, "Foundations of the After Action Review Process," ARI Special Report 42, Institute for Defense Analyses, Alexandria, VA, July 1999; Charlan Nemeth, Keith Brown, and John Rogers, "Devil's Advocate Versus Authentic Dissent: Stimulating Quantity and Quality," *European Journal of Social Psychology* 31, 6 (2001): 707–720; Richard W. Paul and Linda Elder, *Critical Thinking: Tools for Taking Charge of Your Professional and Personal Life* (Upper Saddle River, NJ: Financial Times Prentice Hall, 2002); Karol G. Ross, Gary Klein, Peter Thunholm, John F. Schmitt, and Holly C. Baxter, "The Recognition-Primed Decision Model," *Military Review* (July–August 2004): 6–10; J. Edward Russo and Paul J.H. Schoemaker, "Managing Overconfidence," *Sloan Management Review* 33, 2 (1992): 7–17; Margaret S. Salter and Gerald E. Klein, "After Action Reviews: Current Observations and Recommendations," ARI Research Report 1867, The Wexford Group International Inc., Vienna, VA, January 2007; David M. Schweiger, William R. Sandberg, and Paula L. Rechner, "Experiential Effects Of Dialectical Inquiry, Devil's Advocacy and Consensus Approaches to Strategic Decision Making," *Academy of Management Journal* 32, 4 (1989): 745–772; Charles R. Schwenk, "A Meta Analysis on the Comparative Effectiveness of Devil's Advocacy and Dialectical Inquiry," *Strategic Management Journal* 10, 3 (1989): 303–306; Charles R. Schwenk, "The Cognitive Perspective on Strategic Decision Making," *Journal of Management Studies* 25,1 (1988): 41–55; Winston R. Sieck, Gary Klein, Deborah A. Peluso, Jennifer L. Smith, Danyele Harris-Thompson, and Paul A. Gade, "FOCUS: A Model of Sensemaking," Army Research Institute Technical Report 1200, Klein Associates, Inc., Fairborn, OH, May 2007; U.S. Army, "A Leader's Guide to After-Action Reviews," Training Circular 25-20, 1993, www.acq.osd.mil/dpap/ccap/ cc/jcchb/Files/Topical/After_Action_Report/resources/tc25-20.pdf; Beth Veinott, Gary Klein, and Sterling Wiggins, "Evaluating the Effectiveness of the PreMortem Technique on Plan Confidence," Proceedings of the 7th International ISCRAM Conference—Seattle USA, May 2010, www.iscram.org/ISCRAM2010/Papers/175-Veinott_etal.pdf; Daniel T. Willingham, "Critical Thinking: Why Is It So Hard to Teach?" *Arts Education Policy Review* 109, 4 (2008): 21–32.

2. Paul and Elder, *Critical Thinking*, 25.

3. Klein, "Naturalistic Decision-Making," 457–458; Ross et al., "The Recognition-Primed Decision Model"; Gary Klein, *Streetlights and Shadows*, 90–91.

4. Daniel Kahneman, *Thinking, Fast and Slow* (New York: Farrar, Straus and Giroux, 2011); Bazerman and Moore, *Judgment in Managerial Decision Making*; Dan Ariely, *Predictably Irrational: The Hidden Forces That Shape Our Decision* (New York: HarperPerennial, 2009).

5. Klein, "Naturalistic Decision Making."

6. Kahneman and Klein, "Conditions for Intuitive Expertise."

7. Veinott et al., "Evaluating the Effectiveness of the PreMortem Technique on Plan Confidence."

8. Milkman et al., "How Can Decision Making Be Improved?"

9. Klein, *Seeing What Others Don't*.

10. Beck, *Cognitive Behavior Therapy*.

11. Kegan and Lahey, *Immunity to Change*.

12. Hess and Liedtka, *The Physics of Business Growth*, 80–100.

13. Steve Blank, *The Four Steps to the Epiphany* (Pescadero, CA: K&S Ranch, \
2013); Steve Blank and Bob Dorf, *The Startup Owner's Manual: The Step-By-Step Guide for Building a Great Company* (Pescadero, CA: K&S Ranch, 2012); Eric Ries, *The Lean Startup: How Today's Entrepreneurs Use Continuous Innovation to Create Radically Successful Businesses* (New York: Crown Business, 2011).

14. Hess and Liedtka, *The Physics of Business Growth*, 96–97.

15. Kegan and Lahey, *Immunity to Change*.

16. Ibid., 246.

17. Paul and Elder, *Critical Thinking*, 277–279.

18. U.S. Army, "A Leader's Guide to After-Action Reviews"; Margaret S. Salter and Gerald E. Klein, "After Action Reviews: Current Observations and Recommendations," ARI Research Report 1867, The Wexford Group International, Inc., Vienna, VA, January 2007; Morrison and Meliza, "Foundations of the After Action Review Process."

8. A Conversation with Dr. Gary Klein

1. Interview with Gary Klein via Skype, October 9, 2013.

9. Bridgewater Associates, LP: Building a Learning "Machine"

1. Excerpts from *Principles* and all related materials produced and provided by Bridgewater are protected by copyright and are quoted and reprinted here with express permission from Bridgewater Associates, LP and/or Ray Dalio. The facts in this chapter came from personal interviews with Ray Dalio on July 15 and September 18–19, 2013 and the following sources: Bridgewater Associates, LP Form ADV Uniform Application for Investment Advisor Application, filed March 28, 2013, Securities and Exchange Commission website, www.adviserinfo.sec.gov; John Cassidy, "Mastering the Machine" *New Yorker*, July 25, 2011, www.newyorker.com/reporting/2011/07/25/110725fa_fact_cassidy; Michelle Celarier and Lawrence Delevingne, "Ray Dalio's Radical Truth," *Institutional Investor*, March 2, 2011, www.institutionalinvestor.com/Article/2775995/Research/4079/Overview.html#.UsrzFqU5cds; Ray Dalio, *Principles*, Bridgewater Associates, LP website, www.Bridgewaterater.com/Uploads/FileManager/Principles/Bridgewater-Associates-Ray-Dalio-Principles.pdf; Lucy Kellaway, "Principles for Living We Could Do Without," *Financial Times*, March 23, 2010, www.ft.com/intl/cms/s/0/be8ce2ce-650d-11df-b648-00144feab49a.html; Bess Levin, "Bridgewater Associates: Be the Hyena. Attack the Wildebeest," *Dealbreaker*, May 10, 2010, http://dealbreaker.com/2010/05/bridgewater-associates-be-the-hyena-attack-the-wildebeest/.

Kip McDaniel, "Is Ray Dalio the Steve Jobs of Investing?" *aiCIO*, December 11, 2011, http://ai-cio.com/channel/newsmakers/is_ray_dalio_the_steve_jobs_of_investing_.html; "Ray Dalio: Man and Machine," *Economist*, March 10, 2012, www.economist.com/node/21549968; Kevin Roose, "Pursuing Self Interest in Harmony With the Laws of the

Universe and Contributing to Evolution Is Universally Rewarded," *New York Magazine*, April 10, 2011, http://nymag.com/news/business/wallstreet/ray-dalio-2011-4/.

2. Dalio, *Principles*, 40.

3. Ibid., 6.

4. Cassidy, "Mastering the Machine."

5. McDaniel, "Is Ray Dalio the Steve Jobs of Investing?"

6. Ibid.

7. Ibid.

8. Bridgewater Associates, LP (March 28, 2013), Form ADV.

9. McDaniel, "Is Ray Dalio the Steve Jobs of Investing?"

10. "Ray Dalio: Man and Machine."

11. Dalio, *Principles*, 2.

12. Ibid., footnotes 16, 10.

13. Cassidy, "Mastering the Machine."

14. Dalio, *Principles*, 12.

15. Ibid., 61.

16. Ibid., 12.

17. Stuart Firestein, *Ignorance* (Oxford: Oxford University Press, 2012), 12.

18. Dalio, *Principles*; Ray Dalio, July 15 and September 18–19, 2013, personal interviews.

19. Dalio, *Principles*, 17–21.

20. Dalio, *Principles* 38.

21. Ibid., 22.

22. Ibid., 12.

23. Ibid., 61.

24. Ibid., 18.

25. Ibid., 118.

26. Ibid., 54.

27. Ibid.

28. Ibid.

29. Bridgewater Associates, LP, archive video.

30. Michael B. Parkyn, "Making More Mike Stranks—Teaching Value in the United States Marine Corps," in *Leading with Values: Positivity, Virtue, and High Performance,* ed. Edward D. Hess and Kim S. Cameron (Cambridge: Cambridge University Press, 2006), 213–233; Sgt. Mike Strank and his five weary men were the ones who raised the American flag on Iwo Jima.

31. Dalio, *Principles*, 56–57.

32. Ibid., 56.

33. Excerpted from Principles Nos. 8–19 in Dalio, *Principles*, 58–60.

34. Brad Stone, "The Secrets of Bezos: How Amazon Became the Everything Store," Businessweek.com, October 10, 2013, www.businessweek.com/articles/2013-10-10/jeff-bezos-and-the-age-of-amazon-excerpt-from-the-everything-store-by-brad-stone.

35. Ray Dalio, personal interview, July 15, 2013.

36. Parkyn, "Making More Mike Stranks," 214.

37. Ibid., 232.

38. Personal interviews at the Marine Corps University, 2004.

39. Dalio, *Principles*, 48.

40. Ibid., 89.

41. Ibid.

42. Ibid., 90.

43. Ibid.

44. Ibid., 91.

45. Ibid.

46. Ibid., 92.

47. All names of people in personal conversations are fictional; the conversations in substance are real.

48. Some names and functional job areas have been changed to protect individual privacy.

49. Dalio, *Principles*, 70.

50. Ibid.

10. Intuit, Inc.: "It's Time to Bury Caesar"

1. Most of the facts in this chapter come from Intuit, Inc.'s website, two interviews with Kaaren Hanson, Intuit's vice president of design, which took place in June and September 2013, a site visit to Intuit on June 11, 2013, and the following sources: Scott Cook, "Lessons Learned: CEOs—Get Honest Feedback on Your Performance," Talk at HustleCon 2013 [video file], Intuit Network website, August 26, 2013, http://network. intuit.com/2013/08/26/scott-cook-intuit-4/; Robin Goldwyn Blumenthal, "Don't Write Off Intuit," *Barrons*, September 22, 2011, http://online.barrons.com/article/SB5000142 4053111904706204578006520653753406.html; Deanna Hartley, "The Talent Whisperer: Intuit's Sherry Whiteley," *Talent Management*, March 26, 2013, http://talentmgt.com/ articles/view/the-talent-whisperer-intuit-s-sherry-whiteley; "Catalyst—An Intuit Innovation Experience," Intuit Network website, January 29, 2013, http://network.intuit. com/2013/01/25/innovation-catalyst/; Lucas Mearian, "Intuit forces IT, engineers into room until they get it right," *Computerworld*, October 19, 2012, www.computerworld. com/s/article/9232594/Intuit_forces_IT_engineers_into_room_until_they_get_it_ right?taxonomyId=237&pageNumber=1; Kelly Schalow, "Intuit Inc. Design for Delight Communication Platform," Kelly Schalow website, www.kellyschalow.com/d4d/; Brad Smith, "Three Things Every Leader Should Do in a Meeting," Intuit Network website, July 9, 2013, http://network.intuit.com/2013/07/09/meeting-tips/; Brad Smith, "Five New Year's Resolutions Every Business Leader Should Make," Intuit Network website, January 7, 2013, http://network.intuit.com/2013/01/07/five-new-years-resolutions-every-business-leader-should-make/; Bruce Upbin, "Why Intuit Is More Innovative Than Your Company," *Forbes*, September 24, 2012, www.forbes.com/sites/bruceupbin/2012/09/04/ intuit-the-30-year-old-startup/.

2. Ibid.

3. James L. Heskett, "Scott Cook and Intuit," Harvard Business School Case 396–282, March 1996 (revised January 1997).

4. Intuit, Inc. "Corporate Profile," Intuit, Inc. website, www.about.intuit.com/about_intuit/profile/profile/.

5. Jeanne Liedtka, Andrew King, and Kevin Bennett, *Solving Problems with Design Thinking: Ten Stories of What Works* (New York: Columbia University Press, 2013), 180.

6. Intuit, Inc., "Catalyst—An Intuit Innovation Experience."

7. Ibid.

8. Liedtka et al., *Solving Problems with Design Thinking*; Jeanne Liedtka, Tim Ogilvie, and Rachel Brozenske, *The Designing for Growth Field Book: A Step-by-Step Project Guide* (New York: Columbia University Press, 2014); Jeanne Liedtka and Tim Ogilvie, *Designing for Growth: A Design Thinking Tool Kit for Managers* (New York: Columbia University Press, 2011).

9. Ibid.

10. Kaaren Hanson, personal interview, June 11, 2013.

11. Ibid.

12. Steve Blank, *The Four Steps to the Epiphany* (Pescadero, CA: K&S Ranch, 2013); Steve Blank and Bob Dorf, *The Startup Owner's Manual: The Step-By-Step Guide for Building a Great Company* (Pescadero, CA: K&S Ranch, 2012).

13. Scott Cook, "Leadership in the Innovation Age: Four Principles for Leaders," Intuit Network website, December 3, 2012, http://network.intuit.com/2012/12/03/leadership-in-the-innovation-age-four-principles-for-leaders/.

14. Scott Cook, "Creating a Culture of Experimentation: Ideas and Best Practices," Talk at Lean Startup Conference 2012 [video file], YouTube.com, December 29, 2012, www.youtube.com/watch?v=BoHyuX9ZLus.

15. Brad Smith, "Lean Startup Leadership: It's Time to Bury Caesar," Intuit Network website, November 30, 2012, http://network.intuit.com/2012/11/30/lean-startup-leadership-its-time-to-bury-caesar-2/.

16. "Field Guide to Rapid Experimentation," Presentation transcript, SlideShare, May 2, 2013, www.slideshare.net/IntuitInc/experiment-guide-bookslides.

17. Ibid.

18. Scott Cook, "Lessons Learned: Run Experiments Early," Talk at Hustle-Con 2013 [video file], Intuit Network website, August 14, 2013, http://network.intuit.com/2013/08/14/scott-cook-intuit-3/.

19. Scott Cook, "Lessons Learned: Savor Surprises," Talk at HustleCon 2013 [video file], Intuit Network website, August 7, 2013, http://network.intuit.com/2013/08/07/scott-cook-intuit-2/.

20. Smith, "Three Things Every Leader Should Do in a Meeting."

21. Kaaren Hanson, personal interview, June 11, 2013.

22. Ibid.

23. Cook, "Lessons Learned: CEOs—Get Honest Feedback on Your Performance."

24. Ibid.

25. Jim Collins, *Good to Great: Why Some Companies Make the Leap . . . and Others Don't* (New York: HarperBusiness, 2001).

26. Cook, "Lessons Learned: CEOs—Get Honest Feedback on Your Performance."

27. Smith, "Three Things Every Leader Should Do in a Meeting."

28. Ibid.

29. Brad Smith, "Managing Your Most Precious Resource: Time," Intuit Network website, June 24, 2013, http://network.intuit.com/2013/06/24/improve-time-management/.

11. United Parcel Service, Inc.: Being "Constructively Dissatisfied"

1. This chapter is adapted from Edward D. Hess and Katherine Ludwig, "United Parcel Service, Inc.: The Challenge of Protecting Organizational DNA," UVA-S-0238 (Charlottesville, VA: Darden Business, 2014), an update of Edward D. Hess, "United Parcel Service of America, Inc.," UVA-S-0134 (Charlottesville, VA: Darden Business, 2007), which was adapted from Edward D. Hess, "UPS: Brown's Organic Growth Story," in *The Search for Organic Growth*, ed. Edward D. Hess and Robert K. Kazanjian (New York: Cambridge University Press, 2006), 35–48.

2. From "A Talk with Joe," remarks to the UPS Plant Managers Conference, (1956) in *Jim Casey: Our Partnership Legacy* (United Parcel Service of America, Inc., 1985), 96.

3. Mike Brewster and Frederick Dalzell, *Driving Change: The UPS Approach to Business,* (New York: Hyperion, 2007), 43–44.

4. Hess, "UPS: Brown's Organic Growth Story," 43.

5. Brewster and Dalzell, *Driving Change*, 85.

6. Ibid., 78.

7. Ibid., 137.

8. UPS Corporate Sustainability Report 2012, United Parcel Service, Inc. website, www.responsibility.ups.com/Sustainability.

9. Brewster and Dalzell, *Driving Change*.

10. D. Scott Davis, "Where Trade Crosses Borders, Armies Do Not," September 12, 2011, United Parcel Service, Inc. website, www.ups.com/pressroom/us/speeches?WT.svl=SubNav.

11. Hess, "UPS: Brown's Organic Growth Story," 37.

12. Marcus Wohlsen, "The Astronomical Math behind UPS' New Tool to Deliver Packages Faster," *Wired,* June 13, 2013, www.wired.com/business/2013/06/ups-astronomical-math/.

13. Hess, "United Parcel Service of America, Inc."

14. Wohlsen, "The Astronomical Math behind UPS' New Tool to Deliver Packages Faster."

15. Ibid.

16. United Parcel Service, Inc., "Telematics," United Parcel Service, Inc. website, www.ups.com/content/us/en/bussol/browse/leadership-telematics.html.

17. UPS 2012 Annual Report, United Parcel Service, Inc. website, www.investors. ups.com/phoenix.zhtml?c=62900&p=irol-reportsannual.

18. United Parcel Service, Inc., "Company History 1991–1999," United Parcel Service, Inc. website, www.ups.com/content/us/en/about/history/index.html?WT.svl=SubNav.

19. Hess, "UPS: Brown's Organic Growth Story," 39.

20. UPS 2012 Annual Report.

21. Hess, "UPS: Brown's Organic Growth Story," 43.

22. Ibid.

23. Ibid., 43–44.

24. UPS Corporate Sustainability Report 2012.

25. Ibid.

26. Ibid.

27. Hess, "United Parcel Service of America, Inc."

28. United Parcel Service, Inc., "Benefits," United Parcel Service, Inc. website, https://ups.managehr.com/benefits.htm.

29. Hess, "UPS: Brown's Organic Growth Story," 42.

30. Ibid.

31. UPS Corporate Sustainability Report 2012.

32. Ladan Nikravan, "UPS: Promoting Learning," *Chief Learning Officer*, May 20, 2013, http://clomedia.com/articles/view/ups-promoting-learning.

33. Ibid.

34. United Parcel Service, Inc., "UPS Integrad," United Parcel Service, Inc. website, www.community.ups.com/Safety/Training+For+Safety/UPS+Integrad.

35. UPS 2012 Annual Report.

36. *Jim Casey: Our Partnership Legacy* 4.

Epilogue

1. I learned the three "I's" from a great teacher and friend, Professor Alec Horniman of the University of Virginia Darden School of Business.

Bibliography

Abell, Millie. "Deepening Distributed Learning: Motivating Soldiers to Learn, Grow, Achieve." Paper presented at the Interservice/Industry Training, Simulation & Education Conference (I/ITSEC). National Training Systems Association, 2003.

Algoe, Sara B., and Barbara L. Fredrickson. "Emotional Fitness and the Movement of Affective Science from Lab to Field." American Psychologist 66, 1 (2011): 35–42.

Allodi, Mara W. "The Meaning of Social Climate of Learning Environments: Some Reasons Why We Do Not Care Enough About It." Learning Environments Research 13, 2 (2010): 89–104.

Amabile, Teresa, and Steven Kramer. "How Leaders Kill Meaning at Work." McKinsey Quarterly, January 2012. www.mckinsey.com/insights/leading_in_the_21st_century/how_leaders_kill_meaning_at_work.

Amabile, Teresa, and Steven Kramer. The Progress Principle. Boston: Harvard Business Review Press, 2011.

Amason, Allen C. "Distinguishing the Effects of Functional and Dysfunctional Conflict on Strategic Decision Making: Resolving a Paradox for Top Management Teams." Academy of Management Journal 39, 1 (1996): 123–148.

Ambrose, Susan A., Michael W. Bridges, Michele DiPietro, Marsha C. Lovett, and Marie K. Norman. How Learning Works: Seven Research-Based Principles for Smart Teaching. San Francisco: Wiley, 2010.

Ames, Carole. "Classrooms: Goals, Structures, and Student Motivation." Journal of Educational Psychology 84, 3 (1992): 261–271.

Anderson, John R., Daniel Bothell, Michael D. Byrne, Scott Douglass, Christian Lebiere, and Yulin Qin. "An Integrated Theory of the Mind." *Psychological Review* 111, 4 (2004): 1036–1060.

Andriopoulos, Constantine, and Marianne W. Lewis. "Exploitation-Exploration Tensions and Organizational Ambidexterity: Managing Paradoxes of Innovation." *Organization Science* 20, 4 (2009): 696–717.

Anseel, Frederik, Nico W. Van Yperen, Onne Janssen, and Wouter Duyck. "Feedback Type as a Moderator of the Relationship Between Achievement Goals and Feedback Reactions." *Journal of Occupational and Organizational Psychology* 84, 4 (2011): 703–722.

Argyris, Chris. *Organizational Traps: Leadership, Culture, Organizational Design.* Oxford: Oxford University Press, 2010.

Argyris, Chris. "Teaching Smart People How to Learn." *Harvard Business Review* 69, 3 (1991): 99–109.

Ariely, Dan. *Predictably Irrational, Revised and Expanded Edition: The Hidden Forces That Shape Our Decisions.* New York: HarperPerennial, 2009.

Arnsten, Amy F.T. "Enhanced: The Biology of Being Frazzled." *Science* 280, 5370 (1998): 1711–1712.

Ashby, Gregory F., Alice M. Isen, and And U. Turken. "A Neuropsychological Theory of Positive Affect and Its Influence on Cognition." *Psychological Review* 106, 3 (1999): 529–550.

Aspinwall, Lisa G. "The Psychology of Future-Oriented Thinking: From Achievement to Proactive Coping, Adaptation, and Aging." *Motivation and Emotion* 29, 4 (2005): 203–235.

Aspinwall, Lisa G., and Linda Richter. "Optimism and Self-Mastery Predict More Rapid Disengagement from Unsolvable Tasks in the Presence of Alternatives." *Motivation and Emotion* 23, 3 (1999): 221–245.

Baard, Paul P., Edward L. Deci, and Richard M. Ryan. "Intrinsic Need Satisfaction: A Motivational Basis of Performance and Well-Being in Two Work Settings." *Journal of Applied Social Psychology* 34, 10 (2004): 2045–2068.

Badaracco, Joseph L., Jr. *Leading Quietly: An Unorthodox Guide to Doing the Right Thing.* Boston: Harvard Business School Publishing, 2002.

Bakker, Arnold B., and Wilmar B. Schaufeli. "Positive Organizational Behavior: Engaged Employees in Flourishing Organizations." *Journal of Organizational Behavior* 29, 2 (2008): 147–154.

Bandura, Albert. "Personal and Collective Efficacy in Human Adaptation and Change." *Advances in Psychological Science* 1 (1998): 51–71.

Bandura, Albert. "Perceived Self-Efficacy in Cognitive Development and Functioning." *Educational Psychologist* 28, 2 (1993): 117–148.

Bargh, John A., and Tanya L. Chartrand. "The Unbearable Automaticity of Being." *American Psychologist* 54, 7 (1999): 462–479.

Barron, Brigid. "When Smart Groups Fail." *Journal of the Learning Sciences* 12, 3 (2003): 307–359.

Barsade, Sigal G. Lakshmi Ramarajan, and Drew Westen. "Implicit Affect in Organizations." *Research in Organizational Behavior* 29 (2009): 135–162.

Bartone, Paul T. "Resilience Under Military Operational Stress: Can Leaders Influence Hardiness?" *Military Psychology* 18, Suppl (2006): S131–S148.

Bartone, Paul T. "Hardiness Protects Against War-Related Stress in Army Reserve Forces." *Consulting Psychology Journal: Practice and Research* 51, 2 (1999): 72–82.

Bartone, Paul T., Robert R. Roland, James J. Picanoa, and Thomas J. Williams. "Psychological Hardiness Predicts Success in US Army Special Forces Candidates." *International Journal of Selection and Assessment* 16, 1 (2008): 78–81.

Baumard, Philippe, and William H. Starbuck. "Learning from Failures: Why It May Not Happen." *Long Range Planning* 38, 3 (2005): 281–298.

Bazerman, Max H., George F. Loewenstein, and Sally Blount White. "Reversals of Preference in Allocation Decisions: Judging an Alternative Versus Choosing Among Alternatives." *Administrative Science Quarterly* 37, 2 (1992): 220–240.

Bazerman, Max H., and Don A. Moore. *Judgment in Managerial Decision Making*. 7th ed. Hoboken, NJ: Wiley, 2009.

Beck, Judith S. *Cognitive Behavior Therapy*. 2nd ed. New York: Guilford Press, 2011.

Behar, Howard, and Janet Goldstein. *It's Not About the Coffee: Leadership Principles from a Life at Starbucks*. New York: Penguin, 2007.

Berns, Gregory. *Iconoclast: A Neuroscientist Reveals How to Think Differently*. Boston: Harvard Business Review Press, 2008.

Birkinshaw, Julian, Cyril Bouquet, and J.L. Barsoux. "The 5 Myths of Innovation." *MIT Sloan Management Review* 52, 2 (2012). http://sloanreview.mit.edu/article/the-5-myths-of-innovation/.

Blanchette, Isabelle, and Anne Richards. "The Influence of Affect on Higher Level Cognition: A Review of Research on Interpretation, Judgment, Decision Making and Reasoning." *Cognition & Emotion* 24, 4 (2010): 561–595.

Blank, Steve. "Qualcomm's Corporate Entrepreneurship Program—Lessons Learned (Part 2)." SteveBlank.com, January 30, 2013, http://steveblank.com/2013/01/30/qualcomms-corporate-entrepreneurship-program-lesson-learned-part-2/.

Blank, Steve. "Designing a Corporate Entrepreneurship Program—A Qualcomm Case Study (Part 1 of 2)." SteveBlank.com, January 28, 2013, http://steveblank.com/2013/01/28/qualcomm-the-best-corporate-entrepreneurship-program-youve-never-heard-of/.

Blank, Steve. *The Four Steps to the Epiphany*. Pescadero, CA: K&S Ranch, 2013.

Blank, Steve, and Bob Dorf. *The Startup Owner's Manual: The Step-By-Step Guide for Building a Great Company*. Pescadero, CA: K&S Ranch, 2012.

Bloom, Benjamin S. "The 2 Sigma Problem: The Search for Methods of Group Instruction as Effective as One-to-One Tutoring." *Educational Researcher* 13, 6 (1984): 4–16.

Blumenthal, Robin Goldwyn. "Don't Write Off Intuit." *Barron's*, September 22, 2011, http://online.barrons.com/article/SB50001424053111904706204578006520653753406.html.

Bohm, David. *On Dialogue*. Abingdon, Oxon: Routeledge Classics, 2004.

Bohm, David, Donald Factor, and Peter Garrett. "Dialogue: A Proposal." Infed.org, http://infed.org/archives/e-texts/bohm_dialogue.htm.

Bourne, Lyle E., Jr., and Alice F. Healy. *Train Your Mind for Peak Performance: A Science-Based Approach for Achieving Your Goals.* Washington, DC: American Psychological Association, 2013.

Bramesfeld, Kosha D., and Karen Gasper. "Happily Putting the Pieces Together: A Test of Two Explanations for the Effects of Mood on Group-Level Information Processing." *British Journal of Social Psychology* 47, 2 (2008): 285–309.

Bransford, John D., Ann L., Brown, and Rodney R. Cocking, eds. *How People Learn: Brain, Mind, Experience, and School.* Washington, DC: National Academy Press, 2000.

Braudy, Susan. "He's Woody Allen's Not-So-Silent Partner." *New York Times,* August 21, 1977.

Brewster, Mike, and Frederick Dalzell. *Driving Change: The UPS Approach to Business.* New York: Hyperion, 2007.

Bridgewater Associates, LP Form ADV Uniform Application for Investment Advisor Application. Filed March 28, 2013. Securities and Exchange Commission website, www.adviserinfo.sec.gov.

Broadie, Alexander. *The Scottish Enlightenment.* Edinburgh: Birlinn, 2011.

Brookfield, Stephen D. *Teaching for Critical Thinking: Tools and Techniques to Help Students Question Their Assumptions.* San Francisco: Jossey-Bass, 2012.

Brown, Kirk Warren, Richard M. Ryan, and J. David Creswell. "Mindfulness: Theoretical Foundations and Evidence for Its Salutary Effects." *Psychological Inquiry* 18, 4 (2007): 211–237.

Brown, Paul B. "Analyzing Failure Beforehand." *New York Times,* September 22, 2007. www.nytimes.com/2007/09/22/business/media/22offline.html?fta=y&_r=0.

Brown, Tim. "How Do You Build a Culture of Innovation?" *Yale Insights,* May 2013, http://insights.som.yale.edu/insights/how-do-you-build-culture-innovation.

Brynjolfsson, Erik, and Andrew McAfee. *The Second Machine Age: Work, Progress, and Prosperity in a Time of Brilliant Technologies.* New York: Norton, 2014.

Buckingham, Marcus, and Curt Coffman. *First, Break All The Rules: What The World's Greatest Managers Do Differently.* New York: Simon & Schuster, 1999.

Burnison, Gary. "The CEO Pay Circus of 2013." March 21, 2013. Yahoo Finance/The Exchange, http://finance.yahoo.com/blogs/the-exchange/ceo-pay-circus-2013-214028626. html.

Burns, Andrea B., Jessica S. Brown, Natalie Sachs-Ericsson, E. Ashby Plant, J. Thomas Curtis, Barbara L. Fredrickson, and Thomas E. Joiner. "Upward Spirals of Positive Emotion and Coping: Replication, Extension, and Initial Exploration of Neurochemical Substrates." *Personality and Individual Differences* 44, 2 (2008): 360–370.

Burns, William R., Jr. "Developing More Adaptable Individuals and Institutions." IDA-P-4535. Institute for Defense Analysis, Alexandria, VA, February 2010.

Cameron, Kim S. *Practicing Positive Leadership: Tools and Techniques That Create Extraordinary Results.* San Francisco: Berrett-Koehler, 2013.

Cameron, Kim S. *Positive Leadership: Strategies for Extraordinary Performance.* San Francisco: Berrett-Koehler, 2012.

Cameron, Kim, Arran Caza, and David Bright. "Positive Deviance, Organizational Virtuousness, and Performance." Working Paper, University of Michigan Business School, 2002.

Cameron, Kim S., Jane E. Dutton, and Robert E. Quinn, eds. *Positive Organizational Scholarship: Foundations of a New Discipline.* San Francisco: Berrett-Koehler, 2003.

Cameron, Kim S., Carlos Mora, Trevor Leutscher, and Margaret Calarco. "Effects of Positive Practices on Organizational Effectiveness." *Journal of Applied Behavioral Science* 47, 3 (2011): 266–308.

Cameron, Kim S., and Gretchen M. Spreitzer, eds. *The Oxford Handbook of Positive Organizational Scholarship.* New York: Oxford University Press, 2012.

Campbell, Donald J. "Embracing Change: Examination of a 'Capabilities and Benevolence' Beliefs Model in a Sample of Military Cadets." *Military Psychology* 18, 2 (2006): 131–148.

Capodagli, Bill. "Pixar's Eight Beliefs That Create a Culture of Passion." *HRM Today,* October 20, 2010, www.hrmtoday.com/featured-stories/pixar's-eight-beliefs-that-create-a-culture-of-passion/.

Carroll, Michael. *The Mindful Leader: Awakening Your Natural Management Skills through Mindfulness Meditation.* Boston: Trumpeter, 2008.

Cassidy, John. "Mastering the Machine." *New Yorker,* July 25, 2011, www.newyorker.com/reporting/2011/07/25/110725fa_fact_cassidy.

Catalino, Lahnna I., and Barbara L. Fredrickson. "A Tuesday in the Life of a Flourisher: The Role of Positive Emotional Reactivity in Optimal Mental Health." *Emotion* 11, 4 (2011): 938–950.

"Catalyst—An Intuit Innovation Experience." Intuit Network website, January 29, 2013, http://network.intuit.com/2013/01/25/innovation-catalyst/.

Catmull, Ed. "How Pixar Fosters Collective Creativity." *Harvard Business Review* September (2008): 64.

Celarier, Michelle, and Lawrence Delevingne. "Ray Dalio's Radical Truth." *Institutional Investor,* March 2, 2011, www.institutionalinvestor.com/Article/2775995/Research/4079/Overview.html#.UsrzFqU5cds.

Chartrand, Tanya L., and John A. Bargh. "The Chameleon Effect: The Perception–Behavior Link and Social Interaction." *Journal of Personality and Social Psychology* 76, 6 (1999): 893–910.

Chouinard, Yvon. *Let My People Go Surfing.* New York: Penguin Group, 2005.

Chugh, Dolly, and Max H. Bazerman. "Bounded Awareness: What You Fail to See Can Hurt You." *Mind & Society* 6, 1 (2007): 1–18.

Clark, Ruth Colvin. *Building Expertise: Cognitive Methods for Training and Performance Improvement.* San Francisco: Pfeiffer, 2008.

Clifford, Margaret M. "Risk Taking: Theoretical, Empirical and Educational Considerations." *Educational Psychologist* 26, 3–4 (1991): 263–297.

Clifford, Margaret M. "Students Need Challenge, Not Easy Success." *Educational Leadership* 48, 1 (1990): 22–26.

Clifford, Margaret M. "Failure Tolerance and Academic Risk-Taking in Ten-to-Twelve-Year-Old Students." *British Journal of Educational Psychology* 58, 1 (1988): 15–27.

Clifford, Margaret M. "The Effects of Ability, Strategy, and Effort Attributions for Educational, Business, and Athletic Failure." *British Journal of Educational Psychology* 56, 2 (1986): 169–179.

Clifford, Margaret M. "Thoughts on a Theory of Constructive Failure." *Educational Psychologist* 19, 2 (1984): 108–120.

Clifford, Margaret M., and Fen-Chang Chou, "Effects of Payoff and Task Context on Academic Risk Taking." *Journal of Educational Psychology* 83, 4 (1991): 499–507.

Clore, Gerald L., and Jeffrey R. Huntsinger. "How Emotions Inform Judgment and Regulate Thought." *Trends in Cognitive Science* 11, 9 (2007): 393–399.

Clore, Gerald L., and Janet Palmer. "Affective Guidance of Intelligent Agents: How Emotion Controls Cognition." *Cognitive Systems Research* 10, 1 (2009): 21–30.

Cohen, Marvin S., Leonard Adelman, Terry Bresnick, F. Freeman Marvin, Eduardo Salas, and Sharon L. Riedel. "Dialogue as Medium (and Message) for Training Critical Thinking." In *Expertise Out of Context: Proceedings of the Sixth International Conference on Naturalistic Decision Making*, ed. Robert R. Hoffman. New York: Taylor & Francis, 2007: 219–260.

Cohen, Marvin S., Bryan B. Thompson, Leonard Adelman, Terry A. Bresnick, Lokendra Shastri, and Sharon L. Riedel, "Training Critical Thinking for the Battlefield: Volume I: Basis in Cognitive Theory and Research." Army Research Institute Technical Report 00-2. Cognitive Technologies, Inc., Arlington, VA, June 2000.

Cohn, Michael A., and Barbara L. Fredrickson. "In Search of Durable Positive Psychology Interventions: Predictors and Consequences of Long-Term Positive Behavior Change." *Journal of Positive Psychology* 5, 5 (2010): 355–366.

Collins, Jim. *How the Mighty Fall: And Why Some Companies Never Give In.* New York: Jim Collins, 2009.

Collins, Jim. *Good to Great: Why Some Companies Make the Leap . . . and Others Don't.* New York: HarperBusiness, 2001.

Collins, Jim. "Level 5 Leadership: The Triumph of Humility and Fierce Resolve." *Harvard Business Review* 79, 1 (2001): 66–76.

Collins, Jim, and Jerry I. Porras. *Built to Last: Successful Habits of Visionary Companies.* New York: HarperBusiness Essentials, 2002.

Combs, Arthur W. "Affective Education or None at All." *Educational Leadership* 39, 7 (1982): 495–497.

Combs, Arthur W. "Humanism, Education, and the Future." *Educational Leadership* 35, 4 (1978): 300–303.

Combs, Arthur W. "A Perceptual View of the Adequate Personality." In *Perceiving, Behaving, Becoming: A New Focus for Education: Yearbook 1962.* Alexandria, VA: Association for Supervision and Curriculum Development, 1962: 50–64.

Conner, Marcia L., and James G. Clawson. *Creating a Learning Culture: Strategy, Technology, and Practice.* Cambridge: Cambridge University Press, 2004.

Cook, Scott. "Lessons Learned: CEOs—Get Honest Feedback on Your Performance." Talk at HustleCon 2013 [video file]. Intuit Network website, August 26, 2013, http://network.intuit.com/2013/08/26/scott-cook-intuit-4/.

Cook, Scott. "Lessons Learned: Run Experiments Early." Talk at HustleCon 2013 [video file]. Intuit Network website, August 14, 2013, http://network.intuit.com/2013/08/14/scott-cook-intuit-3/.

Cook, Scott. "Lessons Learned: Savor Surprises." Talk at HustleCon 2013 [video file]. Intuit Network website, August 7, 2013, http://network.intuit.com/2013/08/07/scott-cook-intuit-2/.

Cook, Scott. "Creating a Culture of Experimentation: Ideas and Best Practices." Talk at Lean Startup Conference 2012. YouTube website, December 29, 2012, www.youtube.com/watch?v=BoHyuX9ZLus.

Cook, Scott. "Leadership in the Innovation Age: Four Principles for Leaders." Intuit Network website, December 3, 2012, http://network.intuit.com/2012/12/03/leadership-in-the-innovation-age-four-principles-for-leaders/.

Cornelius-White, Jeffrey. "Learner-Centered Teacher-Student Relationships Are Effective: A Meta-Analysis." *Review of Educational Research* 77, 1 (2007): 113–143.

Cornum, Rhonda, Michael D. Matthews, and Martin E.P. Seligman. "Comprehensive Soldier Fitness: Building Resilience in a Challenging Institutional Context." *American Psychologist* 66, 1 (2011): 4–9.

Cors, Rebecca. "What Is a Learning Organization? Reflections on the Literature and Practitioner Perspectives." University of Wisconsin-Madison, May 5, 2003, www.engr.wisc.edu/services/elc/lor/files/Learning_Org_Lit_Review.pdf.

Coutu, Diane L. "The Anxiety of Learning. The HBR Interview." *Harvard Business Review* 80, 3 (2002): 100–106.

Dalio, Ray. Principles. Bridgewater Associates, LP website, www.bwater.com/Uploads/FileManager/Principles/Bridgewater-Associates-Ray-Dalio-Principles.pdf, accessed January 1, 2014.

Damasio, Antonio. *Descartes' Error: Emotion, Reason, and the Human Brain.* New York: Penguin, 1994.

Damasio, Antonio R. "Descartes' Error and the Future of Human Life." *Scientific American* 271, 4 (1994): 144.

Darling, Marilyn J., and Charles S. Parry. "After-Action Reviews: Linking Reflection and Planning in a Learning Practice." *Reflections* 3, 2 (2001): 64–72.

Darling-Hammond, Linda. "Session 1: How People Learn: Introduction to Learning Theory." The Learning Classroom: Theory Into Practice. Annenberg Learner website, www.learner.org/courses/learningclassroom/session_overviews/intro_home1.html, accessed January 15, 2014.

D'Aveni, Richard A. *Hypercompetition.* New York: Free Press, 1994.

Davidson, Richard J., and Sharon Begley. *The Emotional Life of Your Brain: How Its Unique Patterns Affect the Way You Think, Feel, and Live—and How You Can Change Them.* New York: Plume, 2013.

Davidson, Richard J., Jon Kabat-Zinn, Jessica Schumacher, Melissa Rosenkranz, Daniel Muller, Saki F. Santorelli, Ferris Urbanowski, Anne Harrington, Katherine Bonus, and John F. Sheridan. "Alterations in Brain and Immune Function Produced by Mindfulness Meditation." *Psychosomatic Medicine* 65, 4 (2003): 564–570.

Davis, D. Scott. "Where Trade Crosses Borders, Armies Do Not." United Parcel Service, Inc. website, September 12, 2011, www.ups.com/pressroom/us/speeches?WT. svl=SubNav.

de Bono, Edward. *Lateral Thinking: Creativity Step by Step.* New York: Harper Colophon, 1990.

Deci, Edward L. *Why We Do What We Do: Understanding Self-Motivation.* New York: Penguin, 1996.

Deci, Edward L., and Richard M. Ryan. "The 'What' and 'Why' of Goal Pursuits: Human Needs and the Self-Determination of Behavior." *Psychological Inquiry* 11, 4 (2000): 227–268.

de Geus, Arie. *The Living Company.* Boston: Harvard Business School Press, 1997.

De Houwer, Jan, and Dirk Hermans, eds. *Cognition & Emotion: Reviews of Current Research and Theories.* Hove, UK: Psychology Press, 2010.

De Meyer, Arnoud, Christoph H. Loch, and Michael T. Pich. "From Variation to Chaos." *MIT Sloan Management Review* 43, 2 (2002): 60–67.

Deslauriers, Louis, Ellen Schelew, and Carl Wieman. "Improved Learning in a Large-Enrollment Physics Class." *Science* 332, 6031 (2011): 862–864.

Detert, James R., and Amy C. Edmondson. "Implicit Voice Theories: Taken-for-Granted Rules of Self-Censorship at Work." *Academy of Management Journal* 54, 3 (2011): 461–488.

Deutschman, Alan. "The Fabric of Creativity: At W.L. Gore, Innovation Is More Than Skin Deep: The Culture Is as Imaginative as the Products." Fast Company, December 2004. www.fastcompany.com/51733/fabric-creativity.

Deutschman, Alan. "Gore's Text for Innovation: W.L. Gore's New Rules of Business Start with Breaking the Old Rules." Fast Company, December 2004. www.fastcompany. com/51510/gores-text-innovation.

Dewey, John. *Experience & Education.* New York: Touchstone, 1997.

Diamandis, Peter H., and Steven Kotler. *Abundance: The Future Is Better Than You Think.* New York: Free Press, 2012.

Diener, Carol I., and Carol S. Dweck. "An Analysis of Learned Helplessness: Continuous Changes in Performance, Strategy, and Achievement Cognitions Following Failure." *Journal of Personality and Social Psychology* 36, 5 (1978): 451–462.

Doidge, Norman. *The Brain That Changes Itself: Stories of Personal Triumph from the Frontiers of Brain Science.* New York: Penguin, 2007.

Donaldson, Stewart I., Mihaly Csikszentmihalyi, and Jeanne Nakamura, eds. *Applied Positive Psychology: Improving Everyday Life, Health, Schools, Work, and Society.* New York: Routledge, 2011.

Donaldson, Stewart I., and Ia Ko. "Positive Organizational Psychology, Behavior, and Scholarship: A Review of the Emerging Literature and Evidence Base." *Journal of Positive Psychology* 5, 3 (2010): 177–191.

Dreisbach, Gesine, and Thomas Goschke. "How Positive Affect Modulates Cognitive Control: Reduced Perseveration at the Cost of Increased Distractibility." *Journal of Experimental Psychology: Learning, Memory, and Cognition* 30, 2 (2004): 343–353.

Drucker, Peter F. *Managing in the Next Society.* New York: Truman Talley, 2002.

Drucker, Peter F. "Managing Oneself." *Harvard Business Review* 77, 2 (1999): 64–74.

Drucker, Peter F. *Innovation and Entrepreneurship.* New York: HarperBusiness, 1993.

Duckworth, Angela L., Christopher Peterson, Michael D. Matthews, and Dennis R. Kelly. "Grit: Perseverance and Passion for Long-Term Goals." *Journal of Personality and Social Psychology* 92, 6 (2007): 1087–1101.

Duke, Robert A., Amy L. Simmons, and Carla Davis Cash. "It's Not How Much; It's How: Characteristics of Practice Behavior and Retention of Performance Skills." *Journal of Research in Music Education* 56, 4 (2009): 310–321.

Dutton, Jane E. *Energize Your Workplace: How to Create and Sustain High-Quality Connections at Work.* San Francisco: Jossey-Bass, 2003.

Dweck, Carol S. "Even Geniuses Work Hard." *Educational Leadership* 68, 1 (2010): 16–20.

Dweck, Carol S. "Brainology: Transforming Students' Motivation to Learn." *Independent School* 67, 2 (2008): 110–119.

Dweck, Carol S. *Mindset: The New Psychology of Success.* New York: Ballantine Books, 2006.

Dweck, Carol S. "Motivational Processes Affecting Learning." *American Psychologist* 41, 10 (1986): 1040–1048.

Dweck, Carol S., and Ellen L. Leggett, "A Social-Cognitive Approach to Motivation and Personality." *Psychological Review* 95, 2 (1988): 256–273.

Edersheim, Elizabeth Haas. *The Definitive Drucker: Challenges for Tomorrow's Executives—Final Advice from the Father of Modern Management.* New York: McGraw-Hill, 2007.

Edmonson, Amy C. *Teaming: How Organizations Learn, Innovate, and Compete in the Knowledge Economy.* San Francisco: Jossey-Bass, 2012.

Edmonson, Amy C. "Strategies of Learning from Failure." *Harvard Business Review* 89, 4 (2011): 48–55.

Edmondson, Amy C. "The Competitive Imperative of Learning." *Harvard Business Review* 86, 7/8 (2008): 60–67.

Edmondson, Amy C. "Promoting Experimentation for Organizational Learning: The Mixed Effects of Inconsistency." *Rotman Magazine* Winter (2005): 20–23.

Edmondson, Amy C. "Speaking Up in the Operating Room: How Team Leaders Promote Learning in Interdisciplinary Action Teams." *Journal of Management Studies* 40, 6 (2003): 1419–1452.

Edmondson, Amy C. "Framing for Learning: Lessons in Successful Technology Implementation." *California Management Review* 45, 2 (2003): 34–54.

Edmondson, Amy C. "Psychological Safety and Learning Behavior in Work Teams." *Administrative Science Quarterly* 44, 2 (1999): 350–383.

Edmondson, Amy C., Richard Bohmer, and Gary Pisano, "Speeding Up Team Learning." *Harvard Business Review* 79, 9 (2001): 125–134.

Eisenhardt, Kathleen M. "Making Fast Decisions in High-Velocity Environments." *Academy of Management Journal* 32, 3 (1989): 543–576.

Elliot, Andrew J. "A Conceptual History of the Achievement Goal Construct." In *The Handbook of Competence and Motivation*, ed. Andrew J. Elliot and Carol S. Dweck (New York: Guilford, (2005): 52–72.

Elliot, Andrew J., and Marcy A. Church. "A Hierarchical Model of Approach and Avoidance Achievement Motivation." *Journal of Personality and Social Psychology* 72, 1 (1997): 218–232.

Elliot, Andrew J., and Todd M. Thrash. "Approach and Avoidance Temperament as Basic Dimensions of Personality." *Journal of Personality* 78, 3 (2010): 865–906.

Elliott, Elaine S., and Carol S. Dweck. "Goals: An Approach to Motivation and Achievement." *Journal of Personality and Social Psychology* 54, 1 (1988): 5–12.

Emmons, Robert A., and Anjali Mishra. "Why Gratitude Enhances Well-Being: What We Know, What We Need to Know." In *Designing Positive Psychology: Taking Stock and Moving Forward*, ed. Kennon M. Sheldon, Todd B. Kashdan, and Michael F. Steger. New York: Oxford University Press, 2011, 248–264.

Ericsson, K. Anders. *Development of Professional Expertise: Toward Measurement of Expert Performance and Design of Optimal Learning Environments*. New York: Cambridge University Press, 2009.

Ericsson, K. Anders, Ralf Th. Krampe, and Clemens Tesch-Romer. "The Role of Deliberate Practice in the Acquisition of Expert Performance." *Psychological Review* 100, 3 (1993): 363–406.

Facione, Peter A. "Critical Thinking: A Statement of Expert Consensus for Purposes of Educational Assessment and Instruction. Research Findings and Recommendations." 1990. http://eric.ed.gov/?id=ED315423.

Feder, Adriana, Eric J. Nestler, and Dennis S. Charney. "Psychobiology and Molecular Genetics of Resilience." *Nature Reviews Neuroscience* 10, 6 (2009): 446–457.

Fernandez, Alvaro, and Elkhonon Goldberg. *The SharpBrains Guide to Brain Fitness Second Edition: How to Optimize Brain Health and Performance at Any Age*. San Francisco: SharpBrains, 2013.

Ferrari, Bernard T. "The Executive's Guide to Better Listening." *McKinsey Quarterly*, February 2010, www.mckinsey.com/insights/leading_in_the_21st_century/the_executives_guide_to_better_listening.

"Field Guide to Rapid Experimentation." Presentation transcript. SlideShare, May 2, 2013, www.slideshare.net/IntuitInc/experiment-guide-bookslides.

Fine, Charles H. *Clockspeed: Winning Industry Control in the Age of Temporary Advantage*. New York: Basic, 1998.

Finkelstein, Sydney. *Why Smart Executives Fail and What You Can Learn from Their Mistakes*. New York: Portfolio, 2003.

Firestein, Stuart. *Ignorance: How It Drives Science*. Oxford: Oxford University Press, 2012.

Fischer, Kurt W. "Mind, Brain, and Education: Building a Scientific Groundwork for Learning and Teaching." *Mind, Brain, and Education* 3, 1 (2009): 3–16.

Fischer, Kurt W., and Samuel P. Rose. "Growth Cycles of Brain and Mind." *Educational Leadership* 56, 3 (1998): 56–60.

Flavell, John H. "Metacognition and Cognitive Monitoring: A New Area of Cognitive–Developmental Inquiry." *American Psychologist* 34, 10 (1979): 906–911.

Fletcher, Logan, and Peter Carruthers, "Metacognition and Reasoning." *Philosophical Transactions of the Royal Society B: Biological Sciences* 367, 1594 (2012): 1366–1378.

Fraser, Barry J. "Classroom Environment Instruments: Development, Validity and Applications." *Learning Environments Research* 1, 1 (1998): 7–34.

Fredrickson, Barbara L. "Updated Thinking on Positivity Ratios." *American Psychologist* 68, 9 (2013): 814–822.

Fredrickson, Barbara L. *Positivity: Groundbreaking Research Reveals How to Embrace the Hidden Strength of Positive Emotions, Overcome Negativity, and Thrive.* New York: Crown, 2009.

Fredrickson, Barbara L. "The Role of Positive Emotions in Positive Psychology: The Broaden-and-Build Theory of Positive Emotions." *American Psychologist* 56, 3 (2001): 218–226.

Fredrickson, Barbara L., and Christine Branigan. "Positive Emotions Broaden the Scope of Attention and Thought-Action Repertoires." *Cognition & Emotion* 19, 3 (2005): 313–332.

Fredrickson, Barbara L., and M.F. Losada. "Positive Affect and the Complex Dynamics of Human Flourishing." *American Psychologist* 60, 7 (2005): 678–686.

Freeman, Waldo D., and William R. Burns, Jr. "Developing an Adaptability Training Strategy and Policy for the Department of Defense (DoD)." IDA Paper P-4591. Institute for Defense Analyses, Alexandria, VA, August 2010.

Freud, Sigmund. *Beyond the Pleasure Principle.* Translated by James Strachey. Seattle: Pacific Publishing Studio, 2010.

Fulmer, William E. *Shaping the Adaptive Organization: Landscapes, Learning, and Leadership in Volatile Times.* New York: Amacon, 2000.

Gallup, Inc. Q12®Meta-Analysis: The Relationship Between Engagement at Work and Organizational Outcomes 2012. Gallup, Inc. website, www.gallup.com/strategiccoﬂnsulting/126806/q12-meta-analysis.aspx.

Garvin, David A. *Learning in Action: A Guide to Putting the Learning Organization to Work.* Boston: Harvard Business Review Press, 2000.

Garvin, David A. "Building a Learning Organization." *Harvard Business Review* 71, 4 (1993): 78–91.

Garvin, David A., Amy C. Edmondson, and Francesca Gino. "Is Yours a Learning Organization?" *Harvard Business Review* 86, 3 (2008): 109–116.

Gasper, Karen. "Do You See What I See? Affect and Visual Information Processing." *Cognition & Emotion* 18, 3 (2004): 405–421.

Gasper, Karen. "Permission to Seek Freely? The Effect of Happy and Sad Moods on Generating Old and New Ideas." *Creativity Research Journal* 16, 2 & 3 (2004): 215–229.

Gasper, Karen. "When Necessity Is the Mother of Invention: Mood and Problem Solving." *Journal of Experimental Social Psychology* 39, 3 (2003): 248–262.

Gasper, Karen, and Gerald L. Clore. "Attending to the Big Picture: Mood and Global Versus Local Processing of Visual Information." *Psychological Science* 13, 1 (2002): 34–40.

Gazzaniga, Michael S. "Neuroscience and the Correct Level of Explanation for Understanding Mind." *Trends in Cognitive Sciences* 14, 7 (2010): 291–292.

George, Bill. *Authentic Leadership: Rediscovering the Secrets to Creating Lasting Value.* San Francisco: Jossey-Bass, 2003.

Gephart, Martha A., Victoria J. Marsick, Mark E. Van Buren, and Michelle S. Spiro. "Learning Organizations Come Alive." *Training & Development* 50, 12 (1996): 34–45.

Gillies, Robyn M. "Teachers' and Students' Verbal Behaviours During Cooperative and Small-Group Learning." *British Journal of Educational Psychology* 76, 2 (2006): 271–287.

Goh, Swee C., and Gregory Richards. "Benchmarking the Learning Capability of Organizations." *European Management Journal* 15, 5 (1997): 575–583.

Goh, Swee C., and Peter J. Ryan. "The Organizational Performance of Learning Companies: A Longitudinal and Competitor Analysis Using Market and Accounting Financial Data." *Learning Organization* 15, 3 (2008): 225–239.

Goldman-Rakic, P.S. "Cellular Basis of Working Memory." *Neuron* 14, 3 (1995): 477–485.

Goldsmith, Marshall, with Mark Reiter. *What Got You Here Won't Get You There: How Successful People Become Even More Successful.* New York: Hyperion, 2007.

Goleman, Daniel, Richard Boyatzis, and Annie McKee. *Primal Leadership: Unleashing the Power of Emotional Intelligence.* Boston: Harvard Business Review Press, 2013.

Grams, Chris. "The 12 Enemies of Adaptability." Management Innovation eXchange, May 28, 2013, www.mixhackathon.org/hackathon/contribution/12-enemies-organizational-adaptability.

Grant, Heidi, and Carol S. Dweck. "Clarifying Achievement Goals and Their Impact." *Journal of Personality and Social Psychology* 85, 3 (2003): 541–553.

Grant, Paul, Paula R. Young, and Robert J. DeRubeis. "Cognitive and Behavioral Therapies." In *Oxford Textbook of Psychotherapy,* ed. Glen O. Gabbard, Judith S. Beck, and Jeremy Holmes. Oxford: Oxford University Press, 2007: 15–25.

Greenleaf, Robert K. *Servant Leadership: A Journey Into the Nature of Legitimate Power and Greatness.* 25th anniversary edition. New York: Paulist, 2002.

Gunaratana, Bhante. *Mindfulness in Plain English.* Boston: Wisdom, 2011.

Hackett, James P. "Preparing for the Perfect Product Launch." *Harvard Business Review* 85, 4 (2007): 45–50.

Hagel, John, III, and John Seely Brown. "Institutional Innovation: Creating Smarter Organizations to Scale Learning." Deloitte University Press, 2013, http://cdn.dupress.com/wp-content/uploads/2013/03/DUP293_institutional_innovation2.pdf?848e65.

Halpern, Belle Linda, and Kathy Lubar. *Leadership Presence: Dramatic Techniques to Reach Out, Motivate, and Inspire.* New York: Gotham, 2003.

Hamel, Gary. *What Matters Now: How to Win in a World of Relentless Change, Ferocious Competition, and Unstoppable Innovation.* San Francisco: Jossey-Bass, 2012.

Hamel, Gary. "Innovation Democracy: W.L. Gore's Original Management Model." Management Innovation eXchange, December 29, 2010, www.managementexchange. com/story/innovation-democracy-wl-gores-original-management-model.

Hamel, Gary. "Lessons from a Management Revolutionary." WSJ Blogs, March 18, 2010, http://blogs.wsj.com/management/2010/03/18/wl-gore-lessons-from-a-management-revolutionary/.

Hansen, Drew. "11 Lessons from Startups on Creating Hotbeds of Innovation." *Forbes,* December 6, 2012, www.forbes.com/sites/drewhansen/2012/12/06/11-lessons-from-startups-on-creating-hotbeds-of-innovation/.

Hansen, Morten T. *Collaboration: How Leaders Avoid the Traps, Build Common Ground, and Reap Big Results.* Boston: Harvard Business Review Press, 2009.

Hanson, Kaaren. "Creating a Culture of Experimentation." BRITE Conference Presentation. SlideShare, March 4, 2013, www.slideshare.net/IntuitInc/creating-a-culture-of-experimentation.

Hardiman, Mariale M. *The Brain-Targeted Teaching Model for 21st-Century Schools.* Thousand Oaks, CA: Corwin, 2012.

Hargadon, Andrew. *How Breakthroughs Happen: The Surprising Truth About How Companies Innovate.* Boston: Harvard Business School Press, 2003.

Harter, James K., Frank L. Schmidt, and Theodore L. Hayes. "Business-Unit-Level Relationship between Employee Satisfaction, Employee Engagement, and Business Outcomes: A Meta-Analysis." *Journal of Applied Psychology* 87, 2 (2002): 268–279.

Hartley, Deanna. "The Talent Whisperer: Intuit's Sherry Whiteley." Talent Management, March 26, 2013, http://talentmgt.com/articles/view/the-talent-whisperer-intuit-s-sherry-whiteley.

Healey, Alice F., and Lyle E. Bourne. *Training Cognition: Optimizing Efficiency, Durability, and Generalizability.* New York: Psychology Press, 2012.

Healey, Mark P., and Gerard P. Hodgkinson. "Troubling Futures: Scenarios and Scenario Planning For Organizational Decision Making." In *The Oxford Handbook of Organizational Decision Making,* ed. Gerard P. Hodgkinson and William H. Starbuck. New York: Oxford University Press, 2008.

Heath, Chip, and Dan Heath. *Decisive: How to Make Better Decisions in Life and Work.* New York: Crown Business, 2013.

Henson, Kenneth T. "Foundations for Learner-Centered Education: A Knowledge Base." *Education* 124, 1 (2003): 5–16.

Herman, Arthur. *The Cave and the Light: Plato Versus Aristotle, and the Struggle for the Soul of Western Civilization.* New York: Random House, 2013.

Heskett, James L. "Scott Cook and Intuit." Harvard Business School Case 396–282, March 1996 (revised January 1997).

Heskett, James L., W. Earl Sasser, Jr., and Leonard A. Schlesinger. *The Value Profit Chain: Treat Employees Like Customers and Customers Like Employees.* New York: Free Press, 2003.

Heskett, James L., W. Earl Sasser, Jr., and Leonard A. Schlesinger. *The Service Profit Chain: How Leading Companies Link Profit and Growth to Loyalty, Satisfaction, and Value.* New York: Free Press, 1997.

Hess, Edward D. "Growth is the Dynamic Confluence of Strategy, Entrepreneurship, and Values." Case Study UVA-S-0196. University of Virginia Darden School Foundation, Charlottesville, VA, 2011.

Hess, Edward D. *Smart Growth: Building an Enduring Business by Managing the Risks of Growth.* New York: Columbia University Press, 2010.

Hess, Edward D. "Room & Board." Case Study UVA-S-0150. University of Virginia Darden School Foundation, Charlottesville, VA, 2008 (revised 2010).

Hess, Edward D. *The Road to Organic Growth: How Great Companies Consistently Grow Marketshare from Within.* New York: McGraw-Hill, 2007.

Hess, Edward D. "United Parcel Service of America, Inc." Case Study UVA-S-0134. University of Virginia Darden School Foundation, Charlottesville, 2007.

Hess, Edward D. "UPS: Brown's Organic Growth Story." In *The Search for Organic Growth,* ed. Edward D. Hess and Robert K. Kazanjian. New York: Cambridge University Press, 2006.

Hess, Edward D., and Kim S. Cameron, eds. *Leading with Values: Positivity, Virtue & High Performance.* Cambridge: Cambridge University Press, 2006.

Hess, Edward D., and Jeanne Liedtka. *The Physics of Business Growth: Mindsets, System, and Processes.* Stanford: Stanford University Press, 2012.

Hess, Edward D., and Katherine Ludwig. "United Parcel Service, Inc.: The Challenge of Protecting Organizational DNA." Case Study UVA-S-0238. University of Virginia Darden School Foundation, Charlottesville, VA, 2014.

Higgins, E. Tory. *Beyond Pleasure and Pain: How Motivation Works.* New York: Oxford University Press, 2012.

Higgins, E. Tory. "Making a Good Decision: Value from Fit." *American Psychologist* 55, 11 (2000): 1217–1230.

Hinton, Christina, Koji Miyamoto, and Bruno Della-Chiesa. "Brain Research, Learning and Emotions: Implications for Education Research, Policy and Practice." *European Journal of Education* 43, 1 (2008): 87–103.

Hodgins, Holley S. "Motivation, Threshold for Threat, and Quieting the Ego." In *Transcending Self-Interest: Psychological Explorations of the Quiet Ego,* ed. Heidi A. Wayment and Jack J. Bauer. Washington, DC: American Psychological Association, 2008.

Hodgkinson, Gerard P., and Mark P. Healey. "Cognition in Organizations." *Annual Review of Psycholology* 59 (2008): 387–417.

Holyoak, Keith J., and Robert G. Morrison, eds. *The Oxford Handbook of Thinking and Reasoning.* New York: Oxford University Press, 2012.

Howard-Jones, Paul, Skevi Demetriou, Rafal Bogacz, Jee H. Yoo, and Ute Leonards. "Toward a Science of Learning Games." *Mind, Brain, and Education* 5, 1 (2011): 33–41.

Huppert, Felicia A. "Psychological Well-Being: Evidence Regarding Its Causes and Consequences." *Applied Psychology: Health and Well-Being* 1, 2 (2009): 137–164.

Isaacs, William. *Dialogue: The Art of Thinking Together.* New York: Doubleday, 1999.

Isaacs, William. "Taking Flight: Dialogue, Collective Thinking and Organizational Learning." *Organizational Dynamics* 22, 2 (1993): 24–39.

Immordino-Yang, Mary Helen. "Implications of Affective and Social Neuroscience for Educational Theory." *Educational Philosophy and Theory* 43, 1 (2011): 98–103.

Immordino-Yang, Mary Helen. "The Smoke Around Mirror Neurons: Goals as Socio-cultural and Emotional Organizers of Perception and Action in Learning." *Mind, Brain, and Education* 2, 2 (2008): 67–73.

Immordino-Yang, Mary Helen, and Antonio Damasio. "We Feel, Therefore We Learn: The Relevance of Affective and Social Neuroscience to Education." *Mind, Brain and Education* 1, 1 (2007): 3–10.

Immordino-Yang, Mary Helen, and Lesley Sylvan. "Admiration for Virtue: Neuroscientific Perspectives on a Motivating Emotion." *Contemporary Educational Psychology* 35, 2 (2010): 110–115.

Innosight LLC. "Creative Destruction Whips through Corporate America." INNOSIGHT Executive Briefing. Innosight LLC website, Winter 2012, www.innosight.com/innovation-resources/strategy-innovation/upload/creative-destruction-whips-through-corporate-america_final2012.pdf.

Intuit, Inc. "Corporate Profile." Intuit, Inc. website, www.about.intuit.com/about_intuit/profile/profile/, accessed January 1, 2014.

Isaacs, William N. "Toward an Action Theory of Dialogue." *International Journal of Public Administration* 24, 7–8 (2001): 709–748.

Isen, Alice M. "A Role for Neuropsychology in Understanding the Facilitating Influence of Positive Affect on Social Behavior and Cognitive Processes." In *Handbook of Positive Psychology*, ed. C.R. Snyder and Shane J. Lopez. New York: Oxford University Press, 2002.

Isen, Alice M. "An Influence of Positive Affect on Decision Making in Complex Situations: Theoretical Issues with Practical Implications." *Journal of Consumer Psychology* 11, 2 (2001): 75–85.

Isen, Alice M., Kimberly A. Daubman, and Gary P. Nowicki. "Positive Affect Facilitates Creative Problem Solving." *Journal of Personality and Social Psychology* 52, 6 (1987): 1122–1131.

Isen, Alice M., and Johnmarshall Reeve. "The Influence of Positive Affect on Intrinsic and Extrinsic Motivation: Facilitating Enjoyment of Play, Responsible Work Behavior, and Self-Control." *Motivation and Emotion* 29, 4 (2005): 295–323.

Janssen, Onne, and Nico W. Van Yperen. "Employees' Goal Orientations, the Quality of Leader-Member Exchange, and the Outcomes of Job Performance and Job Satisfaction." *Academy of Management Journal* 47, 3 (2004): 368–384.

Jha, Amishi P., Jason Krompinger, and Michael J. Baime. "Mindfulness Training Modifies Subsystems of Attention." *Cognitive, Affective, & Behavioral Neuroscience* 7, 2 (2007): 109–119.

Jha, Amishi P., Elizabeth A. Stanley, Anastasia Kiyonaga, Ling Wong, and Lois Gelfand. "Examining the Protective Effects of Mindfulness Training on Working Memory Capacity and Affective Experience." *Emotion* 10, 1 (2010): 54–64.

Jim Casey: Our Partnership Legacy. United Parcel Service of America, Inc., 1985.

Johnson, Kareem J., Christian E. Waugh, and Barbara L. Fredrickson. "Smile to See The Forest: Facially Expressed Positive Emotions Broaden Cognition." *Cognition & Emotion* 24, 2 (2010): 299–321.

Jordan, Silvia, Martin Messner, and Albrecht Becker. "Reflection and Mindfulness in Organizations: Rationales and Possibilities for Integration." *Management Learning* 40, 4 (2009): 465–473.

Jourard, Sydney M. *The Transparent Self*. New York: Van Nostrand Reinhold, 1971.

Joyce, William, Nitin Nohria, and Bruce Roberson. *What Really Works: The 4 + 2 Formula for Sustained Business Success*. New York: HarperBusiness, 2003.

Judge, Timothy A., Amir Erez, Joyce E. Bono, and Carl J. Thoresen. "The Core Self-Evaluations Scale: Development of a Measure." *Personnel Psychology* 56, 2 (2003): 303–331.

Kabat-Zinn, Jon. *Mindfulness for Beginners: Reclaiming the Present Moment—And Your Life*. Boulder, CO: Sounds True, 2012.

Kabat-Zinn, Jon. "Mindfulness-Based Interventions In Context: Past, Present, and Future." *Clinical Psychology: Science and Practice* 10, 2 (2003): 144–156.

Kahneman, Daniel. *Thinking, Fast and Slow*. New York: Farrar, Straus and Giroux, 2011.

Kahneman, Daniel. "Bias, Blindness and How We Truly Think (Part 1)." Bloomberg website, October 24, 2011, www.bloomberg.com/news/2011-10-24/bias-blindness-and-how-we-truly-think-part-1-daniel-kahneman.html.

Kahneman, Daniel. "A Short Course in Thinking about Thinking." Edge Master Class, Rutherford California. Edge.org, July 20–22, 2007, www.edge.org/events/the-edge-master-class-2007-a-short-course-in-thinking-about-thinking.

Kahneman, Daniel, and Gary Klein. "Conditions for Intuitive Expertise: A Failure to Disagree." *American Psychologist* 64, 6 (2009): 515–526.

Kahneman, Daniel, Dan Lovallo, and Olivier Sibony. "Before You Make That Big Decision." *Harvard Business Review* 89, 6 (2011): 50–60.

Karpicke, Jeffrey D., and Janell R. Blunt. "Retrieval Practice Produces More Learning than Elaborative Studying with Concept Mapping." *Science* 331, 6018 (2011): 772–775.

Karpicke, Jeffrey D., and Henry L. Roediger. "The Critical Importance of Retrieval for Learning." *Science* 319, 5865 (2008): 966–968.

Kegan, Robert, and Lisa Laskow Lahey. *Immunity to Change: How to Overcome It and Unlock the Potential in Yourself and Your Organization*. Boston: Harvard Business Review Press, 2009.

Kellaway, Lucy. "Principles for Living We Could Do Without." *Financial Times*, March 23, 2010, www.ft.com/intl/cms/s/0/be8ce2ce-650d-11df-b648-00144feab49a.html.

Kelley, Tom, and David Kelley. *Creative Confidence: Unleashing the Creative Potential within Us All*. New York: Crown Business, 2013.

Kent, Alexis. "Synchronization as a Classroom Dynamic: A Practitioner's Perspective." *Mind, Brain, and Education* 7, 1 (2013): 13–18.

King, Patricia Margaret Brown, and Karen Strohm Kitchener. *Developing Reflective Judgment: Understanding and Promoting Intellectual Growth and Critical Thinking in Adolescents and Adults.* San Francisco: Jossey-Bass, 2004.

Kirby, Julia, and Thomas A. Stewart. "The Institutional Yes. The HBR Interview: Jeff Bezos." *Harvard Business Review* 85, 10 (2007): 74–82.

Klein, Gary. *Seeing What Others Don't: The Remarkable Ways We Gain Insights.* New York: PublicAffairs, 2013.

Klein, Gary. *Streetlights and Shadows: Searching for the Keys to Adaptive Decision Making.* Cambridge: MIT Press, 2011.

Klein, Gary. "Naturalistic Decision-Making." *Human Factors* 50, 3 (2008): 456–460.

Klein, Gary. "Performing a Project PreMortem." *Harvard Business Review* 85, 9 (2007): 18–19.

Klein, Gary, Roberta Calderwood, and Donald Macgregor." Critical Decision Method for Eliciting Knowledge." *Systems, Man and Cybernetics* 19, 3 (1989): 462–472.

Klein, Gary, Neil Hintze, and David Saab. "Thinking Inside the Box: The ShadowBox Method for Cognitive Skill Development." In *Proceedings of the 11th International Conference on Naturalistic Decision Making,* ed. H. Chaudet, L. Pellegrin and N. Bonnardel. Arpege Science Publishing, 2013, www.ndm11.org/proceedings/papers/ndm11.pdf.

Klein, Gary, Brian Moon, and Robert R. Hoffman. "Making Sense of Sensemaking 2: A Macrocognitive Model." *Intelligent Systems,* 21, 5 (2006): 88–92.

Klein, Gary, and Linda Pierce. "Adaptive Teams." Klein Associates, Inc., Fairborn OH, June 2001, http://oai.dtic.mil/oai/oai?verb=getRecord&metadataPrefix=html&identifier=ADA467743.

Knoop, Hans Henrik. "Education in 2025: How Positive Psychology Can Revitalize Education." In *Applied Positive Psychology: Improving Everyday Life, Health, Schools, Work, and Society,* ed. Stewart I. Donaldson, Mihaly Csikszentmihalyi and Jeanne Nakamura. New York: Routledge, 2011.

Knowles, Malcolm S., Elwood F. Holton III, and Richard A. Swanson. *The Adult Learner: The Definitive Classic in Adult Education and Human Resource Development.* Burlington, MA: Elsevier, 2005.

Kok, Bethany E., Lahnna I. Catalino, and Barbara L. Fredrickson. "The Broadening, Building, Buffering Effects of Positive Emotions." In *Positive Psychology: Exploring the Best in People,* Volume 2: *Capitalizing on Emotional Experiences,* ed. Shane J. Lopez. Westport, CT: Praeger, 2008: 1–19.

Kolb, David A. *Experiential Learning: Experience as the Source of Learning and Development.* Englewood Cliffs, NJ: Prentice Hall, 1984.

Konnikova, Maria. *Master-Mind: How to Think Like Sherlock Holmes.* New York: Viking, 2013.

Korsgaard, M. Audrey, and Bruce M. Meglino. "Beyond the Individualistic Self: A Framework for Prosocial Motives and Judgments." In *Transcending Self-Interest: Psychological Explorations of the Quiet Ego. Decade of Behavior,* ed. Heidi A. Wayment and Jack J. Bauer. Washington, DC: American Psychological Association, 2008.

Kort, Barry, and Rob Reilly. "Analytical Models of Emotions, Learning and Relationships: Towards an Affect-Sensitive Cognitive Machine." Paper presented at the Conference on Virtual Worlds and Simulation, 2002, http://affect.media.mit.edu/projectpages/lc/vworlds.pdf.

Kort, Barry, Rob Reilly, and Rosalind W. Picard. "An Affective Model of Interplay between Emotions and Learning: Reengineering Educational Pedagogy-Building a Learning Companion." Proceedings of IEEE International Conference on Advanced Learning Technologies, 2001. IEEE Computer Society Press, 2001, http://ieeexplore.ieee.org/xpl/login.jsp?tp=&arnumber=943850amp;&url=http%3A%2F%2Fieeexplore.ieee.org%2Fxpls%2Fabs_all.jsp%3Farnumber%3D943850.

Kosslyn, Stephen M., and G. Wayne Miller. *Top Brain, Bottom Brain: Surprising Insights into How You Think*. New York: Simon & Schuster, 2013.

Kozlowski, Steve W.J. "Training and Developing Adaptive Teams: Theory, Principles, and Research." In *Making Decisions Under Stress: Implications for Individual and Team Training*, ed. Janis A. Cannon-Bowers and Eduardo Salas. Washington, DC: American Psychological Association, 1998: 111–153.

Kumar, Vijay. "A Process for Practicing Design Innovation." *Journal of Business Strategy* 30, 2 & 3 (2009): 91–100.

Kurzweil, Ray. *How to Create a Mind: The Secret of Human Thought Revealed*. New York: Penguin Books, 2013.

Lai, Emily R. "Collaboration: A Literature Overview." Pearson Research Report, 2011, http://images.pearsonassessments.com/images/tmrs/Collaboration-Review.pdf.

Lambrechts, Frank J., Rene Bouwen, Styn Grieten, Jolien P. Huybrechts, and Edgar H. Schein. "Learning to Help through Humble Inquiry and Implications for Management Research, Practice, and Education: An Interview with Edgar H. Schein." *Academy of Management Learning & Education* 10, 1 (2011): 131–147.

Lane, Anthony. "The Fun Factory. Life at Pixar." *New Yorker*, May 16, 2011, www.newyorker.com/reporting/2011/05/16/110516fa_fact_lane.

Langer, Ellen J. *The Power of Mindful Learning*. Cambridge, MA: Perseus, 1997.

The Learning Classroom: Theory Into Practice, Support Materials. Annenberg Learner website, www.learner.org/courses/learningclassroom/support_pages/index.html, accessed January 15, 2014.

Leary, Mark R., Claire E. Adams, and Eleanor B. Tate. "Hypo-Egoic Self-Regulation: Exercising Self-Control by Diminishing the Influence of the Self." *Journal of Personality* 74, 6 (2006): 1803–1832.

Lenfle, Sylvain, and Christoph Loch. "Lost Roots: How Project Management Came to Emphasize Control Over Flexibility and Novelty." *California Management Review* 53, 1, Fall (2010): 32–55.

Lester, Paul B., Sharon McBride, Paul D. Bliese, and Amy B. Adler. "Bringing Science to Bear: An Empirical Assessment of the Comprehensive Soldier Fitness Program." *American Psychologist* 66, 1 (2011): 77–81.

Levin, Bess. "Bridgewater Associates: Be the Hyena. Attack the Wildebeest." Dealbreaker, May 10, 2010, http://dealbreaker.com/2010/05/bridgewater-associates-be-the-hyena-attack-the-wildebeest/.

Lieberman, Matthew D. *Social: Why Our Brains Are Wired to Connect.* New York: Crown, 2013.

Liedtka, Jeanne, Andrew King, and Kevin Bennett. *Solving Problems with Design Thinking: Ten Stories of What Works.* New York: Columbia University Press, 2013.

Liedtka, Jeanne, and Tim Ogilvie. *Designing for Growth: A Design Thinking Tool Kit for Managers.* New York: Columbia University Press, 2011.

Liedtka, Jeanne, Tim Ogilvie, and Rachel Brozenske. *The Designing for Growth Field Book: A Step-by-Step Project Guide.* New York: Columbia University Press, 2014.

Liker, Jeffrey, and Michael Hoseus. *Toyota Culture: The Heart and Soul of the Toyota Way.* New York: McGraw-Hill, 2008.

Linnenbrink, Elizabeth A., and Paul R. Pintrich. "Achievement Goal Theory and Affect: An Asymmetrical Bidirectional Model." *Educational Psychologist* 37, 2 (2002): 69–78.

Linnenbrink-Garcia, Lisa, Toni Kempler Rogat, and Kristin L.K. Koskey. "Affect and Engagement During Small Group Instruction." *Contemporary Educational Psychology* 36, 1 (2011): 13–24.

Loftus, Elizabeth. "Our Changeable Memories: Legal and Practical Implications." *Nature Reviews Neuroscience* 4, 3 (2003): 231–234.

Lopez, Shane J., and C.R. Snyder, eds. *The Oxford Handbook of Positive Psychology.* 2nd ed. New York: Oxford University Press, 2009.

Losada, Marcial. "The Complex Dynamics of High Performance Teams." *Mathematical and Computer Modelling* 30, 9 (1999): 179–192.

Losada, Marcial, and Emily Heaphy. "The Role of Positivity and Connectivity in the Performance of Business Teams a Nonlinear Dynamics Model." *American Behavioral Scientist* 47, 6 (2004): 740–765.

Lovallo, Dan, and Olivier Sibony. "The Case for Behavioral Strategy." *McKinsey Quarterly* March (2010): 30–43.

Lussier, James W., Scott B. Shadrick, and Michael I. Prevou. "Think Like a Commander Prototype: Instructor's Guide to Adaptive Thinking." No. ARI-Research Product-2003-02. Army Research Institute for the Behavioral and Social Sciences, Alexandria, VA, 2003.

Lutz, Antoine, Heleen A. Slagter, John D. Dunne, and Richard J. Davidson. "Attention Regulation and Monitoring in Meditation." *Trends in Cognitive Sciences* 12, 4 (2008): 163–169.

Lyubomirsky, Sonja, Laura King, and Ed Diener. "The Benefits of Frequent Positive Affect: Does Happiness Lead to Success?" *Psychological Bulletin* 131, 6 (2005): 803–855.

Magretta, Joan, with Nan Stone. *What Management Is: How It Works and Why It's Everyone's Business.* New York: Free Press, 2002.

Mangels, Jennifer A., Brady Butterfield, Justin Lamb, Catherine Good, and Carol S. Dweck. "Why Do Beliefs About Intelligence Influence Learning Success? A Social Cognitive Neuroscience Model." *Social Cognitive and Affective Neuroscience* 1, 2 (2006): 75–86.

Marchand, William R. "Mindfulness-Based Stress Reduction, Mindfulness-Based Cognitive Therapy, and Zen Meditation for Depression, Anxiety, Pain, and Psychological Distress." *Journal of Psychiatric Practice* 18, 4 (2012): 233–252.

Marsick, Victoria J., and Karen E. Watkins. "Demonstrating the Value of an Organization's Learning Culture: The Dimensions of the Learning Organization Questionnaire." *Advances in Developing Human Resources* 5, 2 (2003): 132–151.

Martin, James. "Maria Montessori: Guru for a New Generation of Business Innovators." *Globe and Mail,* April 11, 2012, www.theglobeandmail.com/report-on-business/economy/growth/maria-montessori-guru-for-a-new-generation-of-business-innovators/article4099344/.

Maslow, Abraham H. *Maslow on Management.* New York: John Wiley & Sons, 1998.

Maslow, Abraham H. *Toward a Psychology of Being.* Princeton, NJ: D. Van Nostrand, 1962.

Mauboussin, Michael J. *Think Twice: Harnessing the Power of Counterintuition.* Boston: Harvard Business Review Press, 2009.

Mayer, John D., and Peter Salovey. "What Is Emotional Intelligence?" In *Emotional Development and Emotional Intelligence: Educational Implications,* ed. Peter Salovey and David J. Sluyter. New York: Basic, 1997.

McDaniel, Kip. "Is Ray Dalio the Steve Jobs of Investing?" *aiCIO,* December 11, 2011, http://ai-cio.com/channel/newsmakers/is_ray_dalio_the_steve_jobs_of_investing_.html.

McGregor, Douglas. *The Human Side of the Enterprise.* Annotated ed. New York: McGraw-Hill, 2006.

McInerny, D.Q. *Being Logical: A Guide to Good Thinking.* New York: Random House Trade Paperbacks, 2005.

Mearian, Lucas. "Intuit Forces IT, Engineers into Room Until They Get It Right." *Computerworld,* October 19, 2012, www.computerworld.com/s/article/9232594/Intuit_forces_IT_engineers_into_room_until_they_get_it_right?taxonomyId=237&pageNumber=1.

Meyer, Danny. *Setting the Table: The Transforming Power of Hospitality in Business.* New York: HarperCollins, 2006.

Meyer, Debra K., and Julianne C. Turner. "Re-Conceptualizing Emotion and Motivation to Learn in Classroom Contexts." *Educational Psychology Review* 18, 4 (2006): 377–390.

Meyer, Debra K., and Julianne C. Turner. "Discovering Emotion in Classroom Motivation Research." *Educational Psychologist* 37, 2 (2002): 107–114.

Meyer, Debra K., Julianne C. Turner, and Cynthia A. Spencer. "Challenge in a Mathematics Classroom: Students' Motivation and Strategies in Project-Based Learning." *Elementary School Journal* 97, 5 (1997): 501–521.

Mezirow, Jack. "Learning to Think Like an Adult: Core Concepts of Transformation Theory." In Jack Mezirow and Associates, *Learning as Transformation: Critical Perspectives on a Theory in Progress.* San Francisco: Jossey-Bass, 2000: 3–33.

Mezirow, Jack. "Transformative Learning: Theory to Practice." *New Directions for Adult and Continuing Education* 74 (1997): 5–12.

Michelli, Joseph. *Prescription for Excellence: Leadership Lessons for Creating a World Class Customer Experience from UCLA Health System*. New York: McGraw-Hill, 2011.

Michelli, Joseph. *The New Gold Standard: 5 Leadership Principles for Creating a Legendary Customer Experience Courtesy of the Ritz-Carlton Hotel Company*. New York: McGraw-Hill, 2008.

Milkman, Katherine L., Dolly Chugh, and Max H. Bazerman. "How Can Decision Making Be Improved?" *Perspectives on Psychological Science* 4, 4 (2009): 379–383.

Morrison, John E., J.D. Fletcher, Franklin L. Moses, and Eric J. Roberts. "The Army Science of Learning Workshop." ARI Research Note 2007-02. U.S. Army Research Institute for the Behavioral and Social Sciences, Arlington, VA, 2007.

Morrison, John E., and Larry L. Meliza. "Foundations of the After Action Review Process." ARI Special Report 42. Institute for Defense Analyses, Alexandria, VA, July 1999.

Motley Fool. "The 20 Smartest Things Jeff Bezos Has Ever Said." InsiderMonkey, September 10, 2013, www.insidermonkey.com/blog/amazon-com-inc-amzn-the-20-smartest-things-jeff-bezos-has-ever-said-240742/2/.

Mueller, Jennifer S., Shimul Melwani, and Jack A. Goncalo. "The Bias Against Creativity Why People Desire but Reject Creative Ideas." *Psychological Science* 23, 1 (2012): 13–17.

Mueller-Hanson, Rose A., Susan S. White, David W. Dorsey, and Elaine D. Pulakos. "Training Adaptable Leaders: Lessons from Research and Practice." ARI Research Report 1844. Personnel Decisions Research Institutes, Inc., Arlington, VA, 2005.

Murayama, Kou, and Andrew J. Elliot. "The Joint Influence of Personal Achievement Goals and Classroom Goal Structures on Achievement-Relevant Outcomes." *Journal of Educational Psychology* 101, 2 (2009): 432–447.

Naqvi, Nasir, Baba Shiv, and Antoine Bechara. "The Role of Emotion in Decision Making: A Cognitive Neuroscience Perspective." *Current Directions in Psychological Science* 15, 5 (2006): 260–264.

Neff, Kristin D. "Self-Compassion: Moving Beyond the Pitfalls of a Separate Self-Concept." In *Transcending Self-Interest: Psychological Explorations of the Quiet Ego. Decade of Behavior*, ed. Heidi A. Wayment and Jack J. Bauer. Washington, DC: American Psychological Association, 2008.

Nembhard, Ingrid M., and Amy C. Edmondson. "Making It Safe: The Effects of Leader Inclusiveness and Professional Status on Psychological Safety and Improvement Efforts in Health Care Teams." *Journal of Organizational Behavior* 27, 7 (2006): 941–966.

Nemeth, Charlan, Keith Brown, and John Rogers. "Devil's Advocate versus Authentic Dissent: Stimulating Quantity and Quality." *European Journal of Social Psychology* 31, 6 (2001): 707–720.

Newberg, Andrew, and Mark Robert Waldman. *Words Can Change Your Brain: 12 Conversation Strategies to Build Trust, Resolve Conflict, and Increase Intimacy*. New York: Hudson Street, 2012.

Niemiec, Christopher P., Richard M. Ryan, and Kirk Warren Brown. "The Role of Awareness and Autonomy in Quieting the Ego: A Self-Determination Theory Perspective." In *Transcending Self-Interest: Psychological Explorations of the Quiet Ego*, ed. Heidi A. Wayment and Jack J. Bauer. Washington, DC: American Psychological Association, 2008.

Nikravan, Ladan. "UPS: Promoting Learning." May 20, 2013, http://clomedia.com/articles/view/ups-promoting-learning.

Nutt, Paul C. "Expanding the Search for Alternatives During Strategic Decision-Making." *Academy of Management Executive* 18, 4 (2004): 13–28.

Nutt, Paul C. "Surprising but True: Half the Decisions in Organizations Fail." *Academy of Management Executive* 13, 4 (1999): 75–90.

Oaksford, Mike, Frances Morris, Becki Grainger, and J. Mark G. Williams. "Mood, Reasoning, and Central Executive Processes." *Journal of Experimental Psychology: Learning, Memory, and Cognition* 22, 2 (1996): 476–492.

O'Reilly, Charles A., III, and Jeffrey Pfeffer. *Hidden Value: How Great Companies Achieve Extraordinary Results with Ordinary People*. Boston: Harvard Business School Press, 2000.

Parkyn, Michael B. "Making More Mike Stranks—Teaching Value in the United States Marine Corps." In *Leading with Values: Positivity, Virtue, and High Performance*, ed. Edward D. Hess and Kim S. Cameron. Cambridge: Cambridge University Press, 2006: 213–233.

Patrick, Helen, Avi Kaplan, and Allison M. Ryan. "Positive Classroom Motivational Environments: Convergence Between Mastery Goal Structure and Classroom Social Climate." *Journal of Educational Psychology* 103, 2 (2011): 367–382.

Patrick, Helen, Julianne Turner, Debra Meyer, and Carol Midgley. "How Teachers Establish Psychological Environments during the First Days of School: Associations with Avoidance in Mathematics." *Teachers College Record* 105, 8 (2003): 1521–1558.

Patterson, Kerry, Joseph Grenny, Ron McMillan, and Al Switzler. *Crucial Conversations: Tools for Talking When Stakes Are High*. New York: McGraw-Hill, 2012.

Paul, Richard W., and Linda Elder. *Critical Thinking: Tools for Taking Charge of Your Professional and Personal Life*. Upper Saddle River, NJ: Financial Times Prentice Hall, 2002.

Pawlak, Robert, Ana Maria Magarinos, Jerry Melchor, Bruce McEwen, and Sidney Strickland. "Tissue Plasminogen Activator in the Amygdala is Critical for Stress-Induced Anxiety-Like Behavior." *Nature Neuroscience* 6, 2 (2003): 168–174.

Pearlstein, Steve. "How the Cult of Shareholder Value Wrecked American Business." *Washington Post*, September 6, 2013, www.washingtonpost.com/blogs/wonkblog/wp/2013/09/09/how-the-cult-of-shareholder-value-wrecked-american-business/.

Pekrun, Reinhard, Andrew J. Elliot, and Markus A. Maier. "Achievement Goals and Discrete Achievement Emotions: A Theoretical Model and Prospective Test." *Journal of Educational Psychology* 98, 3 (2006): 583–597.

Pentland, Alex "Sandy." "The New Science of Building Great Teams." *Harvard Business Review* 90, 4 (2012): 60–69.

Pessoa, Luiz. "Emergent Processes in Cognitive-Emotional Interactions." *Dialogues in Clinical Neuroscience* 12, 4 (2010): 433–448.

Pessoa, Luiz. "Emotion and Attention Effects: Is It All a Matter of Timing? Not Yet." *Frontiers in Human Neuroscience* 4 (2010): 172.

Pessoa, Luiz. "How Do Emotion and Motivation Direct Executive Control." *Trends in Cognitive Sciences* 13, 4 (2009): 160–166.

Pessoa, Luiz. "On the Relationship Between Emotion and Cognition." *Nature Reviews/ Neuroscience* 9 (2008): 148–158.

Peters, Thomas J., and Robert H. Waterman, Jr. *In Search Of Excellence: Lessons from America's Best-Run Companies.* New York: Warner, 1984.

Pfeffer, Jeffrey. *The Human Equation: Building Profits by Putting People First.* Boston: Harvard Business Review Press, 1998.

Phelps, Elizabeth A. "Emotion and Cognition: Insights from Studies of the Human Amygdala." *Annual Review of Psychology* 57 (2006): 27–53.

Pickett, Linda, and Barry Fraser. "Creating and Assessing Positive Classroom Learning Environments." *Childhood Education* 86, 5 (2010): 321–326.

Pintrich, Paul R. "A Motivational Science Perspective on the Role of Student Motivation in Learning and Teaching Contexts." *Journal of Educational Psychology* 95, 4 (2003): 667–686.

Porath, Christine L., and Amir Erez. "Overlooked but Not Untouched: How Rudeness Reduces Onlookers' Performance on Routine and Creative Tasks." *Organizational Behavior and Human Decision Processes* 109, 1 (2009): 29–44.

Porath, Christine, Gretchen Spreitzer, Cristina Gibson, and Flannery G. Garnett. "Thriving at Work: Toward its Measurement, Construct Validation, and Theoretical Refinement." *Journal of Organizational Behavior* 33, 2 (2012): 250–275.

Posner, Michael I., and Gregory J. DiGirolamo. "Cognitive Neuroscience: Origins and Promise." *Psychological Bulletin* 126, 6 (2000): 873–889.

Powell, Thomas C. "Neurostrategy." *Strategic Management Journal* 32, 13 (2011): 1484–1499.

Powell, Thomas C., Dan Lovallo, and Craig R. Fox. "Behavioral Strategy." *Strategic Management Journal* 32, 13 (2011): 1369–1386.

Pulakos, Elaine D., Sharon Arad, Michelle A. Donovan, and Kevin E. Plamondon. "Adaptability in the Workplace: Development of a Taxonomy of Adaptive Performance." *Journal of Applied Psychology* 85, 4 (2000): 612–624.

Pulakos, Elaine D., Neal Schmitt, David W. Dorsey, Sharon Arad, Walter C. Borman, and Jerry W. Hedge. "Predicting Adaptive Performance: Further Tests of a Model of Adaptability." *Human Performance* 15, 4 (2002): 299–323.

Rao, Hayagreeva, Robert Sutton, and Allen P. Webb. "Innovation Lessons from Pixar: An Interview with Oscar-Winning Director Brad Bird." *McKinsey Quarterly,* 2008, www.mckinsey.com/insights/innovation/innovation_lessons_from_pixar_an_interview_with_oscar-winning_director_brad_bird.

Rao, Jay, and Joseph Weintraub. "How Innovative Is Your Company's Culture." *MIT Sloan Management Review* 54, 3 (2013). http://sloanreview.mit.edu/article/how-innovative-is-your-companys-culture/.

"Ray Dalio: Man and Machine." *Economist*, March 10, 2012. www.economist.com/node/21549968.

Reilly, Rob. "The Science Behind the Art of Teaching Science: Emotional State and Learning." Proceedings of Society for Information Technology & Teacher Education International Conference 2004. AACE, Chesapeake, VA, www.editlib.org/p/13311.

Ries, Eric. *The Lean Startup: How Today's Entrepreneurs Use Continuous Innovation to Create Radically Successful Businesses*. New York: Crown Business, 2011.

Ritchhart, Ron, and David N. Perkins. "Learning to Think: The Challenges of Teaching Thinking." In *The Cambridge Handbook of Thinking and Reasoning*, ed. Keith J. Holyoak and Robert G. Morrison. Cambridge: Cambridge University Press, 2004.

Ritter, Steve. "The Research behind the Carnegie Learning® Math Series." Carnegie Learning website, www.carnegielearning.com/whitepapers/, accessed January 1, 2014.

Robertson, Ivan T., and Cary L. Cooper. "Full Engagement: The Integration of Employee Engagement and Psychological Well-Being." *Leadership & Organization Development Journal* 31, 4 (2010): 324–336.

Robinson, Ken. *Out of Our Minds: Learning to Be Creative*. Chichester, West Sussex: Capstone, 2011.

Rodriguez, Tori. "Creativity Predicts a Longer Life." *ScientificAmerican*, September 9, 2012, www.scientificamerican.com/article.cfm?id=open-mind-longer-life.

Rodriguez, Vanessa. "The Human Nervous System: A Framework for Teaching and the Teaching Brain." *Mind, Brain, and Education* 7, 1 (2013): 2–12.

Rogers, Carl. *The Carl Rogers Reader*. Editors Howard Kirschenbaum and Valerie Land Henderson. New York: Houghton Mifflin, 1989.

Roose, Kevin. "Pursuing Self Interest in Harmony with the Laws of the Universe and Contributing to Evolution Is Universally Rewarded." *New York Magazine*, April 10, 2011. http://nymag.com/news/business/wallstreet/ray-dalio-2011-4/.

Roser, Matthew, and Michael S. Gazzaniga. "Automatic Brains—Interpretive Minds." *Current Directions in Psychological Science* 13, 2 (2004): 56–59.

Ross, Karol G., Gary Klein, Peter Thunholm, John F. Schmitt, and Holly C. Baxter. "The Recognition-Primed Decision Model." *Military Review* July–August (2004): 6–10.

Rothwell, William J. *The Workplace Learner: How to Align Training Initiatives with Individual Learning Competencies*. New York: AMACON, 2002.

Russo, J. Edward, and Paul J.H. Schoemaker, "Managing Overconfidence." *MIT Sloan Management Review* 33, 2 (1992): 7–17.

Ryan, Richard M., and Kirk Warren Brown. "Why We Don't Need Self-Esteem: On Fundamental Needs, Contingent Love, and Mindfulness." *Psychological Inquiry* 14, 1 (2003): 71–76.

Ryan, Richard M., and Edward L. Deci. "Intrinsic and Extrinsic Motivations: Classic Definitions and New Directions." *Contemporary Educational Psychology* 25, 1 (2000): 54–67.

Ryan, Richard M., and Edward L. Deci. "Self-Determination Theory and the Facilitation of Intrinsic Motivation, Social Development, and Well-Being." *American Psychologist* 55 (2000): 68–78.

Salovey, Peter, John D. Mayer, and David Caruso. "The Positive Psychology of Emotional Intelligence." In *Oxford Handbook of Positive Psychology*, 2nd ed., ed. Shane J. Lopez and C.R. Snyder. New York: Oxford University Press, 2009: 237–248.

Salter, Chuck. "Marissa Mayer's 9 Principles of Innovation." Fast Company, February 20, 2008, www.fastcompany.com/702926/marissa-mayers-9-principles-innovation.

Salter, Margaret S., and Gerald E. Klein, "After Action Reviews: Current Observations and Recommendations." ARI Research Report 1867. The Wexford Group International Inc., Vienna, VA, January 2007.

Schacter, Daniel L. "The Seven Sins of Memory: Insights from Psychology and Cognitive Neuroscience." *American Psychologist* 54, 3 (1999): 182–203.

Schacter, Daniel L., and Donna Rose Addis. "The Cognitive Neuroscience of Constructive Memory: Remembering the Past and Imagining the Future." *Philosophical Transactions of the Royal Society B: Biological Sciences* 362, 1481 (2007): 773–786.

Schalow, Kelly. "Intuit Inc. Design for Delight Communication Platform." Kelly Schalow website, www.kellyschalow.com/d4d/, accessed January 1, 2014.

Schein, Edgar H. *Humble Inquiry: The Gentle Art of Asking Instead of Telling*. San Francisco: Berrett-Koehler, 2013.

Schein, Edgar H. *Helping: How to Offer, Give, and Receive Help*. San Francisco: Berrett-Koehler, 2009.

Schein, Edgar H. "From Brainwashing to Organizational Therapy: A Conceptual and Empirical Journey in Search of 'Systemic' Health and a General Model of Change Dynamics. A Drama in Five Acts." *Organization Studies* 27, 2 (2006): 287–301.

Schein, Edgar H. "Taking Culture Seriously in Organization Development: A New Role for OD?" Working Paper 4287-03, 2003, http://dspace.mit.edu/bitstream/handle/1721.1/1834/4287-03.pdf?sequence=1.

Schoemaker, Paul J.H. "Multiple Scenario Development: Its Conceptual and Behavioral Foundation." *Strategic Management Journal* 14, 3 (1993): 193–213.

Schon, Donald A. *The Reflective Practitioner: How Professionals Think in Action*. New York: Basic, 1993.

Schultz, Howard, and Dori Jones Yang. *Pour Your Heart Into It: How Starbucks Built a Company One Cup at a Time*. New York: Hyperion, 1997.

Schultz, Wolfram. "Behavioral Dopamine Signals." *Trends in Neurosciences* 30, 5 (2007): 203–210.

Schultz, Wolfram. "Behavioral Theories and the Neurophysiology of Reward." *Annual Review of Psychology* 57 (2006): 87–115.

Schunk, Dale H. "Self-Regulated Learning: The Educational Legacy of Paul R. Pintrich." *Educational Psychologist* 40, 2 (2005): 85–94.

Schwabe, Lars, Oliver T. Wolf, and Melly S. Oitzl. "Memory Formation Under Stress: Quantity and Quality." *Neuroscience & Biobehavioral Reviews* 34, 4 (2010): 584–591.

Schwarz, Norbert. "Situated Cognition and the Wisdom of Feelings: Cognitive Tuning." In *The Wisdom in Feeling*, ed. L. Feldman Barrett and P. Salovey. New York: Guilford, 2002: 144–166.

Schweiger, David M., William R. Sandberg, and Paula L. Rechner. "Experiential Effects of Dialectical Inquiry, Devil's Advocacy and Consensus Approaches to Strategic Decision Making." *Academy of Management Journal* 32, 4 (1989): 745–772.

Schweinle, Amy, Debra K. Meyer, and Julianne C. Turner. "Striking the Right Balance: Students' Motivation and Affect in Elementary Mathematics." *Journal of Educational Research* 99, 5 (2006): 271–294.

Schwenk, Charles R. "A Meta-Analysis on the Comparative Effectiveness of Devil's Advocacy and Dialectical Inquiry." *Strategic Management Journal* 10, 3 (1989): 303–306.

Schwenk, Charles R. "The Cognitive Perspective on Strategic Decision Making." *Journal of Management Studies* 25, 1 (1988): 41–55.

Seelig, Tina. "The Science of Creativity." Fast Company, April 17, 2002, www.fastcompany.com/1834334/science-creativity.

Sekerka, Leslie E., and Barbara L. Fredrickson. "Establishing Positive Emotional Climates to Advance Organizational Transformation." In *Research Companion to Emotion in Organizations*, ed. Neal M. Ashkanasy and Cary Lynn Cooper. Cheltenham, UK: Edward Elgar, 2008: 531–545.

Sekerka, Leslie E., and Barbara L. Fredrickson. "Creating Transformative Cooperation through Positive Emotions." 2007. http://sekerkaethicsinaction.com/docs/pdfs/Sekerka-Fredrickson%20Transformation%20Chapter%20Web%201-07.pdf.

Seligman, Martin E.P. *Flourish: A Visionary New Understanding of Happiness and Well-Being*. New York: Free Press, 2011.

Senge, Peter. *The Fifth Discipline: The Art & Practice of the Learning Organization*. New York: Currency Doubleday, 1990.

Shadrick, Scott B., Brian T. Crabb, James W. Lussier, and Thomas J. Burke. "Positive Transfer of Adaptive Battlefield Thinking Skills." ARI Research Report 1873. U.S. Army Research Institute for the Behavioral and Social Sciences, Arlington VA, July 2007.

Shansky, Rebecca M., and Jennifer Lipps. "Stress-Induced Cognitive Dysfunction: Hormone-Neurotransmitter Interactions in the Prefrontal Cortex." *Frontiers in Human Neuroscience* 7 (2013): 123.

Shapiro, Shauna L., Kirk Warren Brown, and John A. Astin. "Toward the Integration of Meditation Into Higher Education: A Review of Research Evidence." *Teachers College Record* 113, 3 (2011): 493–528.

Sheldon, Kennon Marshall, Todd Kashdan, and Michael F. Steger, eds. *Designing Positive Psychology: Taking Stock and Moving Forward*. Oxford: Oxford University Press, 2011.

Shook, John. "How to Change a Culture: Lessons From NUMMI." *MIT Sloan Management Review* 51, 2 (2010): 42–51.

Sieck, Winston R., Gary Klein, Deborah A. Peluso, Jennifer L. Smith, Danyele Harris-Thompson, and Paul A. Gade. "FOCUS: A Model of Sensemaking." Army Research Institute Technical Report 1200. Klein Associates, Inc., Fairborn, OH, May 2007.

Simon, Herbert. "What Is an 'Explanation' of Behavior?" *Psychological Science* 3, 3 (1992): 150–161.

Simon, Hermann. *Hidden Champions of the Twenty-First Century: Success Strategies of Unknown World Market Leaders.* New York: Springer, 2009.

Sims, Peter. "What Google Could Learn from Pixar." HBR Blog Network, August 6, 2010, http://blogs.hbr.org/2010/08/what-google-could-learn-from-p/.

Smith, Brad. "Three Things Every Leader Should Do in a Meeting." Intuit Network website, July 9, 2013, http://network.intuit.com/2013/07/09/meeting-tips/.

Smith, Brad. "Managing Your Most Precious Resource: Time." Intuit Network website, June 24, 2013, "http://network.intuit.com/2013/06/24/improve-time-management/.

Smith, Brad. "Five New Year's Resolutions Every Business Leader Should Make." Intuit Network website, January 7, 2013, http://network.intuit.com/2013/01/07/five-new-years-resolutions-every-business-leader-should-make/.

Smith, Brad. "Lean Startup Leadership: It's Time to Bury Caesar." Intuit Network website, November 30, 2012, http://network.intuit.com/2012/11/30/lean-startup-leadership-its-time-to-bury-caesar-2/.

Sommer, Svenja C., and Christoph H. Loch. "Selectionism and Learning in Projects with Complexity and Unforeseeable Uncertainty." *Management Science* 50, 10 (2004): 1334–1347.

Spreitzer, Gretchen, and Christine Porath. "Creating Sustainable Performance." *Harvard Business Review* 90, 1 (2012): 92–99.

Sternberg, Robert. "Intelligence, Competence and Expertise." In *The Handbook of Competence and Motivation*, ed. Andrew J. Elliot and Carol S. Dweck. New York: Guilford, 2005: 15–30.

Stiglitz, Joseph E. "Industrial Policy and Creating a Learning Society." IEA/World Bank Roundtable, Pretoria, July 2012, www.iea-world.org/docs/Stiglitz.pdf.

Stone, Brad. "The Secrets of Bezos: How Amazon Became the Everything Store." Businessweek.com, October 10, 2013, www.businessweek.com/articles/2013-10-10/jeff-bezos-and-the-age-of-amazon-excerpt-from-the-everything-store-by-brad-stone.

Stone, Brad. "Amazon, the Company That Ate the World." Businessweek.com, September 28, 2011, www.businessweek.com/magazine/the-omnivore-09282011.html.

Stone, Douglas, Bruce Patton, and Sheila Heen. *Difficult Conversations: How to Discuss What Matters Most.* New York: Penguin, 1999.

Storbeck Justin, and Gerald L. Clore. "On the Interdependence of Cognition and Emotion." *Cognition & Emotion* 21, 6 (2007): 1212–1237.

Sullivan, Gordon R., and Michael V. Harper. *Hope Is Not a Method: What Business Leaders Can Learn from America's Army.* New York: Broadway, 1997.

Sutton, Robert I. *Good Boss, Bad Boss: How to Be the Best . . ., and Learn from the Worst.* New York: Business Plus, 2010.

Tahirsylaj, Armend S. "Stimulating Creativity and Innovation through Intelligent Fast Failure." *Thinking Skills and Creativity* 7, 3 (2012): 265–270.

Tannen, Deborah. *That's Not What I Meant! How Conversational Style Makes or Breaks Your Relations with Others.* New York: HarperCollins, 2011.

Tannen, Deborah. "Conversational Style". In *Psycholinguistic Models of Production*, ed. Hans W. Dechert and Manfred Raupach. Norwood, NJ: Ablex, 1987: 251–267.

Tavris, Carol, and Elliot Aronson. *Mistakes Were Made (But Not By Me)*. Orlando: Harcourt, Inc., 2007.

Taylor, William C., and Polly LaBarre. "How Pixar Adds a New School of Thought to Disney." *New York Times*, January 29, 2006, www.nytimes.com/2006/01/29/business/yourmoney/29pixar.html?pagewanted=all&_r=0.

Tillson, John C., Waldo D. Freeman, William R. Burns, John E. Michel, Jack A. LeCuyer, Robert H. Scales, and D. Robert Worley. "Learning to Adapt to Asymmetric Threats." IDA-D-3114. Institute for Defense Analyses Alexandria VA, August 2005.

Tishman, Shari, Eileen Jay, and David N. Perkins. "Teaching Thinking Dispositions: From Transmission to Enculturation." *Theory Into Practice* 32, 3 (1993): 147–153.

Tucker, Anita L., and Amy C. Edmondson. "Why Hospitals Don't Learn from Failures." *California Management Review* 45, 2 (2003): 55–72.

Tversky, Amos, and Daniel Kahneman. "Judgment Under Uncertainty: Heuristics and Biases." *Science* 185 (1974): 1124–1131.

United Parcel Service, Inc. "Benefits." United Parcel Service, Inc. website, accessed December 4, 2013.

United Parcel Service, Inc. "Company History 1991–1999." United Parcel Service, Inc. website, accessed October 11, 2013.

United Parcel Service, Inc. "Telematics." United Parcel Service, Inc. website, accessed December 9, 2013.

United Parcel Service, Inc. "UPS Integrad." United Parcel Service, Inc. website, accessed October 11, 2013.

Upbin, Bruce. "Why Intuit Is More Innovative Than Your Company." *Forbes*, September 24, 2012, www.forbes.com/sites/bruceupbin/2012/09/04/intuit-the-30-year-old-startup/.

UPS 2012 Annual Report. United Parcel Service, Inc. website, www.investors.ups.com/phoenix.zhtml?c=62900&p=irol-reportsannual.

UPS Corporate Sustainability Report 2012. United Parcel Service, Inc. website. www.responsibility.ups.com/Sustainability.

U.S. Army, "The U.S. Army Learning Concept for 2015." TRADOC Pam 525-8-2. January 20, 2011, www.tradoc.army.mil/tpubs/pams/tp525-8-2.pdf.

U.S. Army. "A Leader's Guide to After-Action Reviews." Training Circular 2520, 1993, www.acq.osd.mil/dpap/ccap/cc/jcchb/Files/Topical/After_Action_Report/resources/tc25-20.pdf.

USAID. After-Action Review Technical Guidance. PN-ADF-360. February 2006, http://usaidlearninglab.org/library/after-action-review-technical-guidance-0.

Van Eemeren, Frans H., and Rob Grootendorst. "Fallacies in Pragma-Dialectical Perspective." *Argumentation* 1 (1987): 283–301.

Van Looy, Bart, Thierry Martens, and Koenraad Debackere. "Organizing for Continuous Innovation: On the Sustainability of Ambidextrous Organizations." *Creativity and Innovation Management* 14, 3 (2005): 208–221.

Van Yperen, Nico W., Andrew J. Elliot, and Frederik Anseel. "The Influence Of Mastery-Avoidance Goals on Performance improvement." *European Journal of Social Psychology* 39, 6 (2009): 932–943.

Van Yperen, Nico W., and Edward Orehek. "Achievement Goals in the Workplace: Conceptualization, Prevalence, Profiles, and Outcomes." *Journal of Economic Psychology* 38, C (2013): 71–79.

Van Yperen, Nico W., and Lennart J. Renkema. "Performing Great and the Purpose of Performing Better Than Others: On the Recursiveness of the Achievement Goal Adoption Process." *European Journal of Social Psychology* 38, 2 (2008): 260–271.

Vance, Ashlee. "Netflix, Reed Hastings Survive Missteps to Join Silicon Valley's Elite." Businessweek.com, May 9, 2013, www.businessweek.com/articles/2013-05-09/netflix-reed-hastings-survive-missteps-to-join-silicon-valleys-elite.

Vance, Ashlee. "Elon Musk, the 21st Century Industrialist." Businessweek.com, September 13, 2012, www.businessweek.com/articles/2012-09-13/elon-musk-the-21st-century-industrialist.

VandeWalle, Don. "Development and Validation of a Work Domain Goal Orientation Instrument." *Educational and Psychological Measurement* 57, 6 (1997): 995–1015.

Veenman, Marcel VJ, Bernadette H.A. M Van Hout-Wolters, and Peter Afflerbach. "Metacognition and Learning: Conceptual and Methodological Considerations." *Metacognition and Learning* 1, 1 (2006): 3–14.

Veinott, Beth, Gary Klein, and Sterling Wiggins. "Evaluating the Effectiveness of the PreMortem Technique on Plan Confidence." Proceedings of the 7th International ISCRAM Conference, Seattle USA, May 2010, www.iscram.org/ISCRAM2010/Papers/175-Veinott_etal.pdf.

Walberg, Herbert J., and Rebecca C. Greenberg. "Using the Learning Environment Inventory." *Educational Leadership* 54, 8 (1997): 45–49.

Watson, David, Lee A. Clark, and Auke Tellegen. "Development and Validation of Brief Measures of Positive and Negative Affect: The PANAS Scales." *Journal of Personality and Social Psychology* 54, 6 (1988): 1063–1070.

Wayment, Heidi A., and Jack J. Bauer, eds. *Transcending Self-Interest: Psychological Explorations of the Quiet Ego*. Washington, DC: American Psychological Association, 2008.

Weick, Karl, and Katherine Sutcliffe. *Managing the Unexpected: Assuring High Performance in an Age of Complexity*. San Francisco: Jossey-Bass, 2001.

Weinstein, Netta, Kirk W. Brown, and Richard M. Ryan. "A Multi-Method Examination of the Effects of Mindfulness on Stress Attribution, Coping, and Emotional Well-Being." *Journal of Research in Personality* 43, 3 (2009): 374–385.

Welbourne, Theresa M., Diane E. Johnson, and Amir Erez. "The Role-Based Performance Scale: Validity Analysis of a Theory-Based Measure." *Academy of Management Journal* 41, 5 (1998): 540–555.

Werhane, Patricia H. *Adam Smith and His Legacy for Modern Capitalism*. New York: Oxford University Press, 1991.

White, Susan S., Rose A. Mueller-Hanson, David W. Dorsey, Elaine D. Pulakos, Michelle M. Wisecarver, Edwin A. Deagle III, and Kip G. Mendini. "Developing Adaptive

Proficiency in Special Forces Officers." Research Report 1831. Personnel Decisions Research Institutes, Inc., Arlington, VA, 2005.

"Why Cities Keep Growing, Corporations and People Always Die, and Life Gets Faster: A Conversation with Geoffrey West." Edge.org, May 23, 2011, www.edge.org/conversation/geoffrey-west.

Wicks, Andrew C., and Jeffrey S. Harrison. "Stakeholder Theory, Value and Firm Performance." *Business Ethics Quarterly* 23, 1 (2013): 97–124.

Williams, Thomas, Christopher G. Worley, and Edward E. Lawler, III. "The Agility Factor." *Strategy + Business*, April 15, 2013, www.strategy-business.com/article/00188?pg=all.

Willingham, Daniel T. *Why Don't Students Like School? A Cognitive Scientist Answers Questions About How the Mind Works and What It Means for the Classroom.* San Francisco: Jossey-Bass, 2009.

Willingham, Daniel T. "Critical Thinking: Why Is It So Hard to Teach?" *Arts Education Policy Review* 109, 4 (2008): 21–32.

Wisnioski, Matthew. "'Change or Die!': The History of the Innovator's Aphorism." *Atlantic*, December 12, 2012, www.theatlantic.com/technology/archive/2012/12/change-or-die-the-history-of-the-innovators-aphorism/266191/.

W.L. Gore & Associates, Inc. "What We Believe: Our Beliefs and Principles." W.L. Gore & Associates, Inc. website, www.gore.com/en_xx/careers/whoweare/whatwebelieve/gore-culture.html, accessed January 1, 2014.

Wohlsen, Marcus. "The Astronomical Math Behind UPS' New Tool to Deliver Packages Faster." *Wired*, June 13, 2013, www.wired.com/business/2013/06/ups-astronomical-math/.

Wright, George, and Paul Goodwin. "Decision Making and Planning Under Low Levels of Predictability: Enhancing the Scenario Method." *International Journal of Forecasting* 25, 4 (2009): 813–825.

Yan, Zheng, and Kurt Fischer. "Always Under Construction." *Human Development* 45, 3 (2002): 141–160.

Yankelovich, Daniel. "The Magic of Dialogue." *Nonprofit Quarterly* Fall 2001, www.gobarton.com/administration/aqip/documents/strategyforum/Yankelovich%20article.pdf.

Yano, Kazuo. "The Science of Human Interaction and Teaching." *Mind, Brain, and Education* 7, 1 (2013): 19–29.

Zaccaro, Stephen J., Deanna Banks, Lee Kiechel-Koles, Cary Kemp, and Paige Bader. "Leader and Team Adaptation: The Influence and Development of Key Attributes and Processes." ARI Technical Report 1256. George Mason University, Fairfax, VA, August 2009.

Index

hiring, 39–40; at Bridgewater, 142–43; for culture fit, 52; by managers, 51–52; proper, 161–62; by test scores, 135; at W. L. Gore & Associates, Inc., 58–59
hitting bottom, 140
holding period, of corporate stocks, 6
Holsen, Jim, 184
honesty, 55, 132–33
HPLO. *See* High-Performance Learning Organization
HR policies, 54
humanistic psychology, 13; fear and, 18
humanness, 12, 114; overcoming, 13–16
humble inquiry, 66–67
humility, 53–54; empathy and, 57; humble inquiry and, 67

IBM, 198
Idea Jams, 167
ideas, 174
Idea step, 171
IDEO, 7, 56–57
ignorance, 104–5, 123–24; illuminating, 196. *See also* not knowing
Ignorance: How It Drives Science (Firestein), 123
Immordino-Yang, Mary Helen, 23
Immunity to Change (Kegan and Laskow), 85
industrial engineering, 183
information, controlling emotions and, 24
initial public offering (IPO), 185
innovation, 3; culture, 167; insight process and, 80; insights, 103; network, 167–68; organizational size and, 103; process, 174
Innovation Catalysts, 167
insights: enabling, 101–2; innovation, 103; managers and, 101; process, 80–81; suppressing, 101
Intel, 102

intellectual arrogance, 81
Intuit, Inc., 7–8, 19–20, 107, 164–65; D4D and, 166–68; insight process and, 80–81
Intuit Fasal, 170–71
IPO. *See* initial public offering
IQ, 36
Isen, Alice M., 26
Israeli Defense Force, 98
issue diagnosis meetings, 128–29
Issue Log Diagnosis Card, 149, *150*
Issues Log, 149

Jaques, Elliott, 147
Jensen, Greg, 133, 158
Jim Casey: Our Legacy of Leadership (Casey), 187
job mobility, 179
Jobs, Steve, 143
Johnson, R. W., Jr., 51
Jordan, Michael, 137
Judgment in Managerial Decision Making (Bazerman & Moore), 15

Kahneman, Daniel, 11–13, 76, 97–98
Kegan, Robert, 85
Kelleher, Herb, 55
Kelley, David, 56–57
Kelley, Tom, 56–57
Klein, Gary, 7, 23, 75–81, 89–105
Knowles, Malcolm S., 10
Kodak, 102
Kopp, Mary Kay, 190
Kuehn, Kurt, 189

Lambe, Patrick, 104–5
Langer, Ellen, 72
language, 68
Laskow, Lisa, 85
Lateral Thinking: Creativity Step by Step (de Bono), 19
law practice, 38
laziness, 11